AF840576

"Trauma related to being LGBTQ or non-binary is sadly all too common, and the field has long needed an in-depth exploration of sexual traumas, especially one designed for practicing social workers. Presented by experienced clinicians, the case studies include people living in other nations and cultures, in the child protection system, those who are immigrants or asylum seekers, and those having struggles with religion, who are seeking psychotherapy to cope with a range of life crises. Enriched by invitations to reflect on each case presented, this casebook is a 'must read' for those dedicated to affirmative practice with LBGTQ and non-binary people who have experienced sexual trauma."

Jeane W. Anastas, PhD, LMSW, ACSW, Professor of Social Work, New York University

"This innovative book offers several rich and in-depth case examples which can be used to deepen both education and clinical supervision. What makes this book distinct is how the editors focused the contributors on 'writing to the question' and considering how to create 'play' in the clinical encounter. For example, instead of bringing a theoretical orientation to the clinical encounter, they encouraged centering not-knowing in order to deeply sit listening for what the client says, who the client is, and what the client needs. The focus on LGBTQ trauma is critical as there are few texts that integrate theory, literature, and practice for this often-invisible population. This book seamlessly provides core readings and questions at the end of each case to allow space for more questioning, learning, understanding, and growing. An impressive compilation of scholars brings together complex, current case contexts, such as undocumented youth, gender-non-conforming, and traumatic experiences, to name a few."

Michelle R. Munson, PhD, LMSW, Professor, New York University Silver School of Social Work

THE SOCIAL WORK AND LGBTQ SEXUAL TRAUMA CASEBOOK

This inspiring text offers a collection of case studies from expert clinical social workers who work closely with survivors of LGBTQ-related sexual trauma.

The book covers a wide range of topics, such as gender and sexual minority asylum seekers, the embodiment of queer identity, the role of religion, regionality in the LGBTQ experience, and effective use of gay affirmative therapy. Each chapter is framed by key questions that encourage students and mental health practitioners to "think through" the specific needs and challenges of LGBTQ individuals who have experienced sexual trauma. Additional resources include an example of effective supervision and an example of a case conceptualization.

Drawing on the importance of narrative social work and the record of experience it provides, *The Social Work and LGBTQ Sexual Trauma Casebook* is an essential text for students and clinical social workers working with LGBTQ survivors of sexual trauma.

Miriam Jaffe, PhD, LSW, is an assistant teaching professor of graduate composition in the Rutgers University Writing Program. She specializes in issues of autobiography and life-writing.

Megan Conti, LCSW, DSW, is a specialist in sexual trauma. She practices through a psychodynamic, feminist lens with clients aged 3–75 in both community-based mental health agencies and in private practice.

Jeffrey Longhofer, PhD, LCSW, is an associate professor of social work at Rutgers University. He is the author of *A-Z of Psychodynamic Practice* and co-author of *On Being and Having a Case Manager.* His clinical practice focuses on children, adolescents, and adults.

Jerry Floersch, LCSW, PhD, is an associate professor of social work at Rutgers University. He is the author of *Meds, Money, and Manners: The Case Management of Severe Mental Illness* and co-author of *Qualitative Methods for Practice Research*. His clinical practice focuses on adolescents and adults.

THE SOCIAL WORK AND LGBTQ SEXUAL TRAUMA CASEBOOK

Phenomenological Perspectives

Edited by Miriam Jaffe, Megan Conti, Jeffrey Longhofer, and Jerry Floersch

Routledge
Taylor & Francis Group
NEW YORK AND LONDON

First published 2020
by Routledge
52 Vanderbilt Avenue, New York, NY 10017

and by Routledge
2 Park Square, Milton Park, Abingdon, Oxon, OX14 4RN

Routledge is an imprint of the Taylor & Francis Group, an informa business

© 2020 Taylor & Francis

The right of Miriam Jaffe, Megan Conti, Jeffrey Longhofer, and Jerry Floersch to be identified as the authors of the editorial material, and of the authors for their individual chapters, has been asserted in accordance with sections 77 and 78 of the Copyright, Designs and Patents Act 1988.

All rights reserved. No part of this book may be reprinted or reproduced or utilised in any form or by any electronic, mechanical, or other means, now known or hereafter invented, including photocopying and recording, or in any information storage or retrieval system, without permission in writing from the publishers.

Trademark notice: Product or corporate names may be trademarks or registered trademarks, and are used only for identification and explanation without intent to infringe.

Library of Congress Cataloging-in-Publication Data
A catalog record for this title has been requested

ISBN: 978-1-138-35103-5 (hbk)
ISBN: 978-1-138-35104-2 (pbk)
ISBN: 978-0-429-43553-9 (ebk)

Typeset in Bembo
by codeMantra

CONTENTS

CONTRIBUTORS

Edward J. Alessi, LCSW, PhD, is an associate professor at the Rutgers School of Social Work. His research aims to improve understanding of stress and trauma among lesbian, gay, bisexual, and transgender (LGBT) populations and enhance clinical practice with LGBT and other marginalized populations. In June 2017, he was named Rutgers Chancellor's Scholar, an award created to support faculty excellence at the Associate Professor level. His research has been published in journals such as *Psychological Trauma, Child Abuse & Neglect, Psychotherapy, Psychotherapy Research*, and *The Journal of Sex Research*. Dr. Alessi's current projects examine how stress and trauma influence the integration experiences of LGBT immigrants, asylum seekers, and refugees in the United States, Canada, and Europe. He served as guest editor for the *Clinical Social Work Journal's* first special issue on Clinical Practice with LGBTQ Populations. Dr. Alessi has also been recognized for his teaching. He was awarded the Rutgers University Presidential Fellowship for Teaching Excellence in 2017. In addition, he received the Outstanding Professor of the Year Award four years in a row (2013–2016). A clinical social worker since 2001, he has worked primarily in outpatient mental health and has been an independent practitioner since 2004.

Roxanna Ast, LSW, PhD candidate, Rutgers University, is a New Jersey-based bi-national, International Social Worker and researcher who spent many years living, studying, and working in the Middle East, United Kingdom, and most recently the United States. As a social worker, her direct practice has involved working with immigrants, refugees, and asylum seekers who have experienced various forms of trauma including: rape, sexual assault, torture, war-based violence, human trafficking, and child abuse. She worked closely with interdisciplinary teams to help immigrants and refugees integrate into new communities and ensure they receive psychological treatment and support for their trauma. As a researcher, she has focused mainly on help seeking behavior of survivors of violent crimes, perceptions of violent crimes among Middle Eastern and immigrant populations, and intersection identities, especially among the refugee and immigrant populations. In addition, her research includes evaluation research specifically focusing on social service programs and interventions that are put in place to support immigrants and trauma survivors in their journey.

Megan Conti (co-editor), DSW, LCSW, received her Bachelor's Degree (BA) in Political Science and Latin American and Latino Studies from the College of the Holy Cross and her Masters in Social Work (MSW) from Fordham's Graduate School of Social Service with a dual major in clinical practice and administration. Megan also completed two years of post-graduate training from the Ackerman Institute for the Family before receiving her Doctorate in Clinical Social Work (DSW) from Rutgers University. Megan's career has focused largely on community-based practice at both outpatient mental health facilities and in non-profit family services organizations as a clinician, supervisor, and administrator. In addition to direct practice, Megan has experience teaching Clinical Practice Courses with a specialization in children, youth, families, and women. Her scholarship focuses on utilizing queer theory and post-modernism to challenge dominant knowledge and practice paradigms, as well as integrating macro concepts into micro social work practice through critical social work methods. She has been published in *Psychoanalytic Social Work*, and she edited and contributed to *The Social Work and Sexual Trauma Casebook*, which is forthcoming from Routledge Press.

Jerry Floersch, (co-editor) LCSW, PhD, Associate Professor, Rutgers University School of Social Work, is a 1998 graduate of the University of Chicago School of Social Service Administration. After earning the Masters degree in social work from the University of Kansas, he worked as a social worker in drug and alcohol, hospital, mental health, and community settings. He administered a mental health crisis service and played a key role in developing and implementing housing policies and programs for the adult severely mentally ill. He is the author of Meds, Money, and Manners: The Case Management of Severe Mental Illness, published by Columbia University Press (2002), where, utilizing ethnographic and socio-historical methods, he examined the rise of community support services, the rise of the case manager and case management, and the limits of management models in providing services. He is a recent NIMH K08 recipient (2004–2009) for training in and development of qualitative methods to study youth subjective experience of psychotropic treatment. His work on psychotropic treatment focuses on the meanings adolescents and young adults make of their medication treatment, including social and psychological "side effects." In 2008, he was recipient of a Case Western Reserve University Presidential

Research Initiative award, where as the PI, he led a two-year investigation of college student use of mental health services, including psychiatric medications. His new book, with Jeffrey Longhofer and Paul Kubek, *On Having and Being a Case Manager*, builds on earlier work in this field by exploring a clinical method for case management practice. He is currently conducting a multisite study of college student use of psychiatric medications. His latest book is with Oxford University Press: *Qualitative Methods for Practice*.

Eric Hartman, LCSW, DSW, works in full-time private practice in New York City. After receiving his Master of Social Work degree from New York University (NYU), he worked for six years at the Ali Forney Center, a community-based organization that serves homeless and street-involved LGBTQ youth. He studied in an intensive clinical training program for seven years at the Psychoanalytic Psychotherapy Study Center in NYC, and received his certificate in 2013. Subsequently, he earned his Doctor of Social Work (DSW) from Rutgers University in 2016, where his research interests included the investigation of gay male embodiment and the impact of heterosexism on how gay men experience their bodies. His article titled, "The Queer Utility of Narrative Case Studies in Clinical Social Work Research and Practice" was published in the September 2017 issue of Clinical Social Work Journal. He co-edited that special issue of the journal and co-authored the introductory article. He also co-authored a book chapter titled "Incorporating minority stress theory into clinical practice with sexual minority populations" with Edward Alessi in a forthcoming book titled *Social work practice with the LGBTQ community: Exploring practice and policy factors* published by Oxford University Press.

Russell Healy, BA (Drew University), **MSW** (Rutgers University), and **DSW** (Rutgers University), has over 25 years of clinical experience. He has worked along the continuum of care from in-patient treatment to outpatient counseling. Currently, he maintains a private practice and teaches for the Rutgers School of Social Work's Office of Continuing Education on LGBTQ issues. Russell's most recent work is in research and advocacy for transgender youth. He has been a consultant and writer for social work textbooks.

Erica Goldblatt Hyatt, DSW, LCSW, MBE, is an administrator, clinician, educator, and author. She is currently the Assistant Director of the Doctorate of Social Work at Rutgers University and is a three-time graduate of the University of Pennsylvania as well as a graduate of McGill University. A notable figure in thanatology, Dr. Goldblatt Hyatt is the author of the only self-help book available for bereaved teen siblings, entitled *Grieving for the Sibling You Lost* (New Harbinger Publications, 2015). She is a special editor for aging at the journal, *Reflections: Narratives of Professional Helping*, and a peer reviewer for several academic publications. She has published both academically and commercially on topics of death, dying, and bereavement. A nationally-recognized speaker, Dr. Goldblatt Hyatt is also a passionate advocate for women's reproductive rights and has been featured in media campaigns by Planned Parenthood of Pennsylvania as well as repeatedly welcomed at press conferences alongside Pennsylvania Governor Tom Wolf. She maintains two sites of clinical practice: one in Society Hill, Philadelphia, working with women who have terminated desired pregnancies due to fetal anomaly, as well as individuals coping with a fear of death. The other is in Northeast Philadelphia, where she works with adolescents experiencing a variety of forms of grief, loss, and questioning of their religious experiences and upbringing. She is particularly fascinated by the concept of identity and how it develops across traumatic life experiences.

Miriam Jaffe (co-editor), LSW, PhD (English) (Rutgers University), was the Director of the Doctorate in Social Work Writing Program at Rutgers University and has returned to the English department, where she teaches graduate level writing. She combines her expertise in composition and the case study method with her clinical social work practice experience to produce educational materials for clinical social workers and students of clinical social work. She is the lead editor of two previous casebooks—*Social Work and K-12 Schools* and *Social Work and Sexual Trauma* (Routledge, 2017). She is also the author of "Case and Frame: Teaching Case Study Composition" (Journal of Clinical Social Work, 2016). She currently practices at The Center for Therapy and Counseling and teaches writing skills at Rutgers University. Her areas of interest include life writing, narrative activism, and cultural theory.

Michael Jarrette-Kenny, DSW, LCSW (Rutgers University), is a clinical social worker and psychotherapist. He is currently employed as a clinician in Wyckoff, NJ providing individual and group counseling services for adults, couples, children, and families. He started his social work career in 1998 as a support counselor for developmentally disabled adults at The Arc of Bergen and Passaic counties. Upon completing his MSW in 2004, he began working on an acute inpatient psychiatric unit at Bergen Regional Medical Center and as a screener for Care Plus NJ's Psychiatric Emergency Screening Program. He has completed advanced training in hypnosis at the New York Milton H. Erickson Society for Psychotherapy and Hypnosis (NYSEPH) and in EMDR. His areas of interest include the integration of hypnosis and mindfulness approaches in the treatment of complex trauma.

Sarilee Kahn, LSW, PhD, an assistant professor at the McGill University School of Social Work, studies the intersection of psychological trauma, culture, migration status, and religion for individuals holding stigmatized identities. As a practitioner, she has worked with conflict-affected individuals, and survivors of torture and gender-based violence in North America, Afghanistan,

Iraq, Bosnia, Liberia, and Sierra Leone. Her research highlights the experiences of individuals seeking refugee status on the basis of gender, sexual orientation and/or gender identity, and the migration pathways for LGBTQ refugees fleeing to Europe, the United States, and Canada. She holds Masters degree in Social Work and Public Health from Columbia University and earned a PhD in Social Work from New York University.

Jeffrey Longhofer (co-editor), PhD, LCSW, is an associate professor of social work at Rutgers University where is he is also curriculum director of the clinical doctoral degree, DSW. He holds graduate degrees in anthropology and social work. He did his postgraduate training in child development and psychoanalysis and adult psychoanalysis at the Cleveland Psychoanalytic Center and the Hanna Perkins Center (Cleveland, OH). He is a clinical social worker, applied anthropologist, and psychoanalyst, whose research focuses on mental health practice, mental health case management, psychiatric medication, and the roles that stigma and shame play in the social and psychological dynamics of practitioner/client interactions. His career has been shaped by a concern for developing and disseminating *experience-near* analyses of human experience with the creative use of research methods from the allied disciplines of anthropology, social work, and psychoanalysis. He has three recent books: Columbia University Press (2010): *On Having and Being a Case Manager: A Relational Method for Recovery;* Oxford University Press (2013), Qualitative Methods for Practice; Palgrave MacMillan (2015), A to Z for Psychodynamic Practice. He has a forthcoming book, with Jerry Floersch, *Social Work After Neoliberalism and the Managerial State: What is to be Done?*

Karie McGuire, LCSW, DSW, received her Bachelor of Science degree in Public Health from Rutgers New Brunswick. She began her career as a sexual health educator and became an AmeriCorps service member at the Rutgers Camden School of Social Work Healthy Futures Future Program. She worked for the Rutgers Future Scholars Program before going back to school where she earned a Masters degree in Social Work. Karie has worked the past three and a half years with the DreamCatcher Program, the statewide victim service provider for victims of all forms of human trafficking in New Jersey. Starting as a care manager and then moving to the role of supervisor, Karie leads the team in crisis intervention, case management, clinical services, trainings for the community, and partnering with law enforcement. Karie also works at Cooper University Hospital as a per diem medical social worker. In the past, Karie worked as an adjunct professor for Wilmington University in the Child Advocacy Program teaching courses around responding to child maltreatment and trauma. Karie's interests include helping clients gain access to mental health services and healthcare, crisis work, human trafficking prevention/intervention, and sexual health.

Tracy M. Norris, DSW, LCSW-R, BA in Sociology (The City College of New York), MSW (Columbia University), and (DSW) Doctorate in Clinical Social Work (Rutgers University) is a psychodynamic psychotherapist and a clinical social worker. Tracy currently works as the Director for the Nathaniel Community Success (NCS) alternative-to-incarceration (ATI) and behavioral health treatment program for justice-involved individuals with mental illness at the Center for Alternative Sentencing and Employment Services (CASES). Tracy also works as a psychotherapist at the Advanced Center for Psychotherapy and is a Psychoanalytic candidate at the National Institute for the Psychotherapies. Tracy is the sole owner of the copyright in "Applied Intersectionality in the Case of a Black Lesbian: An Example of Clinical Supervision" which has been licensed to the publisher of this book.

Sandra Van Nest, LCSW, DSW, has a private practice in New Jersey where she provides psychotherapy to children and adults. After completing her Master of Social Work at Radford University, she worked in rural non-profit agencies advocating for children and families facing domestic and sexual violence. While life eventually carried Sandra to suburban New Jersey with a shift in her career toward children with developmental delays and their families, she finds that her practice is still informed and influenced by her early training on the needs and strengths of rural communities. All communities, whether a building in an urban area, a suburban block, or a rural county have unique cultures, service brokering leaders, and a certain amount of protectiveness of the status quo. Sandra is a graduate of the Doctorate of Social Work program at Rutgers University. She consults at local, state, and national organizations of interdisciplinary teams of professionals who work with children and families.

Antonio Quirindongo Jr. is a Licensed Associate Counselor (LAC) and National Certified Counselor (NCC), with a BA in Psychology & Communication from Rutgers University and an MA in Counseling from The College of New Jersey, with concentration in Marriage, Couple, and Family Counseling and Therapy (MCFCT). Alongside offering individual, couples, and family therapy services, Antonio provides free, confidential HIV Testing & Counseling for a wide variety of clients over the age of 13. For Jaffe's podcast on LGBTQ sexual trauma and HIV, which is featured on the Routledge Digital Resources site, Antonio graciously provided personal content and clinical expertise from the field. Antonio's profound contribution to this project gives a dignified voice to the populations he serves at a local clinic in his community. With passion and empathy, Antonio dedicates his life's work through advocating for equality, love, health, and happiness of, not just his clients, but of all people because everyone is deserving and worthy of an extraordinary life.

INTRODUCTION

Writing to a Question: What is LGBTQ Sexual Trauma?

Miriam Jaffe and Jeffrey Longhofer

Writing to a question is a style of writing that complicates a topic or subject. This genre of writing does not seek to completely answer a specific question, nor does it seek to confirm a specific theory. It seeks, foremost, to complicate a theory-to-practice and practice-to-theory reality. Moreover, writing to a question for practitioners has an added dimension: it complicates matters by virtue of the swampy ground that characterizes practice. It can be asserted that a theory-to-practice and practice-to-theory reality is one of ambiguity. In writing to a question, the case material of the practitioner works to complicate and explicate ambiguity. The reaction one should have at the end of reading this kind of writing is "Wow, that is complicated." Or, "I have never thought of it that way before."

In contrast, writing to a theory likely leads to: "Oh, that is how that theory works." Or, "I see now what that theory is getting at." The power, thus rationale, of these two social work writing genres is that the respective conclusions must produce different reader/audience effects. Writing to a question is our acknowledgment of ambiguity and a sense of not knowing the "is" of our client's problem/situation/circumstance/context. The aim is to demonstrate the complexity of our work; in sum, it works against any type of reductive thinking or answer.

In the academy and elsewhere, we are trained to relate our thoughts and questions to what others have argued or written; we are expected to write in response to others. Too often, however, this kind of writing leads to tedious mimicry. The challenge for contemporary critical thinkers is to find a way to add something new to what has already been said. Many new scholarly writers (especially those trained in and committed to a particular practice paradigm) come to the practice of writing with an answer in mind. And they tend to use

[a] theory as ciphers or filters, reducing the meaning and significance of complicated cases, events, and symptoms, to formulaic and predictable narratives and outcomes. This *reuse* of theory will not lead to innovation, complication of ideas, or compelling narratives. Here, we have asked our contributors to practice a different kind of writing: *writing to a question*. And while this is not a substitute for *writing to a theory*, it is meant to offer a way of priming the imagination.

One of the great struggles of living is to find a way to exist between too much theory, too many ideas and judgments, and too few. Both are potential hazards and both may lead to ponderous prose, limited narratives, and impoverished lives. In clinical practice, we are told "to start where the client is." This, we assume, means tuning our instrument (our ears, principally) to the voices and gestures of those around us and to listen with a special kind of attention: not from where we're located, conceptually, judgmentally, or legally. Wilfred Bion (1967), in his essay "Without Memory and Desire," argues that one must approach each therapy hour with a suspension of memory and desire. This suspension creates what Winnicott referred to as "transitional" spaces, where play and creativity reside. In his mind, creativity and play have something in common: they happen in a space between our inner and outer worlds. In his words, play and creativity takes

> place neither strictly in our imagination, nor in the truly external world (i.e., all that is out of our control), playing happens in that space where our imagination is able to shape the external world without the experience of compliance, climax, or too much anxiety.
>
> *(Winnicott, 1971, p. 70)*

With Bion and Winnicott in mind, we believe that writing to a question requires that practitioner-scholars consider the following:

1 *Writing to the question* encourages posing questions "without memory and desire." Here, the purpose is to let your imagination take you to places not dictated by your theory. In good clinical practice, this is precisely what you do. You listen to your clients, sometimes for long periods of time, and very gradually you begin to form a picture, a story emerges, about their lives (and yours). Think of the many times in your clinical practice when narratives have been hastily constructed, with fragments of data and big chunks of theory. Satisfying? Accurate? *Writing to a question* encourages us to remain close to the human experience.

2 *Writing to the question* encourages thinkers to pose questions about *what is?* These are always ontological questions (i.e., about what we take to be real or knowable, the nature or quality of being). If I ask a question about dreaming, using only neuroscience, I will be led down one very

> narrow path, and it will not likely include the dreamer's experience of dreaming. If I ask a question about dreaming using Freud's repressive thesis, I will be led down yet another path, sometimes equally narrow. If I ask a question about dreaming using cognitive theory, I will be led down another path. Writing to a question forces us to ask: what is the dream, especially from the perspective of the dreamer? When we ask questions in this way, we find ourselves imagining and exploring in a mode of play.

The question that *Social Work and LGBTQ Sexual Trauma* addresses—*What is LGBTQ Sexual Trauma?*—came to us as we finished a collection on *Social Work and Sexual Trauma*, which elided possible differences between hetero-normative sexual trauma and queer experiences of sexual trauma. In this book, expert social workers in the field offer cases of LGBTQ sexual trauma to help us answer this question. We do not believe that there is one answer. In the following chapters, the reader will find an array of possible answers.

★ ★ ★ ★ ★

The first section of this book lays the groundwork for the three main points of conversation that recur throughout the chapters. Thus, we begin with a case dependent on the recognition of intersectionality and the questioning of categories, two themes which extend throughout the collection of voices here. Intersectionality, the consideration of how social and political discrimination and/or privilege overlap with gender and sexuality, helps us to think about how all the parts of a person come together to form a whole. However, in Miriam Jaffe's chapter, "Queering Trauma Therapy: The Case of Ariel, a Gender Non-Binary Undocumented Latina Immigrant in the US," the too many categories with which Ariel had to balance and contend—non-normative gender, sexuality, and citizen status, to name a few—left her fragmented, not whole. Jaffe's therapeutic work with Ariel would include challenging the need for categories, thus "queering" or perhaps undermining the notion of categories altogether. Jaffe uses the historic links between "queer" and "Jewish" to provide Ariel with a language for feeling Other and a narrative of transgenerational trauma.

Chapter 2, "The Devil You Know: Emerging Queer Identity as Traumatic Loss in a Religious Community," by Erica Goldblatt Hyatt, directly addresses the third main theme that reverberates throughout each chapter: religion. Goldblatt Hyatt describes her work with Jerrod, a gay male who struggles with his relationship to a church and Christian community. Goldblatt Hyatt finds that at the intersection—or what some might describe as a violent collision—of religion and queer identity, there is grieving for the part of the self that dies when one is forced to be either/or instead of both, so to speak. While most of the later chapters expose the deep wounds inflicted, sometimes self-inflicted, in the name of the Lord, Goldblatt Hyatt offers a model of treatment that helps Jerrod to integrate the queer and religious parts of himself.

In the third chapter, Sarilee Kahn and Edward Alessi, start off an exploration of the foundational three themes of this book—intersectionality, the questioning of categories, and religion—by providing transnational perspective. Specifically, Kahn and Alessi discuss how these issues manifest in LGBTQ asylum seekers. A growing body of evidence finds that LGBTQ asylum seekers flee their countries of origin after suffering psychological abuse and physical and sexual violence, often beginning in childhood. Perpetrated by family, community members, and state actors, multiple forms of victimization often continue throughout the life cycle. In order to gain protection guaranteed in the *Refugee Convention*, LGBTQ claimants arriving in a host country must prove a "well-founded fear of persecution" based upon their membership in a sexual or gender minority group (LaViolette, 2009). Consequently, claimants must construct a trauma narrative, often disclosing sexual abuse histories for the first time and at a time when they may not be psychologically ready to do so. Clinicians may also have to help LGBTQ asylum seekers prepare their trauma narrative. However, this places the clinician's precept of "do no harm" in tension with judicial necessity; evidence suggests that lack of choice over whether, when, and how to disclose sexual trauma may engender significant psychological distress. In order to address this tension, the authors propose a trauma-informed, human rights practice framework, built upon the theoretical foundations underpinning Testimony Therapy and Trauma-Informed Cognitive Behavioral Therapy to help practitioners guide LGBTQ asylum seekers through sexual abuse history disclosures. To illustrate the clinical utility of this framework, Kahn and Alessi zoom in to a case study involving a gay asylum seeker from Iran.

Zoomed out, their work helps define the transnational experience of LGBTQ sexual trauma and methods for treatment; while regional influences contextualize each case, one might find thick threads of connection between tacks on the world map. While writing to a question, people choose the questions they ask by thinking about the meaning behind the relationship between points of information. For example, one might choose to zoom in on the subject of "testimony" in Iran as it relates to other forms of "testimony" in this book. The reason it is so important, we believe, for readers to do their own connective thinking, is because we work off the premise that case studies are prone to the errors of subjectivity. The editors do not presume to be experts in vicarious experience.

As we considered the intention and pedagogy behind writing to a question, we decided to provide unframed, raw case material for our readers to ponder themselves. After all, our hope is to invite other voices into discussion of each author's ideas, and in recognition that the ideas collected here may become considered truer than others because they appear in print, we thought the inclusion of first person testimonies would flip some power dynamics in two important ways: (1) they allow those who experienced LGBTQ sexual trauma to speak for themselves, to offer personal definitions of what LGBTQ sexual trauma meant to them, without any clinical or editorial overlay, and (2) they allow readers to think through their own sets of lenses. To those ends, we were extremely fortunate to benefit from the expert interview and translation skills of Roxanna Ast, who provided us with the book's first interlude, which includes "Tara's Story" and "Sam's Story." These stories, told in anonymity for the survivors' own protection, are more remarkable than any of our own words can say.

Stories that exist beyond what words are able to express often live inside the body. The literal "embodiment" of LGBTQ identity is the topic the unifies the second section of this volume. In Chapter 4, "Straight on the Streets and Gay for the Stay: The Emerging Bisexuality of a Trafficked Female," Karie McGuire examines her work with victims of human trafficking. Research shows that there is a large number of homeless LGBTQ youth who are vulnerable to trafficking because they are constantly moving and in transit in large cities; the fetishization of LGBTQ youth also makes them targets for pimps. It was when Angela, McGuire's client, was "safe" in jail, however, that her bisexuality emerged. Without much "conscious" time to develop her own sexuality throughout her teenage years, given that Angela often dissociated while victimized, life off the streets allowed her the chance to develop her sexual identity in a way she never could before. However, once drawn back to the streets, Angela would engage in reenactments of past victimizations with men. She would dissociate from her body to the point of not being able to remember her actions. Angela felt attracted to both men and women, but her encounters with men almost always led to dissociation and disembodiment, her means to cope with the trauma of being trafficked during her most formative years of development.

In "Trauma, Fantasy, and Identity Development in a Transgender Client: The Case Study of Alex," Chapter 5, Megan Conti explores how the embodied experience of transgendered individuals is unique in the sense that a transgender individual often experiences formative periods of development in a body that does not match her gender identity, an experience that can be traumatic and can manifest itself in myriad ways throughout the developmental cycle. How a transgender individual navigates this experience of trauma is unique and important for understanding psychosexual development and the formation of an embodied identity. Using the case of Alex, Conti explores how one transman, prior to coming out as trans, expressed his deep gender dysphoria through dreams and dissociative fantasies that centered around sexual trauma—dreams that, through analysis, never formulated into any disclosure of an actual event of sexual trauma and which, after coming out as trans and beginning the transition, dissipated when the client was able to experience himself and his world in a new way.

In Chapter 6, Eric Hartman's "On Losing and Finding My Sissy Body: A Psychoanalytic-Phenomenological Perspective on the Trauma of Growing Up Gay," continues with the theme of embodiment and the complexity of growing up as a sexual minority in a heterosexist culture. A review of the literature shows a gap in the scholarship about how proto-gay boys develop through embodied, intersubjective experience and how that development shapes the lived bodily experiences of adult gay men. Hartman argues why this scholarship is necessary, proposes the need for more first-personal accounts of gay childhood development, and provides special emphasis on the developmental trajectory of effeminate boys who grow up to identify as gay men. The sissy body is then explored through the lens of trauma and dissociation in the shame-based processes of defeminization. Hartman, who closes his chapter with a case vignette from his own training analysis, discusses the effects of foundational formative experiences for gay men in a hetero-normative world.

At this point in the book, we offer another interlude in which we share two more pieces of primary source material: "Applied Intersectionality in the Case of a Black Lesbian: An Example of Clinical Supervision," by Tracy M. Norris, and "Steve's Story: A Case Conceptualization," by Jeffrey Longhofer. Norris's recording of herself leading supervision as a Black supervisor gives early career clinicians an idea of what a supervision session might look like with a seasoned psychotherapist; moreover, we learn that cultural competence of LGBTQ folk means nothing if it is informed only by white privilege or straight privilege. In a world of white privilege, supervision, and one might say even social work generally, has been driven institutionally by white privilege and straight privilege. Norris's example helps readers to confront these issues head on.

Longhofer's example of a case conceptualization suggests that we confront another issue head on: queer identity is not always analogous to sexual or gender trauma. Although this book is about LGBTQ sexual trauma, the salience of Longhofer's case conceptualization is that it represents that the point that being gay is not in and of itself traumatic. When Longhofer creates a safe space for his client Steve, Steve thrives during his emerging sexuality. Longhofer's case conceptualization illustrates how writing up detailed case notes produces fruitful reflection, one deeper than standard case notes. His writing will inspire readers, we hope, to devote the necessary time actively listening during session and then the necessary time to write in reflection afterward. Clearly, the time Longhofer spent listening and reflecting was key to the safe space made manifest in his therapeutic alliance with Steve.

In the aftermath of traumatic formative experiences, individuals often manifest an ambivalent attitude toward interpersonal relationships; a general lack of faith and ability to trust others and even themselves. In cases involving sexual abuse, this attitude may extend to the experience of their own sexual identity. This sense of distrust represents a particular challenge to the development of the therapeutic relationship, the common factor that is the foundation of most effective psychotherapeutic interventions. Section Three takes up the confusing world of attachment as it relates to LGBTQ sexual trauma. Chapter 7 "(Mis)taken Judgement: The Social Construction of Loyalty and Love for a Lesbian in Rural Appalachia," by Sandra Van Nest, shows how Lila, a 16-year-old lesbian survivor of incest and corrective rape from rural Appalachia, longs to return home to "daddy," the perpetrator of her abuse. Meanwhile, Lila just wanted to "be true" to her girlfriend. Though Lila had always known that she would date girls, this was her first relationship, and she wanted to do it right. However, when she explained this to her father, his ongoing sexual molestation of her escalated. Lila's father forced her to have intercourse with him. To Lila, the desire to be faithful in her new romantic relationship was the impetus to disclose to a teacher that her home life was full of incest and abuse. Lila's father believed that it was his job to show her the ways of men and women, which she obviously did not understand since she said she wanted to be with a girl. As a clinical case manager, Van Nest's job was to help Lila and her family through the court system and child protective service system. In this rural community, there were few therapeutic options, and many barriers to overcome: geography, isolation, and ignorance. Van Nest examines rural social work and the role of the case manager using a systems perspective with the frame of social construction.

Chapter 8, by Michael Jarrette-Kenny, presents the phenomenological experience of both patient and therapist, addressing these issues of sexual identity formation and interpersonal functioning as they intersect with attachment and trauma history. Jarrette-Kenny introduces us to Richard, a 43-year-old white male, who presented with acute anxiety issues after leaving a 19-year relationship with a much older man. During the treatment process, it became apparent that the presenting symptoms reflected the tumultuous circumstances of his childhood and teenage years, a period in which he experienced frequent emotional and physical abuse at the hands of his fundamentalist Christian parents and sexual abuse from peers and other adults. The author, operating from an eclectic, integrative perspective, advocates interventions informed by contemporary attachment theory and a humanistic, LGBTQ affirmative framework in regards to issues of sexuality. Jarrette-Kenney's chapter shows how an expert clinician navigates a complex case while practicing gay affirmative therapy.

Since the 1990s, "gay affirmative therapy" (GAT) has been considered best practice when working with clients whose internalized homophobia manifests in self-destructive behavior, depressive symptoms, or interferes with living a full, vital life. While not a primary therapeutic approach in cases complicated by substance abuse, sexual compulsivity, or depression, GAT can be integrated into whatever primary treatment model the clinician employs. Successful incorporation of GAT involves accurate assessment, timing, intention, and modality. In the closing chapter, "Effective Use of Gay Affirmative Therapy in a Forensic Case of Sexual Trauma," Russell Healy presents the case of Hal to demonstrate successful integration of GAT. Assessment concerns, such as readiness to experience/confront shame, and conceptual issues, such as how secrets and traumatic childhood events can reinforce internalized homophobia and cause it to function as a defense mechanism, are the focus here. Additionally, Healy considers matters of modality: is GAT more effective in a group setting, and if so, which group culture(s) work best? If the primary therapeutic setting is individual, how does the clinician understand their role in the client's life-space, and does therapist orientation matter? Finally, he investigates the therapist's use-of-self: how does the clinician attend to, and use, experience in work with clients whose internalized homophobia presents complex manifestations? These questions, to which Healy writes, apply to all of the chapters. Yet the context of working with Hal in connection to a forensic investigation of Hal's alleged sexual offense provides insight into the vast array of clinical social work scenarios in which therapists must understand the intricacies of LGBTQ sexual trauma.

* * * * *

This volume serves practitioners and students interested in understanding LGBTQ issues. Our goal in framing each chapter with pre-reading and post-reading questions is to inspire practitioners and students themselves to begin to *think* and *write* to the questions they face while working in this understudied and complex realm. Thus, *Social Work and LGBTQ Sexual Trauma* is an invitation to join this conversation in classrooms, supervision groups, and through self-reflection. While some of the case material is among the most heart-wrenching narrative to grasp, ultimately, we offer these chapters with supreme hope that "listening" through close reading is a way to engage in what we do not know without having to pretend that there are right answers at the ready. These are stories to feel with, and although we must tolerate the ambiguities of feeling, it is feeling—and empathy—that will drive compassionate care.

Section One

1

QUEERING TRAUMA THERAPY

The Case of Ariel, a Gender Non-Binary Undocumented Latina Immigrant in the US

Miriam Jaffe

Pre-Reading Questions

1. What does the verb "to queer" mean to you? How can one "queer" therapy?
2. What does "Gender Non-Binary" mean to you? Do you know any other terms that might correspond to "Gender Non-Binary"?
3. Given the title of this chapter, what kind of "trauma" might Ariel's particular intersectionality produce?

In "Queers are like Jews, Aren't They? Analogy and Alliance Politics," Janet R. Jakobsen explored the historical relationship between "Jewish" and "Queer." She found that "the similarities and differences of the two categories are not fully separable. They are overlapping–intertwined even–but not co-extensive" (p. 77). One extension of her argument, the whole of which is too important in its complexity for me to gloss here, reveals the negative connotations of the "Jewish" and "Queer" pairing: "Jews" and "Queers" are different, reviled, abstract threats, complicit in subversive activity (Jakobsen, 2003). However, for the purposes of this case study, I am more interested in Jakobsen's idea that a "Jewish" and "Queer" alliance has advantageous possibilities if managed with constant curiosity about individual autonomy. Specifically, I am taken by Jakobsen's idea that a positive correlation between "Jewish" and "Queer" emerges as "a space of difference that didn't just produce a new identity…but might also allow us to remain in the space of difference itself, without being trapped in identity" (p. 92).

In my psychotherapy work with Ariel, a gender non-binary, undocumented Latina, age 25, I contextually used Jewishness to form an alliance and to create an alternate space where Ariel could escape the chronicity of anxiety, which was symptomatic of traumatic stress. Here, I present a case study of our human experience.

The Case of Ariel

"Ariel. That's a Hebrew name. Old Testament." Ariel sat before me at our first meeting. I made this comment as a point of connection and also as a point of curiosity. My name is Hebrew and Old Testament in origin, and I am an American-Jew. Ariel identified as an undocumented Latina gender non-binary "human" who preferred "she/her" pronouns. In Hebrew, Ariel means lion of God—a male name, though you'd never know it from Disney's *Little Mermaid*. My name, Miriam, means "sea of bitterness," and I never thought it fit me. Immediately, I felt that we would challenge categories.

"My parents are very religious," Ariel said. They had converted from Catholicism to Jehovah's Witness soon after they had come to the United States. Ariel was struggling with her faith, which denounced her non-binary identity, and she was not out to either of her parents when we met. Later, she and her mother would develop a tacit understanding of the situation.

She initially came into treatment, however, because she was in mourning; her first love, Olivia, had hung herself after a particularly meaningful visit with Ariel.

We spent our first months together talking about the suicide. Ariel cycled the same loop of self-blame and uncertainty for miles and miles. She scrolled through her phone during sessions, reading me intimate text messages, including the one from the night before the suicide. Everything had seemed fine, status quo, so to speak. Ariel never noticed any warning signs. She showed me a picture of herself with Olivia in front of the LOVE monument in Philadelphia from a day together that seemed full of possibility and freedom. There had been no note with the suicide. And Ariel had no explanation; she imagined that Olivia had financial problems or that Olivia's family would never have accepted their same-sex relationship. "Maybe she died because I made her hopeful or happy for the first time. Maybe she couldn't take it."

For some reason, I responded allegorically. I told Ariel the storyline of a film in which the main character feels guilty being happy after surviving the Holocaust. The main character was in the resistance, and he had watched his closest comrade die beside him on a mission—but he had no choice but to keep fighting. Initially, I thought Ariel had come to therapy to rid herself of survivor's guilt. Ariel was compelled to keep on fighting, to keep on being alive. For insurance purposes, I'd diagnosed Ariel with PTSD, even before I'd heard the story of her border crossing. But I hoped that our work could move beyond that label. I hoped that Ariel could once again feel full of possibility and freedom, that I had could help her build a self-LOVE monument without the traditional barriers of metal sculpture.

Border Crossing

After some time, Ariel told me about her early childhood. She and her family had migrated from Mexico to the United States. They came in two waves. First, her father, mother, and two older siblings crossed the border; she knew little about the crossing because she was distant from her father and two older siblings into adulthood. Ariel had a twin brother, Meyer, who had been her closest confidant. They had been left together with an Aunt and Uncle in Mexico who kept Ariel and Meyer in a dark room with a TV and a mattress; the Aunt and Uncle stole all the money and gifts that Ariel's parents sent to them from the States. Once, Ariel saw her cousin riding a new bike that her parents had meant for her. Ariel and Meyer stayed like this from age four until they were six, years when primary attachment figures are all-important and attachment styles are formed (Bowlby, 2008).

Then, their mother suddenly appeared to accompany Ariel and Meyer on their border crossing. She had raised enough money to pay a smuggler. Ariel remembers the journey vividly: Ariel spent days stuffed under the false bottom of a flatbed truck with her mother and brother. "Keep quiet," her mother said as they bumped wildly through the turbulent desert.

Right at the border, Ariel developed hypothermia. "The temperatures drop quickly in the desert at night," Ariel told me,

> and I almost died. My mom broke away from the camp to seek a border agent. Better to be caught then to have me die, she thought. She never found an agent. But she was punished. Once we got over the border, we had to stay in a house somewhere for a few weeks. And there she was punished for trying to save my life.

Without words, Ariel said that her mother had been raped. I didn't ask how many times. I didn't ask anything. I felt a knowing and a not knowing.

By the time Ariel and her twin came "home" to the East Coast, their dad and older siblings had developed alcoholism. Their own personal histories had been fraught. The alcoholism was the reason that the family began to attend the Kingdom Hall of the Jehovah's Witnesses, a sect that forbids drinking and the celebration of man-made holidays. Ariel respected the power of the sect because it had saved her mom from abuse by her now sober dad. But she struggled because the sect also forbade homosexuality, and she'd known since age ten that she was not attracted to males. Moreover, Ariel had never felt, exactly, that she was fully or only a girl. Only her brother Meyer knew this information, but he believed in the sect's dictates enough to lose respect for Ariel over time. Losing Meyer was more painful than Olivia's suicide; after all, Meyer had stepped in to help Ariel during middle school and high school, a period of seven years when she was bullied—and assaulted—incessantly. Even though she had never come out, the boys that were her comrades in elementary school turned against her when they realized she often wanted to be like them instead of "liking" them as potential boyfriends. Ariel told me about the horribly violent experiences of her formative years with nonchalance—and only toward the end of our two years of treatment, as if those years had been comparatively easier; I suspected that Ariel often dissociated and willed away huge chunks of her memory.

Shannon E. Wyss (2004) wrote that while the statistics are too few, it appears that 9% of heteronormative youth are bullied at school compared to 50% of youth on the LGBTQ spectrum, who experience name calling, beatings, rape, and sometimes even murder. Wyss (2004) cited that teachers rarely intervene because they believe that queer teens bring it on themselves:

> As a result, many LGBTQ students spend their time in school not learning but quite literally trying to survive... On reaching puberty, girls are no longer supposed to be friends with genetic males, are expected to date heterosexually, and are supposed to conform to heterosexual norms of beauty... which can be quite painful.
>
> *(p. 710)*

Part of Wyss's point is that youth who experience queer phobia are considered high-risk for maladaptive behaviors and mental illness. But Ariel would reveal nothing close to a hint of maladaptivity, if it was there.

The Undocumented Closet

I must pause in this narrative to describe Ariel's appearance: her dark hair was short, but long enough to be feminine. We spent a lot of time talking about her hair and her desire to shave the sides: "But that won't be appropriate," she explained, her right knee held tight over her left knee, suddenly, as if she had transformed into someone wearing a short skirt, her ankle twirling, as if her leather flats were stilettos. Ariel's manner of dress was impeccably professional. She worked a full-time office job in the same field she was pursuing part-time at community college, yet she looked like she could have been the boss: structured suits, sometimes with feminine ruffles, always in dark powerful colors. Her body was tiny and child-like, but she accessorized with distracting oversized costume jewelry. Most noticeable was her perfect smile: bright white teeth in a row like soldiers, guarding anything that might come out of her mouth. She was always smiling, even when she told me about the suicide and the border crossing. Ariel's demeanor—the consistent smile, specifically—made me more curious than anything she had verbally disclosed.

*****

> I didn't know that I was undocumented until my senior year. I'd earned a merit placement at a summer program that offered a college scholarship for urban minority students who demonstrated potential. They needed my social security number to give me the money at the end, and that's when my mom told me that I didn't have one. I think she thought it was better that I didn't know until I needed to. Anyway, long story short, I became a DREAMer. Now the president is threatening to end DACA, so everything is up in the air again.

she said with an unnerving calm. The daylight pouring in through the blinds created a shadow that looked like bars over her face. "Many nights, I wake up sweating, and I can't feel my hands. And sometimes, I can't feel my tongue, and my chest hurts," she reported. "It feels like I am going to die." But Ariel rarely went to the doctor. She was scared of needles, and moreover, she was scared of deportation:

> Federal, state, and local laws have created a state of fear among undocumented immigrants that they could be deported from the United States at any time, necessitating that they constantly hide information about their status and avoid the purview of authorities.
>
> *(Villazor, 2013, p. 6)*

Going to the hospital, for Ariel, was worse than the repeated experience of severe anxiety, which made her feel near death every time.

However, Ariel's eternal smile and flawless appearance, not to mention her work ethic and familial piety, betrayed none of her anxiety. She fit the DREAMer narrative, which is "built upon a discourse of exceptionalism and privatized notions of citizenship" and "emphasize[s] the respectability and worthiness of some to remain within;" Ariel's appearance of success was not only protecting the secret of her non-binary identity, but it was also an appeal to neoliberal nativist policies, the invisible walls off the undocumented nightmare, which "criminalize immigrants" and preserve rhetorics that exclude people of color (Cisneros & Gutierrez, 2018, p. 85). She felt pressure to be a model minority figure.

About a year into our relationship, Ariel began a serious romance with Jael, the daughter of a Jewish plastic surgeon. "Their house was built from scratch just for them. They designed it. And they want to take us out to dinner and an opera," Ariel said, describing Jael's family. Ariel also showed me videos and pictures of them together from her phone. In one of the videos, Jael and Ariel were leaning against the back of Jael's bright red sports car. Jael was flaunting her long curly hair and pivoting to find her best selfie angle. Jael's face, photo ready, was caked in makeup. Ariel was a natural beauty with skin like a dark pear, but it seemed to me that she was always wearing a mask. Goffman's (1959) seminal idea that people consciously use cultural assumptions to portray the direct opposite of their hidden selves popped into my head as I learned about their relationship.

"Wait… Her vanity license plate reads J.A.P.?" I asked dramatically.
"Yes, those are her initials."

"Do you know what that means? What J.A.P. means?" I shifted into a sort of stereotypical Jewish accent, which came off both accusingly and comedically. I often overplayed my Jewishness, if that is possible, in order to sooth potential cultural tension. Also, I often taught Ariel Yiddish words as a way of helping her to express complex emotions.

"Oh, like a Japanese person?" Ariel laughed her quiet laugh at me. "Jael said that she and her family are, like, the most liberal people in America. Her mom is an inner-city public school teacher."

"Well, that's cool, but," I shifted back to myself, "it means Jewish American Princess, which can be derogatory. It's like a spoiled brat, kind of." Ariel googled Urban Dictionary immediately and started laughing again, confirming that Jael fit the definition, but not totally. I was distracted because during our dialogue about this, Ariel kept laughing through her teeth. I never believed that she was actually laughing. Her laugh reminded me of my daughter's antique doll, which has a string at the neck that when pulled, produces a mechanical giggle in response. Ariel's "laughter" was prompted by a thick noose of institutionally driven "hidden assaults" to civil and human rights that DREAMers endure; she was gagged from the start of her American life by the "benign language of assimilation" (Yoshino, 2007, p. 295). Together, Ariel and I explored how she used her "laughter" to control what people really knew about her, and without any expectation that I could change this coping mechanism, I told Ariel my own version of how the "JAP" came to be:

> Jews' sought their way out of oppression after oppression, for better or for worse, through upward social mobility, and in America, and in most places, money felt like safety, even though it never really was. It is just a facade. A way of trying to fit in. But it's not the whole story.

I used this moment to explain transgenerational trauma using my family's holocaust history, but for the purposes of this chapter, I turn to Tihamer Baku and Katalin Zana (2018), who say what I was hoping to establish:

> Traumatic experience deeply shocks the traumatized person's feeling of security in the world…Traumatized persons may create an internal world where sufferings are elaborated only in a selective manner. In this intra-subjective process, felt threats to security gain a permanent quality that

> keep individuals in a condition of permanent readiness. This experience will express itself in the body, in memory, and in actions, and thus form an atmosphere that can become transgenerational...Survivors wordlessly make family members witnesses to their experiences, against their intention and without either the survivor or the family having any clear insight into the process.
>
> *(p. 273)*

From a more narrative version of this expert definition, we decoded Ariel's attraction to Jael and Jael's performance of a Jewish-American Princess identity.

> Jael is perfect: she looks like a model the way she does her make-up, she's so self-assured, she's so strong in grad school that she's already landed a job, so she's going into life without any debt, and plus she's got a trust fund. It's like she has nothing to worry about, but you know, she does worry, I think, somewhere in there, which is why she's pushing herself so hard to look perfect and be perfect when she doesn't even have to. We have the same work ethic.

Baku and Zana (2018) go on to say that "second and third generations" (Jael's and then my generations) "living in this atmosphere experience the world as split...This split appears also at the relational level: loneliness as well as mature, well-functioning object relations can be present in parallel" (p. 274). I wondered if I had unwittingly used my own my own splitting—and then un-splitting—to demonstrate my transgenerational trauma; in our dialogues, I exposed parts of my deep personal pain to Ariel. On one occasion, I got swept into myself, and tangential to whatever initial point we had been discussing, I told her about my recurring dream that I must escape Nazis by jumping from roof to roof. I told her about my own experiences of waking up in a freezing cold sweat from the sound of my own moaning. I suppose that I was trying to normalize or destigmatize the body's natural stress responses, but I cannot vividly remember my intentions. In hindsight, its feels right that I should have crossed any borders between us as a way to show that though I may be a therapist, I am also simply a human who can and must function with boundaries and also, in the moments I deem necessary, without artifice. Ultimately, I only remember that Ariel's smile disappeared for a while, her mouth hanging open, letting me in.

"Performative Contradictions"

In "Documenting the Undocumented: Toward a Queer Politics of No Borders," Melissa Autumn White (2014) critiqued "how the control and regulation of mobility and identity function as central technologies of capitalist sovereignty" (p. 979) using Judith Butler's famous line: "there is something inevitable about the performative contradiction that emerges through the entanglement of tactics and imaginaries" (p. 978). Ariel's "performative contradictions" should have bothered me given that they seemed to reinforce her own oppression, especially because I was deeply entrenched in a news cycle that presented the "Undocuqueer Movement" as the only hope for radical change: "Undocuqueer, as a political entity, specifically addresses intersectional oppression and serves as a mode through which to question the processes that create and maintain exclusionary norms" (Cisneros & Gutierrez, 2018, p. 85). The Undocuqueer activists, unlike Ariel, were out and performing their intersectionality. Ariel would never come out to her own father, and she had no interest in engaging her aggressors. I had to ask: was Ariel's behavior maladaptive?

Austen and Goodman (2017) argued, according to the minority stress model, that gender non-conforming adults have an "increased risk for negative outcomes and maladaptive behaviors," including suicide, especially due to internalized stigma (pp. 827–828). During my assessment of Ariel's behavior, I was careful not to make assumptions about why Ariel was careful about behaviors that some might call "covering" or "passing" (Goffman, 1959; Yoshino, 2007). After all, as Wyss (2004) cited, "most of the work in gender attribution is done not by those who display gender but by those who interpret it" (p. 712). Had I mentioned to Ariel the news about Undocuqueer activists, I would have been tacitly suggesting that she participate in the system that created borders as her strategy to erase them (White, 2014). Had I asked questions about surgical options as a "cure" for "gender dysphoria"—concepts which Ariel never brought up—I would have been making economic assumptions as well as speaking from the privileged rhetoric of normativity (Austen & Goodman, 2017). Everyday, Ariel was up against national borders, gender borders, sexuality borders; therefore, my role was to be fluid.

In their review article, "Non-binary or genderqueer genders," Richards et al. (2016) noted the historicity of this sea change among mental health clinicians. With the release of the DSM-5 came the annihilation of the "Gender identity Disorder" diagnosis, which the APA replaced with "gender dysphoria" in recognition that having a different gender identity is not a disorder; the authors also argued that "it is the discrimination rather than the membership of this specific group [non-binary or genderqueer] which is psychopathogenic" (p. 97). While I wholeheartedly agree with the sentiment that discrimination is psychopathogenic, I question how Richards et al. use the words "specific group." In my role as therapist, I was still on the fence about whether or not Ariel's behaviors were maladaptive, but in my role as a Jewish person, I felt that I completely understood Ariel's conflicting needs to have a body that was safe in a land yet utterly beyond borders. Even though I belong to a specific group as a Jew, I would also be shunned, as I have been, from within my own group for various and sundry reasons. Part of the problem for Ariel was that she had to pretend to want to be a part of a group, even though she had come to accept, as part of our work together, that "group" may just be an extension of the word border.

I worried aloud in supervision about Ariel's conception of borders because I felt it reflected her surface level attachment to Jael. I also brought up examples of Ariel's attachment to her phone. In the most salient example, Ariel was examining the socioeconomic differences between herself and Jael.

"When Jael thinks Mexico, she thinks Cancun. She thinks luxury resort." Then Ariel pulled up a picture of the house her family still owned in Mexico. It was a squat brick structure, one room, maybe, and without glass windows. "Everyone knows our house," Ariel said, "because there is a payphone in front of it." She stared at the picture on the screen of her iPhone. "I don't want to go back there." She held onto her phone throughout the session, as if a wi-fi connection was as dear as life itself.

By now, we weren't talking about Olivia's suicide anymore. In fact, during one meaningful session, Ariel posted a sort of eulogy on social media, and then, in my presence, she deleted Olivia's social media pages and old phone number. She took a deep breath, moved very close to me, and deleted their entire chain of text messages. It felt like a time to say *Kaddish*, the mourner's prayer. We sat in silence, almost touching, for the rest of that session. She almost cried on my shoulder, but I didn't invite her to. "Don't take away Ariel's coping skills," my supervisor said to me sternly as I lamented over the session.

> If she needs to put her walls up, then maybe that is how she will get through life after the severity of her complex trauma. Your job is not to break down her walls here, Miriam. Only she can do that, and only if she is really ready. She's got a lot to lose if she reveals her truth–her housing with mom and dad, for one. The intensity of the pain when it gets to the surface, for two. Maybe a deep connection with another person is just too much for her to handle right now.

Walls, Walls, I thought to myself, and the Trumpian chant *Build that wall!* started ringing in my ears. However, I soon realized that Ariel had broken down a sort of wall in search of attachment: she had deleted something that was kept safe behind the screen of her phone, and she came close to me for comfort as she let the memories leave the phone and enter her own body. While Dahms (2015) found that smartphone screens helped to connect the activists of the undocuqueer movement and that social media created a supportive online queer community, Ariel's slow release of social media's "weak ties" led to "strong ties" when the screen was put down (Gladwell, 2010). In other words, she began to perseverate less on memory, unreliable commitment, and facade and more on the real people around her; she was finding safe spaces, including the therapy room, in which she could free herself enough to trust in our therapeutic alliance.

Jewish/Queer Trauma Therapy

Carolyn Stevenson (2008) calls psychotherapy a "queer–meaning unconventional–space" in which the therapist must take "emotional risks" with countertransference in order to "create a more expansive space" (pp. 243–244). In the case of Ariel, my self-disclosure about my own Jewish experience was risky because, at times, I found myself drawing from a reservoir of Jewish experience as a means to help Ariel think connectively about trauma. Although I had set out to ignore Jewish stereotypes, Ariel and I made frequent references to the brand of insecurity and neuroticism made culturally acceptable by certain Jewish pop culture figures, and she talked about the "balls" of "badass Jews" like Ruth Bader Ginsburg; Ariel wanted to achieve some elusive assuredness and self-confidence. After all, our main topic of conversation for the next year was Ariel's crippling anxiety over everything, including her relationship with Jael. If Jael didn't answer a text immediately, Ariel was sure that Jael was either dead or cheating. I pointed out that Ariel might have come to expect either abandonment or death given her family's migration story and experience of Olivia's suicide. But the worst of Ariel's issues concerned Jael's privilege, sense of entitlement, and, frankly, ignorance. It was March of 2018, when the news was a dark cloud over Ariel's DACA status. Jael had assumed that Ariel was a citizen, but Jael's mom had begun probing. Ariel felt forced to come out to Jael and her parents about being undocumented.

She was full of shame and felt that Jael's rich Jewish family would never accept her, even though they somehow accepted their daughter's homosexuality. To add insult to injury, Jael had then chastised Ariel when she had told her dad, Dr. P, that she attended community college. "Why didn't you just say one of the state schools around here? Then it would be easier for us to just get married and get you out of this mess." Jael was clueless. And Ariel didn't want pity or rescue or money. She wanted Jael to serve as a life partner. Ariel was also a little clueless: one of the main reasons she liked Jael—aside from her good looks—was that Jael liked authentic Mexican food. I often sense a lack of depth in their relationship, but I held back my judgment.

"I bet Jael's family immigrated here from Europe not too long ago," I said to Ariel. "And I bet that her family has a ton of respect for your work ethic. Jews had to fight for their place here, too, you know." We spent a lot of time on cultural differences. Ariel didn't understand how free Jael felt filling plate after plate at buffets, for example. Ariel didn't understand the importance of Jewish holidays after having been banned from those kinds of celebrations as a Jehovah's Witness. "If it is true that Jael's family is nervous about your relationship for any reason," I said, "it is probably just that you're not Jewish. I'm stereotyping here about Jewish continuity, but my guess is that what they care most about is having Jewish grandchildren." For many reasons, that was tough for Ariel to swallow.

"My body certainly isn't birthing any babies," she said. That was the first time, ever, that she lost the smile.

> I'm biologically female, I guess. But I don't feel like a girl. I don't feel like a boy. I don't feel like any of the words I've googled to try to figure out who I am. I had another one of those crazy panic attacks last week, where I can't feel my hands and I'm dizzy, like a heart attack, but it happened during the day. It's because I went into a trans chat room, and everyone was complaining about hating their body parts and their hormone shots. One girl showed the scars after her top surgery. I don't want any knives or needles. That's not gonna fix what is inside.
>
> "What is inside?"

"I don't know. But I'm not a girl, and I'm not a boy. I started crying because it would be easier, in a way, if I were trans. Instead, I'm nothing, nothing that can be fixed."

"You're not nothing. You're so many things. You're super smart. You're so hard working," I said, my words missing the mark. I sense that I should have asked: "Why do you need to be fixed? Is there any small way that you can accept yourself the way you are?" But I didn't say that.

And for the first time, Ariel spoke without the nervous laugh.

> I'm not interested in the categories. I don't want to have to explain myself to anyone. Not to my parents. Not to Jael's parents. Not to whoever is reading my DACA extension application. I'm Ariel. I'm a person. If Jael wants to have kids, I'll be the best…

She started to say "father" and paused. "I'll be a parent who loves unconditionally." Time was up. She got up, walked out quickly, and I didn't hear from Ariel for three months.

Ariel's hiatus gave me some time to do my homework about gender nonbinary individuals. I easily found a host of terms: androgynous, mixed gender, bigender, gender fluid, pangender, genderqueer, and trigender (Richards et al., 2016). But I didn't find a name for the work we were doing until I found Sophie Croisy's (2008) work on the creolization of trauma theory. Creolization is the "process of transverse dynamics that endlessly reworks and transforms the cultural patterns of varied social and historical experiences and identities" (Bluntansky & Sourieau, 1998, p. 3). In the name of creolization (and with a nod to post colonial theory), Croisy (2008) challenged traditional psychoanalytical concepts about self/identity and argued that "trauma theories should let themselves be transformed again and again by the testimonies of those who have lived through trauma" (p. 133); she also argued that "creolization promotes the idea of constant cultural mutation, of cultural sharing" (p. 135).

The cultural sharing between me and Ariel went something like this: I gave her a framework to preserve memory through my modeling of Jewish memory, genealogical memory in "diaspora," the state of constant migrancy. She ultimately didn't feel the need move past her mourning. She could accept her symptoms, thereby reducing her symptoms, because there was no either-or binarism, no sick-well binarism, just the choice to remember. Ariel gave me the freedom to recognize and feel deeply that not everything needs a name or has a name that fits.

The last time I saw Ariel, it was the end of the summer, and Ariel came in with a beach tan that contrasted with the skin under the tiny hairs that had been shaved above her ears. Her smile was there, but softer. "Jael and I are moving in together." I think she came in to say goodbye.

Many Conclusions

There is no takeaway here. In other words, this is a case about which I am still thinking, still unfolding, even though Ariel is no longer in my life.

While creolization is one lens through which to view my experience with Ariel, and the queering of psychotherapy another, for now I believe that something else was happening: what I call "Jewish/Queer trauma therapy." This lens feels more like layers of lenses, like an antique optometrist's tool. In its layers of words, "Jewish/Queer Trauma" forms an intersectional specificity relevant to the therapeutic relationship that Ariel and I formed.

One connection I see more clearly through these layered lenses considers our overlapping senses of statelessness as linked with our femininity. While I am a privileged documented citizen of the US, the transgenerational memory of Jewish wandering in exile makes me feel implicitly unsafe, especially amid the rising awareness of white supremacist and neo Nazi factions. I feel especially worried for my children. I wonder: "What do my 'papers' mean if a century ago, my own family escaped Siberia on 'acquired' passports that bear someone else's surname, my 'legal' name today? And," like a typical Jewish mother, "how will I protect my children?" In "Freud, Bluher, and the Secessio Inversa: Mannerbunde, Homosexuality, and Freud's Theory of Cultural Formulation," Jay Geller (2003) wrote that Freud and Bluher's dialogue reveals Bluher's thinking that "Jewish statelessness and survival are connected to their effeminacy. That is, the Jews have devoted themselves exclusively to the woman's realm of the family and have focused upon the woman-associated reproductive instinct" (p. 118). This idea helps me to imagine Ariel's resistance to utilizing her body's reproductive potential if, after all, there may be "survival" but no world of safety waiting for the unborn stateless. I can also imagine that Ariel's idealization of "badass" Jewish women with "balls," or even of me, might have inspired Ariel to develop her own kind of queering, her own understanding that "papers" and official categories are in flux like humans, constantly shape-shifting and ever-adaptive rather than maladaptively stuck.

Another connection I recognize through the lenses of "Jewish/Queer Trauma" is precisely a sense that survival is contingent upon shape shifting. In "Passing Like Me," Daniel Itzkovitz (1999) called this shape shifting "chameleonism," citing the famous train car scene from James Weldon Johnson's Autobiography of an Ex-Colored Man (1917) in which the Jewish character displays a sort of "When in Rome," non-committal identity (p. 36). Ariel's "smile" and superficiality were small parts of her chameleonism, her outward playing along with the expectations for her roles. As a Jewish therapist, perhaps I overplayed my own role as a Jewish woman—like the caricatures in Yiddish theater—in order to show that I knew how to play the game, too. I validated that performance could be key to survival. Yet I also provided a healing space, in the room, inside myself where I held her trauma each week, and in relation to my own trauma—as if my Jewishness was a framework for how to have both trauma and love without one choking out the other. It was a space where she could stop performing and where she could feel free enough to make choices about her relationship to her body. Moreover, she could walk out of the space of her own accord. When Ariel told me that her "body would not be birthing babies," the time she stopped smiling and walked out for three months, she put a hard stop to the kind of shape shifting that childbirth and perhaps even mothering would require. She exhibited empowerment in her shift out of play.

Finally, for now, I return to Jakobsen's ideas in recognition of the pitfalls of my layered lenses and to recover of hope that these pitfalls are avoidable. In short, Jakobsen (2003) pointed out the problem with pairing "Jewish" and "Queer" is that "The two terms are not simply equivalent and they cannot necessarily be interchanged" (p. 82); so, if a Jewish/Queer analogy exists, it must emphasize that each traumatized or transgenerationally traumatized human has a unique oppression to which no other human oppression can compare, especially so as to avoid appropriation and historical specificity. Moreover, in order for an alliance of the sort I propose here to work, therapy must be guided toward individual autonomy. After all, there must remain the possibility that the very categories the words "Jewish" and "Queer" signify are themselves unstable, shifting with context and in relation to one another: "Unlike the relations of analogy where one term effectively elides or even replaces that to which it is analogized, in this conceptualization both terms remain present" (Jakobsen, 2003, p. 91). In my work with Ariel, the "Jewish/queer" alliance allowed Ariel to reframe her non-binary, undocumented experience as one in which she was not trapped all the time because I did not try to "replace" her experience; I simply offered up my own and listened to hers so that she could define her experience to herself.

Just as a case study write-up of clinical work with an individual is, according to Talal Al-Rubaie (2002), "transferable" but not "generalizable," I do not expect that "Jewish/Queer Trauma Therapy" would ever perfectly overlay a different case. Yet what I hope is most transferable here is that the therapist can feel permission to open up the possibilities of a trauma alliance in which both patient and practitioner can help each other to heal.

Close Reading Questions

1. Define Yoshino's phrase "benign language of assimilation" in your own words. Why does Jaffe agree that this kind of language can be dangerous?
2. Why do Richards et al. call discrimination against queer people "psychopathogenic" in their discussion of changes to DSM relating to gender dysphoria?
3. White writes about "how the control and regulation of mobility and identity function as central technologies of capitalist sovereignty." What does White mean? Why is this idea important to Jaffe's decision to queer trauma therapy?

Prompts for Writing

1. Which "performative contradictions" do you notice in yourself? How could they help you to make sense of a client who seems self-contradictory for survival?
2. Conduct research on the theory of "transgenerational trauma." Do you recognize this kind of trauma in yourself and/or others around you? Do you have any clients who may be experiencing this type of trauma?
3. As a clinician, what interventions would you make to address the astounding and disproportionate bullying that queer people experience. Look at the article by Wyss listed in the references to get started.
4. Listen to the podcast featuring Antonio Quirindongo, a clinician at a free HIV testing clinic, on the Routledge Digital Resources website. Write about the immigrant experience with healthcare in connection to Ariel's experience.

References

Al-Rubai, T. (2002). The rehabilitation of the case-study method. *European Journal of Psychotherapy, Counseling & Health, 5*(1), 31–47.

Baku, T., & Zana, K. (2018). The vehicle of transgenerational trauma: The transgenerational atmosphere. *American Imago, 75*(2), 271–285.

Bluntansky, K., & Sourieau, M. (1998). *Caribbean creolization*. Gainesville: University Press of Florida.

Bowlby, J. (2008). *Attachment*. New York, NY: Basic Books.

Cisneros, J., & Gutierrez, J. (Spring 2018). What does it mean to be undocuqueer? Exploring (i)legibility within the intersection of gender, sexuality, and immigration status. *QED: A Journal in GLBTQ Worldmaking, 5*(1), 84–102.

Croisy, S. (2008). Michelle Cliff's non-western figures of trauma. *The AnaChronist, 13*, 131–156.

Dahms, B. (2015). Queering citizenship: Undocuqueer and immigration reform. *Dialogo, 18*(2), 79–89.

Geller, J. (2003). Freud, Bluher, and the Secessio Inversa: Mannerbunde, homosexuality, and Freud's theory of cultural formation. In D. Boyarin, D. Itzkovitz, & A. Pellegrini (Eds.), *Queer theory and the Jewish question* (pp. 90–120). New York, NY: Columbia University Press.

Goffman, E. (1959). *The presentation of self in everyday life.* New York, NY: Doubleday.

Gladwell, M. (2010). Small change: Why the revolution will not be tweeted. *The New Yorker*, October 4.

Itzkovitz, D. (1999). Passing like me. *The South Atlantic Quarterly, 98*(1–2), 35–57.

Jakobsen, C. (2003). Queers are like Jews, aren't they? Analogy and alliance politics. In D. Boyarin, D. Itzkovitz, & A. Pellegrini (Eds.), *Queer theory and the Jewish question* (pp. 64–89). New York, NY: Columbia University Press.

Richards, C., Bourman, W. P., Seal, L., Barker, M. J., Nieder, T. O., & T'Sjoen, G. (2016). Non-binary or genderqueer genders. *International Review of Psychiatry, 28*(1), 95–102.

Stevenson, C. (2008). Psychotherapy: A queer space. *Smith College Studies in Social Work, 78*(2–3), 243–262.

Villazor, R. C. (2013). The undocumented closet. *North Carolina Law Review, 92*(1), 1–74.

White, M. A. (2014). Documenting the undocumented: Toward a queer politics of no borders. *Sexualities, 17*(8), 976–997.

Wyss, S. E. (2004). "This was my hell": The violence experienced by gender non-conforming youth in US high schools. *International Journal of Qualitative Studies in Education, 17*(5), 709–730.

Yoshino, K. (2007). *Covering: The hidden assault to our civil rights.* New York, NY: Random House Trade Paperbacks.

2

THE DEVIL YOU KNOW

Emerging Queer Identity as Traumatic Loss in a Religious Community

Erica Goldblatt Hyatt

Pre-Reading Questions

1. How might the experience of bereavement relate to queer individuals' processing of individuation?
2. What is internalized homophobia? How might it manifest as a part of one's spiritual or religious experience?
3. Can you imagine a spiritual or religious space that would be safe for queer individuals? What would it look it? What might a safe spiritual or religious space look like in therapy?

Jerrod shifted awkwardly across from me. He tapped his fingers on the ceramic edge of his coffee cup and inhaled the steam rising toward his face. I didn't know him well, but I knew who he was. In our small, conservative Christian community, almost everybody has met or is at least familiar with everybody else.

As a former professor of psychology at the tiny local college mostly populated by members of the community church, Jerrod was a fixture. He was active in student government. He produced the annual community art exhibition that partnered church members and students as they worked together on religiously-inspired pieces for display. He was one of the religious studies majors that flocked together in the dining hall at lunch, peppering our minister-professors with theological questions. We never interacted much while I worked at the College, but we both knew of the other.

I have a bit of a unique reputation in my community. A secular Jewish girl from Canada, I arrived at the beginning of 2011 after marrying into the

Church. I met my husband Will in a neighboring state while I was working in a community agency as a trauma therapist: I saw him in a picture on my boss' desk and was struck by his tall, lanky appearance. Will was at the time an auto mechanic with a Mohawk and pierced ears plugged with circular gages. He was the opposite of what should appeal to a good Jewish girl, and I was captivated. I found a way to be introduced, and after a few weeks of dating, Will told me about the mystic Christian community where he was raised.

The Church of Will's origin was founded upon the theological writings of an 18th century scientist and mystic who claimed to have his "spiritual eyes opened" by Jesus Christ. Its followers believed that all existing scripture was metaphorical in origin: The Garden of Eden, for example, was actually a metaphor for human development. Furthermore, the sect believed that the spiritual world is all around us, and they proffered extensive doctrine about what happens when we die. Because I spent the first few years as a social worker in end of life environments, I was intrigued by this theology. By the time Will and I were married, we moved to the state where the headquarters of the church was housed in a suburban town, and I was hired at the local college. I became pregnant toward the end of my first year teaching, and our baby was diagnosed with a rare and deadly fetal anomaly. Will and I made the heartbreaking decision to terminate the pregnancy, and this choice created rumor and controversy in the community, where its most conservative members believed that abortion was murder. As I began to feel increasingly like an outsider, I grew frustrated in my position at the college, and sought a position at a larger, more liberal, college. I remained active in our community as a private psychotherapist, and established a reputation for helping to treat other self-described "outsiders" (Goldblatt Hyatt, 2020).

Jerrod, on the other hand, seemed about as "insider" as a resident of the community could get, and I wondered why he had asked to meet with me. I raised my eyebrows in surprise when he took a deep breath and said, "I'm probably not who you think I am. I'm living a lie."

It was this statement that began an exploration of Jerrod's challenges developing and maintaining an identity as a gay man born and raised in a conservative Christian environment. Surprisingly, the clinical work that I conducted with Jerrod and soon grew to encompass the experiences of other queer members of our community validated a theory I conceived nearly a decade earlier to understand the ways grieving adolescent siblings coped and formed identity after the loss of a brother or sister (Goldblatt Hyatt, 2011).

Of note, in this chapter I will utilize the term "queer" to encapsulate the wide range of LGTBQIA, gender expansive, and gender creative client presentations. I am aware that a single case study is not generalizable to an entire population, and that each member of the queer community may experience unique demographic features that complicate any one individual presentation. My hope is that my theoretical orientation and description of practice will provide a useful starting point for clinicians working with similar queer-identified youth who have been raised in a conservative Christian environment, and that readers should feel free to add, detract from, and critique my perspective as we seek to provide the most healing of services for the communities we see.

This chapter extends an argument that I initially applied to the bereavement processes of adolescent siblings (Goldblatt Hyatt2, 2020), rooted in a social studies of childhood perspective. My theoretical orientation developed from Graham's (2011) exposition of how the study of childhood has shifted in recent years. According to Graham (2011), in the past, children were viewed as static recipients of adult intervention and expected to progress through sequential stages of development according to a trajectory espoused by white, Eurocentric theorists. However, the modern social studies of childhood movement argues that children are active negotiators of identity, in which numerous intersectional aspects including gender, socioeconomic status, resources, external social forces, and more allow social workers to appreciate them as active participants in the construction and reconstruction of their identities, moving both within and across groups to create a sense of self (Graham, 2011). I have previously argued that in the case of sibling bereavement, just as experimentation with substances, clothing styles, and social groups may occur in adolescence, teens may "try on" multiple coping mechanisms in order to establish a sense of self (Goldblatt Hyatt2, 2020). In this chapter, I propose that queer teens from conservative religious environments may attempt to individuate in a similar fashion. My queer clients have experienced a struggle with identity, self-expression, and transition to adulthood, which may be appreciated as an experience of bereavement. Raised in a religion condemning same-sex marriage and espousing the sinful nature of queerness, these teens preliminarily experimented with multiple coping styles in order to find safe, socially-sanctioned ways to self-express. I extend the adolescent sibling bereavement coping model by applying it to queer youth who, through therapy, may reinvest in their religion in order to achieve identity synthesis and meaning. Jerrod's case represents a composite of three individuals that presented to therapy with symptoms of depression, self-harm, and risky or impulsive behavior relating to coming out and struggling with potentially abandoning their religion of origin. In identifying as queer, this population faced a dual form of anticipatory grief that results from the loss of family support as well as struggling with separating from their religious community. Some teens, like Jerrod, may feel pulled toward remaining openly queer in their community of origin despite persecution due to a desire for the familiarity and consistency the religion provides, as well as opportunities to speak out and create safe space for people like them. Others may find meaning by engaging in more open and accepting religious and spiritual institutions of practice. None of the adolescents I worked with in my clinical practice have, as of yet, turned to atheism as a permanent solution, though many considered it.

If social workers can better understand the unique loss challenges experienced by queer adolescents in conservative communities and how they may engage in different elements of coping to address these experiences, we can better address the population and guide them as they seek to narrate meaning in their lives and disengage, reengage, or seek new engagement in religion.

Literature Review

There is certainly no dearth of literature exploring the identity development experiences of queer youth. Most seminal and familiar to scholars, Cass' (1979) theoretical work on homosexual identity formation consists of six stages building on an Eriksonian psychosocial perspective. Cass' (1979) model includes multiple sub-paths, including confusion, comparison, tolerance, acceptance, pride, and synthesis. Like Erikson's (1964) stages, Cass' (1979) stages are epigenetic and build upon each other, though, also like Erikson's model, they do not consider exigent factors impacting adolescent identity development including sociocultural, economic, or mentorship and other resource factors. Furthermore, Cass' (1979) linear model precludes the possibility of other approaches. Cass' (1979) model represented an important development in the approach to queer identity, but it also neglected to consider the role of religion as it impacts identity formation, however, Wood and Conley (2013) argued that during the identity tolerance stage, queer individuals may be more vulnerable to loss of religion or spirituality in their lives if they experience negative experiences such as spiritual abuse, in which they are threatened with eternal and spiritual consequences by clergy or family. Unfortunately, one's queer self and one's religious or spiritual identities may not fit together.

Empirical research has explored the integration of religious and sexual identities and appears to validate the importance of identity synthesis (Cass, 1984). Ginicola and Smith (2011) have applied Fowler's (1981) six stages of faith development to Cass' (1979) model, noting that the identity comparison phase, when individuals may begin to realize same-sex attractions, aligns with Fowler's (1981) mythic-literal faith, as they begin to adapt the messages from religious and spiritual teachings for themselves. Because, according to Cass (1979), youth may at this time actively search for role models that may not exist in some religious traditions, they may experience alienation and isolation. This may continue across the process of both faith and identity development as queer individuals continue to search for self-acceptance and pride and to eventually confront homonegativity while synonymously and developmentally growing in and attempting to internalize faith (Ginicola & Smith, 2011). The goal of identity synthesis should ideally coalign with Fowler's (1981) stage of universal faith, whereby an individual can accept that the queer component of themselves is one of many important core tenets of identity and honors and co-exists with the faith experiences of individuals from other backgrounds.

However, Ginicola and Smith (2011) acknowledged that this is challenging for most individuals to achieve.

Dahl and Galliher's (2009, 2011, 2012a, 2012b) multiple explorations of the experiences of queer youth formerly affiliated with the Church of Latter Day Saints (LDS) provided a useful comparison to the small, conservative Church explored in this chapter. They also engage youth in faith-based education beginning in childhood. Dahl and Gahliher's (2009) survey of 69 queer individuals found that most participants who did not experience identity conflict were unaffiliated with a religious orientation, preferring spirituality as a more personal pursuit. Of note, some reported living non-integrated, compartmentalized lives where their religious and sexual identities were constantly in conflict. This lack of identity synthesis led them to experience a loss of faith and disillusionment with God (Dahl & Galliher, 2009). A follow-up study explored the correlation between religiosity and sexual orientation conflict and mental health symptoms (Dahl & Galliher, 2010). It appeared that individuals who experienced internalized homophobia and were preoccupied with their own sin and God's judgment of them impacted symptoms (Dahl & Galliher, 2010). However, the authors noted that behavioral religiosity was not associated with mental health outcomes; rather, it was one's individual perceived conflict as well as external experiences that contributed to depressive symptomatology (Dahl & Galliher, 2010). Another study by the same authors explored the outcomes of queer youth raised in a conservative Christian community and found that youth experienced feelings of inadequacy, religious guilt, depressive symptoms, and social strain (Dahl & Galliher, 2012a). However, the authors noted that there were also positive outcomes, including an increased sense of self, acceptance of others, and incorporation of religious values such as service and social support into one's life (Dahl & Galliher, 2012a). A companion study identified details in the identity development process of the youth in the above study, by exploring the impact of religiosity on identity development in queer youth (Dahl & Galliher, 2012b). Respondents identified enjoyable participation with the faith of their origin in their early years, but began to feel different and to attempt to deny same-sex attractions. Some began to question their faith, while others worked to maintain it, even by attempting to change their orientations. Finally, participants redefined their religious values and disengaged from the religious orientation of their childhoods (Dahl & Galliher, 2012b).

The process of accepting the self and honoring one's true sexual orientation can be challenging in small, conservative Christian societies. Research by Dehlin, Galliher, Bradshaw, and Cromwell (2015) explored the experiences of 1493 same-sex attracted current or former Mormons, and researched how they navigated conflict between sexual and religious identity. Findings suggested that initial attempts to deny or compartmentalize one's true sexual identity is unsustainable and yields significant psychosocial costs. An ideal experience involves the integration of both sexual and religious identities, or the complete rejection of the religious identity itself (Dehlin et al., 2015). It was extremely rare for individuals to reject their queer identity (Dehlin et al., 2015).

Interestingly, the Mormon religion offers a variety of approaches to same-sex attraction, whereas the Church in this chapter only offers one: shunning it as sin. Dehlin, Galliher, Bradshaw, and Crowell (2014) explored the impact of different approaches and beliefs in same-sex attraction. These included embracing biological views of same-sex attraction, aligning with psychosocial views such as early childhood trauma as a cause, coping by engaging in church, staying and remaining celibate, and getting married either to a person of the same or alternate sexual orientation. Results indicated that individuals who remained active in the LDS church displayed the lowest levels of self-esteem and higher levels of depression (Dehlin et al., 2014). Well-being was increased in those who married individuals of the same sexual orientation, while those in heterosexual marriages fared more poorly (Dehlin et al., 2015). Thus, despite having more channels to confront and potentially engage with one's queerness, individuals may suffer psychologically if they remain affiliated with a religion that ultimately does not accept their sexual orientation and forces them to deny or minimize it.

With a better understanding of how individuals from small, conservative Christian backgrounds can struggle with maintaining a religious identity and one that honors queerness, the case study below will illustrate Jerrod's attempts to cope with this conflict by assuming different identities in order to find a better fit. Ultimately, through the process of therapy, Jerrod was able to embrace both his true self and maintain a connection to his religion.

Case Content

I was shocked to learn how much Jerrod had been struggling, and as he delved into his attempts to cope with his queer orientation, I felt a surge of empathy. He gently raised the sleeves of his shirt to reveal several rows of superficial self-inflicted cuts running from just above his wrist to his mid-bicep.

The self-harm extended into risky sexual activity. He was finding sexual partners on queer dating apps, and meeting for one-time hookups with individuals he knew little about and would never see again. He admitted that some sexual encounters occurred without any form of protection, and wondered aloud, "Maybe I'm trying to infect myself with HIV. Then I'll be forced to come out." Jerrod, however, expressed a great deal of fear and anxiety connected to contracting the HIV virus. He experienced panic attacks after any sexual encounter, and would administer enemas to himself rationalizing that these would reduce the likelihood of transmission. All this time, he was maintaining his presence in our community as a confident, successful young man with a good reputation. His friends and family were unaware that he was struggling.

As we continued to meet, I learned more about Jerrod's history and when he first realized that he was gay. He identified a turning point in early adolescence when he developed a crush on his best friend and found himself masturbating to fantasies of him. Jerrod felt repulsed, and experienced guilt and regret in the aftermath, recalling that all religious teachings of his childhood imparted by ministers informed that homosexuality was a perversion of marriage. Marriage, in turn, was a sacred bond between men and women, and ultimately brought each individual closer to God. He recalled hearing stories from family members about how gay friends from other religious denominations were not invited to community weddings because having homosexuals present undermined the sanctity of the heterosexual married bond. He even identified a moment where his uncle told him that "being gay is like punching The Lord straight in the face. Just because you *can* do it, does it mean you *should*."

As Jerrod progressed into middle adolescence, he sought to individuate by adapting different coping styles that appeared more socially-sanctioned or were more viable alternatives than coming out as queer. In his description of these attempts to integrate, I began to recognize a very similar coping style to those I observed in bereaved adolescent siblings many years before when I worked in pediatric oncology.

In 2011, I submitted my doctoral dissertation exploring the impact of bereavement on grieving teen siblings and suggested that during such a vulnerable time, when teens are seeking ways to safely individuate from their families of origin, the experience of loss may present a true crisis that causes them to cope in patterns that were validated both by my exploration of the limited research on the topic, as well as my clinical practice experience. I created and described, via case study, different coping styles that, if left without intervention, placed the adolescent at risk for adopting an identity that was rooted in these mechanisms (Goldblatt Hyatt, 2011). I published a self-help book on the topic (Goldblatt Hyatt, 2015). As my clinical encounters with grieving teens progressed, I came to appreciate, most of all, their resilience and how they "tried on" different identities as they coped, reflecting the true flexibility and curiosity that are hallmarks of adolescence. Moving beyond the assertions in my dissertation that argued for coping styles existing on a spectrum, I suggested in a later publication that, in accordance with the social studies of childhood approach, it is not uncommon for bereaved teen siblings to engage in a more fluid process whereby, depending on the context, relationship, and other psychosocial factors, bereaved teen siblings may display different coping styles in different moments reflective of Balk's (2014) concept of ecological niches. Balk (2014) essentially asserted that *who* a teen is in any given moment is reflective of multiple variables with whom the individual interacts, experiences support, and responds.

Jerrod experienced the onset of his homosexuality as a traumatic loss. It reflected the loss of the values, norms, and spiritual teachings of ministers that provided structural support, comfort, concrete direction, and answers for as long as he remembered. He experienced the anticipatory grief of his community's rejection as well as loss related to how he had previously envisioned his life progressing. In an attempt to cope, he displayed the following styles I originally identified in grieving teen siblings:

1. **Hyper-Maturity**. My research on grieving teen siblings suggested that some coped with loss by attempting to grow up too fast, too soon. This phenomenon, coined by Balk (2009), identified that in the aftermath of grief, teenagers may redefine their roles and relationships. This was especially true for teens whose parents were unavailable to support them due to their own feelings of loss (Balk, 2009). During early childhood, Jerrod's father walked out, leaving his mother to care for Jerrod and his brother, who was a newborn. As Jerrod began to identify as queer, his mother was absent attempting to parent his younger brother, who had begun to display some behavioral challenges. Jerrod acknowledged his feelings of anger toward his father, with whom he no longer had a relationship, in multiple sessions. However, he harbored not only resentment for his mother for her absence but also some ambivalence at causing her more distress by being queer. In my prior work, I identified that hyper-mature bereaved siblings coped by attempting to assume aspects of leadership in their lives and communities, in order to protect their parents from further grief. So, too, did Jerrod want to prevent his mother from experiencing further grief by his coming out. He described his initial attempts to cope with the loss by becoming "even smarter, even better, than before." This was an extension of the personality Jerrod had initially established for himself as he grew up in the community, as an engaged, committed boy who sought to learn from mentors like ministers and respected community members. Jerrod informed that he exaggerated this identity by throwing himself into community organizing, taking on several extra credits-worth of work at the College, and interning with a local minister. He told me,

   > I just want to be a grownup already. They know what they're doing, and why they're doing it. They know who they are. I tried to be like the grownups I respected as a kid, and most of those were ministers.

2. **Replicating**. The experience of loss may trigger an identity crisis in adolescents who seek to define and redefine themselves according to their relationships with others (Shipkey, 2008). In earlier work I noted that some grieving teens responded to this by attempting to become more like the sibling who died, replicating their roles, hobbies, and friendships. This provided a sense of predictability and stability. Jerrod, in his loss, found a way to cope by replicating pieces of the identities of friends whom appeared to him as heterosexual, self-confident, and in control.

There was a boy in his class, Jake, whom Jerrod in particular sought to emulate. Jake was an athlete and always provided his opinions in religion class, even if these were controversial. Jerrod had always deferred to the authority of ministers in his life, but after beginning his queer journey, he began to "try on" aspects of Jake, getting more involved in sports, hanging out with athletes, and moving to the back of the religion class beside him, instead of his usual position in the front. He recalled more frequently raising his hand to critique the instructor and offer devil's advocate viewpoints. In maintaining a closer proximity to Jake, Jerrod felt a sense of predictability and stability in his life. He was able to push questions about his sexual orientation aside by associating with Jake and his crew. He confided,

> I always loved acting and the theater, and I really tried to be like Jake as if he were a character in a play. Becoming Jake felt like such a relief from my own crazy head sometimes. The only problem was that sometimes it was hard to stop being Jake. Sometimes I got so caught up in how people looked at me and treated me that I wanted to hide inside myself, like who I was wasn't enough.

True to the patterns I found in replicating bereaved teen siblings, Jerrod strived to become an identity he couldn't possibly fulfill.

3. **Prematurely Individuated**. A third pattern I noticed in bereaved teen siblings that once again extended to Jerrod was an increased sense of introspection, feeling different or marked by loss, and isolation from friend groups. While siblings who have experienced death are reacting to a concrete loss that friends and family know about, Jerrod was responding to the internal loss created by the conflict between his sexual and religious identity. Like some of the teens I worked with, he threw himself into risk-taking activities to create a sense of belonging, such as indulgence in drugs, alcohol, and risky sex. While testing limits and engaging in risky behaviors are not uncommon in adolescence, Jerrod's engagement with these was founded rooted in an attempt to numb his sense of internal loss. At times, Jerrod spent days away from home in the nearby city, drinking all night long and sleeping with strangers, but he never felt fulfilled. He did not enjoy his journeys into the city, but he also felt compelled to leave our community in order to achieve sexual gratification, which ultimately felt hollow, temporary, and increased his anxiety over contracting HIV. He told me that he wished he could find a boyfriend in our community, but this felt impossible.
4. **Resilient**. Nearly all of the teens I worked with, in the long term, achieved resilient coping and identity synthesis as they experimented with different coping styles, engaged in therapy, and found a good fit for themselves. Indeed, when grieving teen siblings experienced protective factors in the

form of mentorship, peer acceptance, skills of tenacity, and family support, they thrived. Certainly, research has reflected this (Collins et al., 2010). Jerrod possessed many protective factors including high academic achievement and opportunities for educational advancement, and skills of responsibility and persistence. However, he also lived a part of a family in crisis with a mother unable to provide support, a sense of internalized homophobia that was reinforced by the community and religious teachings, and increasing isolation. One of my main goals in therapy was to provide support and validation for him as he struggled to explore and accept himself, in the hope that he, too, would achieve resilience.

Course of Therapy

My work with Jerrod was multifaceted, and included elements of the interventions I utilized with bereaved teen siblings, such as cognitive-behavioral, narrative, and existential therapy. However, while the research on religious and sexual identity conflict is expanding, there is little practical assistance available for clinicians looking for therapeutic interventions to assist this group (Etengoff & Daiute, 2014). Thankfully, I located a useful model by conducting an extensive literature review. This model created a useful guide and structural base for the above therapeutic approaches. Entitled the GRACE model (Bozard & Sanders, 2011), the intervention seeks to empower Christian clients to learn how to reclaim religion in order to cope with perceived conflict between religious and sexual identity.

The GRACE model stands for Goal, Renewal, Action, Connection, and Empowerment. I will frame the discussion of my work with Jerrod within the phases of the model, providing detail within each section.

Goals

The first phase of the GRACE model involves an examination of an individual's goals, which consists of assessing religious history, religious and spiritual experiences, and the emotional attachment to these as well as client readiness for therapy (Bozard & Sanders, 2011). Jerrod disclosed that he loved our community because he was born and raised there, and had always felt a close connection with the religious teachings until he began to identify as queer. Although he was increasingly traveling into the city for sexual encounters and was considering applying to graduate school there, he stated that he wished he could come out as gay and not face the consequences of being gay in the community, as well as the fallout on his mother and younger brother. He also knew that he could not deny his homosexuality and was searching to find acceptance within himself. He struggled with living in the closet, knowing what being gay meant in the community, living "with the devil you know," versus coming out and facing the unknown response. I had a thorough understanding of Jerrod's religious history and wanted to honor the pieces of the tradition that he remained attached to, such as the idea of a loving God, while trying to gently battle the internalized homophobia created not by the religious texts he grew up with, but the community's interpretation and dissemination of these. We also set a goal for self-care that included daily affirmations, mindfulness, and elements of CBT for suicide prevention (Stanley et al., 2009) that incorporates coping cards to provide useful cues for other ways to express self-injurious urges.

Renewal

This refers to renewal of hope, in which a client begins to ponder how to integrate both religious and queer identities (Bozard & Sanders, 2011). Renewal includes encouraging the client to even consider different interpretations of scripture that might maintain a connection with religion. At this point, I utilized narrative therapy with Jerrod to narrate his experiences within his faith tradition and focus on describing moments of inclusion, feeling connected to a higher power, and imagining a future for himself where he could continue to feel connected to a higher power. We spent many sessions discussing the differences between being spiritual or religious, and Jerrod's interpretation of spirituality was one in which he lived a life practicing his individual interpretation of religion without a house of worship and maintained a more individual connection to God. Since group worship was central to Jerrod's upbringing, he was uncomfortable with the idea of individual spirituality and longed for the comfort and ritual of institutionalized religion. However, he also struggled with the conservative approach to homosexuality rooted in homophobia that defined many sermons, Sunday school, and other religion-infused classes that he was required to take at the local elementary, middle, high schools, and college. We made much use of CBT approaches to reframe distortions such as catastrophizing, which he frequently engaged in. We roleplayed how he might come out to his mother and close friends, allowing him to experience anxiety but also waves of relief in just getting the words "I'm gay" out of his head and out of his mouth. In just speaking these words, he was able to experience relief, and not fear. Speaking the words aloud empowered him, and we began to create a list of friends and community members that he felt he might want to come out to first. Notably, the very people he held in high esteem, some of the ministers he had known since childhood, were actually those he wanted to talk to first, because he wanted to explore if they could extend God's love to him. He began to feel empowered to challenge them about their message of shunning homosexuality in favor of heterosexual unions while all the while claiming that God loved all of His children universally. He also began to focus on the Christian concept of forgiveness, working to forgive both himself and the people within our community who might not be as compassionate toward him as he would have hoped. We discussed his relationship with and connection to Jesus, whom he felt would embrace him no matter his sexual orientation, because Jerrod was, at his core, a kind and loving person. Though he was raised in a religion with fundamentalist cognitive messages that promoted black and white, all or nothing approaches to living a "good life," he also recognized that one tenet of his religious upbringing remained important, and that was service. Being altruistic and helping others, both as Jesus did but also as Jerrod was taught, created a sense of longitudinal connection between Jerrod, the Church, and Jesus. Whereas he initially imagined himself as withdrawing from the community once he came out, Jerrod began to imagine himself maintaining an investment in community organizing, leading trips to soup kitchens, and connecting college kids and community members. As his perspective began to grow, Jerrod began to appreciate the many shades of grey involved in living life as a gay Christian man.

Action

The first two phases focused on discussion, preparation, and challenging irrational thoughts occurring inside of Jerrod, while promoting self-care and better coping strategies to cultivate a healthier self. The action phase consists of a time when individuals decide whether to remain in their religion, renew their affiliation, or create new opportunities for spiritual engagement (Bozard & Sanders, 2011). For Jerrod, taking action involved planning out and exploring how he wanted to move forward with coming out in the community, and also seeking additional resources to support him. I arranged for him to meet with a psychiatrist, as we were both concerned about his depression and ideation of self-harm. The psychiatrist prescribed a mood stabilizer that Jerrod felt was helpful. Grateful that we live near a large city, we were able to locate a regional support group for queer religious youth at the local Unitarian Universalist (U.U) Church. The U.U. faith promotes itself as open-minded, focused on social justice and equality, and welcoming of diversity (Unitarian Universalist Association, 2019). Even further, some denominations of the U.U. include a "Welcoming Congregations Program," into which queer people are invited and honored. Jerrod began to attend meetings and experience peer support from individuals across other mostly conservative religious backgrounds at different stages of coming out. He was comfortable traveling away from our community to participate in this group, but eventually began to feel empowered as his peers validated and honored his own coming out process, and he began feeling a *connection* with others like him, which is the next component of the GRACE model. We soon began to make a concrete plan for coming out.

Connection

The purpose of connection is to help clients feel a connection with God, as well as community (Bozard & Sanders, 2011). I believe Jerrod's sense of connection began with the therapeutic relationship. Similar to conclusions by Goodrich, Buser, Luke, and Buser (2016) that explored queer clients' perspectives of counseling, therapy was helpful for Jerrod as it promoted self-acceptance as well as an identification with me, his counselor, within a supportive environment. Furthermore, because I was familiar with and lived in the same environment as Jerrod, we shared a common language and recognition of his experiences within the community, preparing for many of them to see his religious and spiritual identities as irreconcilable and could lead to increased feelings of isolation and disenfranchisement (Lomash, Brown, & Galupo, 2018). With a connection between us established, we were able to work closely on connecting him first with complete outsiders in the U.U. peer support group that honored his experience, and then within the community. Jerrod never wavered in his connection with God, though he did question why he was enduring such great suffering. He was comforted by reminding himself that God, too, grieved with him and loved him unconditionally. He began to recognize automatic irrational thoughts focused on eternal punishment or feeling doomed because of his sexuality. The core tenet he was raised with, that "God is Love," sustained him.

Coming out in the community was tricky, but he began by first telling a few childhood friends, who were unconditionally supportive. After a few months of therapy, he began to tell them about his self-harm but not the reasons behind it, though a few had their suspicions. He then disclosed his homosexuality to his mother, who was disappointed. She wondered if his father's leaving the family had caused him to search for love and acceptance in other father figures, and asked him if he might want to try conversion therapies or attempt on his own to shun his feelings. His uncle sent some emails condemning his "behavior" and he brought these to therapy to discuss whether he wanted to respond to these. We spent time processing his deep hurt over his mother's rejection of his sexual orientation, and he talked about potentially moving out of her house as their relationship became strained. He also explored his feelings in the U.U. support group. Jerrod began to feel the urge to self-harm, and we worked on stabilization and refocusing on the support he was receiving from his friends and the U.U. group as well as roleplaying where he had the chance to respond to a pretend version of his uncle. We also brought his mother in for some family sessions, though it was clear she would need a great deal of time, and her own therapy, to face Jerrod's truth with an open mind.

Jerrod decided to move into an apartment with a friend and, a few months after coming out to his mother, wrote an open letter to the community about his sexual orientation on social media. He initially hoped to talk to a few ministers in the community about being gay but experienced a few false starts due to anxiety and fear, so he reconsidered, and we discussed other ways he might want to proceed. He insisted that he no longer wanted to hide his sexuality and wanted to stay in the community, but wanted, most of all, to "be myself." It was apparent that he was truly coming into his own identity, creating goals that were based on his own self and needs without feeling the need to jump across coping strategies as he had in the past. However, he maintained the confidence he learned by emulating Jake in religious class, and felt more prepared to respond to comments or critique on social media than face-to-face, now that he had told significant others that he was gay. We imagined possible responses and roleplayed how he would respond. After he posted the letter, Jerrod felt an enormous sense of *empowerment.*

Empowerment

In the empowerment phase, clients experience success as they work toward their goals (Bozard & Sanders, 2011). Similar to what Bozard and Sanders (2011) propose, despite the experience of some resistance to his coming out, Jerrod was buoyed by the progress he had made and the outpouring of support toward him after posting his letter, which was more plentiful than he had imagined. The letter stimulated lively debates across social media and conversations that may have been harder to have in person. Behind computer screens, community members across ages groups and levels of conservatism joined the debate and engaged in a dialogue that Jerrod began. He was able to express his fear and sadness over the community not being a welcoming place for queer people, and even challenge some ministers who maintained that being gay is a sin. Though he did not change everybody's mind, Jerrod created a conversation and different discussion threads about the experience of being queer popped up so frequently that eventually the community started a social media page for the church and queer alliance. Jerrod was a familiar face in the community, and his story was passed across church members and kids at the high school and college, including a few who were struggling with their own sexual orientations that sought him for advice. At this time, we worked on creating and maintaining appropriate boundaries for him to provide mentorship and guidance while also maintaining mindfulness of his experience working through his newly "out" status. After the initial rush of support and euphoria of coming out, we planned on facing microaggressions and how to cope with subtle elements of discrimination in church, at community events, and other social events where he might encounter more conservative, less open-minded individuals. We continued to work together to explore ways that Jerrod could maintain his individuality and feel welcomed to the extent the community could support him, and ensure that he had appropriate resources on the outside, too.

Jerrod continued to go to church and participate in religious activities, though he frequently became depressed when he felt less than welcomed. He tried to remind himself that he was on a journey of discovery that was pushing both his own conception of self as well as the identity of the community in new directions, and he believed that the change happening was for the better.

Discussion

Jerrod's case represents a composite of the adolescents I have worked with in our conservative religious community who have struggled with coming out and disclosing their queer identities. It should be noted that there was an inordinate amount of pressure on Jerrod as the first young person not only to come out, but to continue residing in a community where so many members followed homonegative interpretations of religious scripture. While Jerrod was held as an example and symbol of hope for other queer adolescents in the community, not everyone has followed the same path, and each have faced discrimination in numerous social venues that caused some to move out or choose other spiritual traditions or religions that are more open-minded. Jerrod's resilience was somewhat rooted in his temperament and true connection to our community through his overwhelming engagement across his childhood.

The intersection of Jerrod's sexual and religious identity mirrors Ginicola and Smith's (2011) fusion of Cass (1979) and Fowler's (1981) models: he was able to achieve identity synthesis as he began to find community with similar peers, internalize the meaning of religious scripture, and move toward self-acceptance. According to Cass (1984), an individual can move through the model through first applying the label of queerness to oneself and develop positive feels about it, a desire to come out to both queer and straight significant others, and maintaining more and more contact with other queer individuals. Jerrod followed this path while also progressing through stages of faith that allowed him to move from blindly accepting the teachings interpreted by others to truly applying them to himself and his own life. In this way, he was able to achieve empowerment and pride and eschew former conceptions of homosexuality as sinful. This allowed him to develop a synthesized and coherent identity, whereas before he experimented with different coping styles across hyper-maturity, replicating, and prematurely individuated. Some of these circumstances allowed him to feel strength and develop skills to help him cope with his journey, while others put him at risk for further psychological and physical injury. The process of therapy provided a safe space to encourage self-acceptance and the adoption of healthy coping mechanisms on his journey to identity.

Key to Jerrod's success was maintaining connection with the elements of his religion that provided avenues for self-love, acceptance, communing with God and Jesus, and service work. Jerrod reflected elements of the above-mentioned studies on queer Mormon youth who struggled with enjoying and engaging in their communities from an early age, but ultimately felt disenfranchised due to their sexual orientation. I do believe that while our community is fairly conservative, there are elements of progressive attitudes scattered across the town that do provide the opportunity for flexibility and tolerance, whereas Mormon communities may not.

Limitations

Jerrod's case is not meant to be generalized to entire populations of queer youth maturing in conservative Christian environments; it is representative of a specific context that may provide mirroring details when compared across other religious and spiritual communities. Certainly, there must exist other coping styles in response to loss that I have not identified, particularly among minority youth and those from nontraditional household environments, as my research on grieving teen siblings explored youth from white, mostly Christian, two-parent households. It is essential to note that Jerrod had also experienced the loss of his father by leaving the family: this was the earliest tangible loss he could remember, and it undoubtedly affected his identity and coping too. A perspective of intersectionality must be emphasized in which the multiple elements of any client's life story are honored in the creation of identity, from race, socio-economic status, experiences of privilege, and more. This case study could, in fact, be expanded into a dissertation or multiple articles exploring the influence of these numerous factors on Jerrod's experience of loss in his community and how these affected coping. Nonetheless, I am hoping that this case study provides some insight and examples of how teens like Jerrod may cope with their queerness in a community that does not condone it, and how applying the GRACE model may be helpful.

Conclusion

Queer adolescents raised in conservative Christian environments may experience the onset of LGBTQIA+ sexual or gender orientation as a traumatic loss due to the potential rejection of community and parental support upon identifying as gay and considering coming out. Interestingly, my exposure to the heteronormative trauma of grieving adolescent siblings caused me to identify a similar coping style among queer youth experiencing the traumatic loss of future heterosexual identity and community, as well as family, support. The anticipation and internalization of this loss may cause such youth to assume or "try on" different identity orientations in order to cope.

How might social work clinicians address such examples of queer sexual trauma and loss? With the goal of promoting identity synthesis and resilience, the GRACE model may provide a useful framework within which clinicians can support the individu and empowerment of queer teens to assist them as they navigate the complex conflict between their religious and sexual or gender identities.

Close Reading Questions

1. How does Jerrod maintain his connection to religion? How does his connection to religion relate to the title of this chapter: "The Devil You Know"?
2. Summarize the GRACE model of treatment. What key elements of GRACE can you take away from this case study?
3. Define hypermaturity, replicating, premature individuation, and resilience in your own words. Pick an example of one of these terms from Goldblatt Hyatt's case study and offer your commentary.

Prompts for Writing

1. What would you tell a client who reported that "being gay is like punching The Lord straight in the face. Just because you *can* do it, does it mean you *should*."
2. Goldblatt Hyatt argues that the process of Jerrod's individuation relates to the experience of bereavement. Why do you think she is motivated to make this connection? What evidence can you cite from the case study to support your answer?
3. Many case studies in this volume address the intersection of religion and queer identity. Pick one or more and write out how you could (or could not) connect the other chapter(s) to Goldblatt Hyatt's chapter.

References

Balk, D. E. (2009). Sibling bereavement during adolescence. In D. Balk & C. A. Corr (Eds.), *Adolescent encounters with death, bereavement, and coping* (pp. 199–214). New York, NY: Springer.

Balk, D. E. (2014). *Dealing with death, dying, and grief during adolescence.* New York, NY: Routledge.

Bozard, Jr., R. L., & Sanders, C. J. (2011). Helping Christian lesbian, gay, and bisexual clients recover religion as a source of strength: Developing a model for assessment and integration of religious identity in counseling. *Journal of LGBT Issues in Counseling, 5*(11), 47–74.

Cass, V. C. (1979). Homosexual identity formation: A theoretical model. *Journal of Homosexuality,* 7(3), 219–235.

Cass, V. C. (1984). Homosexual identity formation: Testing a theoretical model. *The Journal of Sex Research, 20*(2), 143–167.

Collins, K., Connors, K., Donohue, A., Gardner, E., Goldblatt, E., Hayward, A., … Thompson, E. (2010). *Understanding the impact of trauma and urban poverty on family systems: Risk, resilience, and interventions.* Baltimore: University of Maryland.

Dehlin, J. P., Galliher, R. V., Bradshaw, W. S., & Cromwell, K. A. (2014). Psychosocial correlates of religious approaches to same-sex attraction: A Mormon perspective. *Journal of Gay and Lesbian Mental Health, 18*, 284–311.

Dehlin, J. P., Galliher, R. V., Bradshaw, W. S., & Cromwell, K. A. (2015). Navigating sexual and religious identity conflict: A Mormon perspective. *Identity, 15*(1), 1–22.

Dahl, A. L., & Galliher, R. V. (2009). LGBTQ young adult experiences of religious and sexual identity integration. *Journal of LGBT Issues in Counseling, 3*(2), 92–112.

Dahl, A. L., & Galliher, R. V. (2010). Sexual minority young adult religiosity, sexual orientation conflict, self-esteem, and depressive symptoms. *Journal of Gay and Lesbian Mental Health, 14*(4), 271–290.

Dahl, A. L., & Galliher, R. V. (2012a). LGBTQ adolescents and young adults raised within a Christian religious context: Positive and negative outcomes. *Journal of Adolescence, 35*(6), 1611–1618.

Dahl, A. L., & Galliher, R. V. (2012b). The interplay of sexual and religious identity development in LGBTQ adolescents and young adults: A qualitative inquiry. *Identity: An International Journal of Theory and Research, 12*(3), 217–246.

Erikson, E. (1964). *Identity, youth, and crisis*. New York, NY: Norton.

Etengoff, C., & Daiute, C. (2014). Clinicians' perspective of the relational processes for family and individual development during the mediation of religious and sexual identity disclosure. *Journal of Homosexuality, 62*(3), 394–426.

Fowler, James W. (1981). *Stages of faith*. New York: Harper and Row.

Ginicola, M. M., & Smith, C. (2011). The church, the closet, and the couch: The counselor's role in assisting clients to integrate their sexual orientation and religious identity. *Journal of LGBT Issues in Counseling, 5*, 304–326.

Goldblatt Hyatt, E. D. (2020). The outsider-insider perspective. In B. Counselman & A. Redcay (Eds.), *Working with grief and traumatic loss: Theory, practice, personal self-care and reflection for clinicians*. San Diego, CA: Cognella.

Goldblatt Hyatt, E. D. (2020). Shifting identities, shifting meanings: Adolescent siblings and grief. In M. Diaz & B. Shepherd (Eds.), *Narrating practice with children and adolescents*. New York, NY: Columbia University Press.

Goldblatt Hyatt, E. D. (2011). *Development in crisis: Adolescent sibling bereavement* (Doctorate in Social Work (DSW) Dissertations, 11). University of Pennsylvania School of Social Policy and Practice, Philadelphia, PA. Retrieved from https://repository.upenn.edu/edissertations_sp2/11

Goldblatt Hyatt, E. D. (2015). *Grieving for the sibling you lost: The teen's guide to coping with grief and finding meaning after loss*. Oakland, CA: Instant Help Solutions (New Harbinger Publications).

Goodrich, K. M., Buser, J. K., Luke, M., & Buser, T. J. (2016). Spiritual and sexual identity: Exploring lesbian, gay, and bisexual clients' perspectives of counseling. *Journal of Homosexuality, 63*(6), 783–807.

Graham, M. (2011). Changing paradigms and conditions of childhood: Implications for the social professions and social work. *British Journal of Social Work, 41*, 1532–1547.

Lomash, E. F., Brown, T. B., & Galupo, M. P. (2018). "A whole bunch of live the sinner hate the sin": LGBTQ microaggressions experienced in religious and spiritual context. *Journal of Homosexuality, 66*(10), 1–17.

Shipkey, N. (2008). *Impact of sibling death on older adolescents* (Dissertation Abstracts International). AAT 3320524.

Stanley, B., Brown, G., Brent, D., Wells, K., Poling, K., Curry, J., … Hughes, J. (2009). Cognitive-behavioral therapy for suicide prevention (CBT-SP): Treatment model, feasibility, and acceptability. *Journal of the American Academy of Child & Adolescent Psychiatry, 48*(10), 1005–1013.

Unitarian Universalist Association. (2019). *We welcome people with many beliefs*. Retrieved March 28th, 2019 from https://www.uua.org/beliefs/what-we-believe/beliefs

Wood, A. W., & Conley, A. H. (2013). Loss of religious or spiritual identities among the LGBT population. *Counseling and Values, 59*(1), 95–111.

3

WHOSE STORY IS IT, ANYWAY?

Supporting Sexual and Gender Minority Asylum Seekers in the Preparation of Their Trauma Narratives

Sarilee Kahn and Edward J. Alessi

Pre-Reading Questions

1. What is your conception of a Sexual and Gender Minority Asylum Seeker (SGMAS)? What experiences do you imagine a SGMAS might endure? For example, what is "corrective rape"?
2. How would you define the terms complex trauma and retraumatization?
3. What do you think of when you think of testimony? Have you ever testified before?

Arman* sat in the chair in the clinician's office, his gaze toward his feet. Dressed in a dark blue suit and tie, his breath was shallow and his face was devoid of visible emotion. Arman recalled how frustrated his attorney was with his "unwillingness" to reveal the details of traumatic events related to his sexual orientation, which occurred in his country of origin. The attorney was also, according to Arman, tired of pushing him to discuss his same-sex sexual experiences. However, both were necessary to present his sexual orientation-based asylum claim in immigration court. As a result, Arman—a 26-year-old man identifying as gay—was sent to a mental health professional to help with the task of writing his story of persecution. Afraid of disclosing the truth, and also afraid of not disclosing it, Arman sat in silence, waiting to see what the clinician would do or say.

* The name of this patient was changed for purposes of confidentiality.

The case of Arman exemplifies the lived experiences of sexual and gender minority (SGM) individuals we have met in our work. Typically, they come from countries where expressions of non-conforming sexual orientations and/or gender identities may not be protected under the law, or may be, in fact, against the law. Persecution in the absence of state protection may lead some SGM individuals to leave their countries of origin to seek protection in countries such as the United States or Canada. Once in the host country, they may petition for legal protection under asylum law; however, doing so can be extremely challenging and may seriously impact SGM asylum seekers' emotional and psychological well-being. The primary component of proof is a detailed statement that describes the persecution, and, thus, traumatic events, that they suffered in their countries of origin. For asylum seekers like Arman, the act of telling the story may be fraught with complexities not well understood by immigration attorneys who represent them or asylum adjudicators charged with deciding their fate.

Social workers, with our unique perspective of conceptualizing individuals' psychosocial difficulties and strengths within an environment of intersecting systems, may be called upon to intervene. This is usually no easy task. So, how does a social worker serving SGM asylum seekers (SGMAS) facilitate the client's recounting of traumatic stories from childhood onwards, particularly when these stories are likely to involve multiple episodes of physical, emotional, and/or sexual abuse? And how does the social worker align with a trauma-informed approach while also upholding the ethics of social work practice—honoring client empowerment, moving at the client's own pace—when the immigration system demands that SGMAS discuss traumatic events and disclose their sexual and/or gender minority identity? Building upon our proposed framework for clinical practice with SGMAS (Alessi & Kahn, 2017), in this chapter we focus on assisting SGMAS with the construction of the persecution narrative in preparation for their asylum hearings. We illustrate how to do so with the inclusion of a case study. Finally, we close with recommendations for future clinical research to facilitate support for SGMAS. First, however, we provide readers with a brief overview of the scope of violence against SGM individuals and a primer on relevant refugee law.

Scope of the Problem: Violence Against Sexual and Gender Minorities

At present, 75 countries criminalize consensual same-sex sexual activity and relationships; of these, six countries (Iran, Mauritania, Saudi Arabia, Sudan, Yemen, and Iraq) and parts of two others (northern Nigeria and southern Somalia) invoke the death penalty for same-sex sexual behaviors (Carroll, 2016). SGMAS have reported a wide range of persecution, including physical and psychological abuse, extortion, shunning, assault, forced heterosexual marriage, forced participation in conversion therapy, and so-called "corrective" rape (Hopkinson et al., 2017; Shidlo & Ahola, 2013). Berg and Millbank (2009) found a significant level of sexual assaults reports in SGMAS claims in Canada and Australia. In our own research, we have found that it is common for SGMAS to report sexual trauma (Kahn & Alessi, 2018).

Families, community members, clergy, and state actors may perpetrate these acts of violence, and in countries with limited or no legal protections for SGM individuals, such victimization often occurs with impunity (Alessi, Kahn, & Chatterji, 2016; Alessi, Kahn, & Van Der Horn, 2017; Office of the United Nations High Commissioner for Human Rights, 2015). While SGM individuals also encounter violence in, for example, the United States and Canada, those living in countries where rights for SGM people are limited or non-existent usually cannot rely on others for assistance or support. Moreover, attempts to seek help from family members or police may lead to further victimization, forcing SGM individuals to flee their countries of origin to seek protection in host countries (Alessi, Kahn, Wooner, & Van Der Horn, in press).

According to the *Refugee Convention* of 1951 (United Nations), in order to be granted asylum, which is the right to protection and citizenship in a country of refuge, claimants must prove a "well-founded fear of persecution" in their country of origin due to (i) race, (ii) religion, (iii) nationality, (iv) political opinion, or (v) membership in a particular social group. Typically, this fear is based on a past record of persecution due to one of these areas. Of these five areas, membership in a particular social group is currently the basis of claims for SGM individuals fleeing homophobic and transphobic persecution (Musalo, Moore, & Boswell, 2011). To gain asylum in a host country, SGMAS must not only prove a well-founded fear of persecution, they must also prove: (i) that this fear is based on their membership in a sexual or gender minority group, and (ii) that they are, in fact, members of that group (LaViolette, 2009). Asylum claims may be heard by a representative of UNHCR in a country of transit, such as Turkey, a common gateway to European Union countries, the United States, or Canada. Alternatively, the petitioner may appear before an asylum adjudicator within the host country.[1]

Mental Health Impacts of Violence Against Sexual and Gender Minorities

What we know from our own research and that of others is that by the time SGMAS reach the host country, they may be suffering from an array of mental health symptoms associated with long histories of abuse and social marginalization. These experiences may contribute to symptoms of depression, anxiety, posttraumatic stress disorder (PTSD), and complex trauma syndromes (Alessi et al., 2016; Shidlo & Ahola, 2013). More specifically, complex trauma syndromes may result when individuals are exposed to prolonged, repeated traumatic events, particularly situations of interpersonal violence where the balance of power rests disproportionately with the perpetrator. This is the situation, for example, in cases of child abuse, state-sponsored or state-sanctioned violence, and other instances where escape may not be possible (Courtois & Ford, 2012; Herman, 1997; van der Kolk, Roth, Pelcovitz, Sunday, & Spinazzola, 2005). Individuals affected by complex PTSD typically manifest the symptoms of PTSD, according to the diagnosis in the fifth edition of the *Diagnostic and Statistical Manual of Mental Disorders* (American Psychiatric Association, 2013), plus an array of additional symptoms, including (a) severe emotional dysregulation, (b) marked impairment in interpersonal relationships, (c) severe dissociation, (d) chronic impulsivity and suicidality, and (e) high levels of somatization (Cloitre, Koenen, Cohen, & Han, 2002). It is well established that people with complex trauma syndromes, as well as those with PTSD, may re-experience the feelings and sensations associated with past traumatic events when forced to remember them in the present (Cloitre et al., 2009; Courtois & Ford, 2012; Herman, 1997; McCann & Pearlman, 1990). As shown by Bögner, Herlihy, and Brewin (2007), this is a particular risk for these individuals when disclosing their history of sexual violence.

The Implications of Asylum Seeking Processes for SGM Petitioners

The risk of re-traumatization is particularly salient for asylum petitioners. While negative psychological reactions may be mitigated when individuals feel that they have control over their trauma stories and who hears them (Tener & Murphy, 2015), asylum seekers frequently have no such choice or agency. Instead, they must perform according to the standards and the timelines of the immigration regulations of the host country. In the United States, for example, asylum petitioners have one year to construct and submit the persecution narrative; in Canada, that timeline can be as short as 30–60 days. Failure to present a coherent, detailed, and credible narrative may result in an asylum denial, followed by deportation to the country of origin where the individual may be placed at risk of re-victimization (Einhorn & Berthold, 2014; Johnston, Allotey, Mulholland, & Markovic, 2009). Berg and Millbank (2009) found a significant level of sexual assaults reported in SGM asylum claims in Canada and Australia. In our own research, we have found that it is common for SGMAS to report sexual trauma (Kahn & Alessi, 2018). Although it is well established that disclosure of sexual trauma requires sensitivity and support (Johnston et al., 2009), it has not been widely discussed in the literature with respect to SGMAS (Kahn & Alessi, 2018).

In addition to reconstructing the trauma narrative to prove "well-founded fear of persecution" based upon past events, SGMAS must prove that they are members of a sexual or gender minority group. This presents the second major hurdle for those seeking protection in a foreign land. In our previous research (see Alessi et al., 2017), we found that SGMAS have often been conditioned to hide all aspects of their identities in order to survive. Ironically, when filing an asylum claim, petitioners may be forced to come out, or, as Kenji Yoshino (2007) suggests, to "reverse cover" and perform according to Western notions of lesbian, gay, bisexual, transgender, or queer (LGBTQ) identities. While this may be liberating for some SGMAS, for others it can feel imposed and thus burdensome (Kahn & Alessi, 2018). Furthermore, reverse covering is usually happening at the same time that SGMAS are exposing the most intimate details of their sexual to lawyers, adjudicators and other strangers, who may not even speak the same language. In our research, lawyers representing SGM asylum seekers admitted that, in order to help their SGM asylum seeker-clients win their cases, they put pressure on their clients to talk and write about their feelings of sexual attraction and expose graphic descriptions of same-sex sexual encounters (see Kahn & Alessi, 2018). Others admitted that they encouraged their clients to attend Pride Parades and local LGBTQ community events, as well as document their attendance at these events using photographs and social media, because the immigration adjudicators would want to see evidence of such affiliation. This advice was given to SGMAS, even though some were reluctant to come out publicly (Kahn & Alessi, 2018). We also found that coerced coming out during asylum seeking may have negative psychological consequences for some SGMAS, who may struggle to reconcile their sociocultural affiliation with the prevailing mores of the host country (Kahn & Alessi, 2018). For some SGMAS, documenting affiliation with the LGBTQ community in the host country through photographs and social media could be life-threatening, as some fear public exposure and, thus, being discovered by family and community members in their countries of origin (International Commission of Jurists, 2016).

Given that SGMAS must reveal their traumatic pasts, divulge private information about their sex lives, and disclose their sexual orientation and/or gender identity before they may be ready to do so, the remainder of this chapter discusses ways for social workers to assist SGMAS with this process so as to help them feel more in control of their situations. We believe that the Testimony Method (Agger & Jensen, 1990; Cienfuegos & Monelli, 1983) can be used with SGMA. However, before we talk about the Testimony Method, we briefly discuss a trauma-informed, affirmative practice framework that we developed for supporting SGMAS from early migration through resettlement. This framework provides foundational knowledge for addressing the array of interpersonal, intrapersonal, and structural issues at various points during the resettlement process. SGMAS may benefit most from receiving services from social workers and other mental health professionals who can understand and address their complex needs. After discussion of our framework, we discuss the Testimony Method and how it can be used with SGMAS in the midst of the claims process.

A Framework for Clinical Practice with SGMAS

Supporting SGMAS requires that the social worker be grounded in a number of conceptual, ethical, and practice orientations. In addition to skills of trauma-informed practice, the clinician must embody cultural humility and sensitivity, particularly with respect to diverse expressions of sexual orientations and gender identities. Here, an affirmative standpoint is key. This standpoint includes being aware of one's biases and unconscious agendas for clients to come out or align with a specific identity label; categories such as lesbian, gay, bisexual, or transgender may, in fact, have little relevance to clients from traditional cultures (Alessi & Kahn, 2017). For example, in Arman's cultural context, the concept of "gay" did not exist when he was growing up. People with erotic interest for the same sex were referred to in derogatory terms, such as *hamjens-bazi,* which roughly translates to "faggotry." He, like many asylum seekers, learned the term "gay" through connecting with others through the Internet.

In addition, it is important for clinicians to become familiarized with cultural issues and human rights abuses in the client's country of origin. Clinicians working in host countries should also understand the basic requirements of asylum in their country, including time limits for filing claims. Establishing a relationship with the client's immigration attorney is also important to coordinate efforts and prevent undue repetition of the trauma narrative. Further, should the client require language interpretation, it is vital to vet the interpreter not only for professional training and adherence to best practices (e.g., adhering to confidentiality and fidelity of interpretation), but also for negative attitudes toward sexual and/or gender minorities. Should the client feel that the interpreter is homophobic or transphobic, or that aspects of their lives might be shared with others in the client's diaspora community, it will be impossible to establish a safe, holding environment with the clinician. Finally, clinicians should be aware of LGBT-affirmative refugee services as well as grass-root support organizations that provide support and concrete services to SGM asylum seekers, including affirmative clergy or religious groups, housing services, and food banks. Clinicians should take a compassionate stance, employ harm reduction strategies, and maximize access to resources for SGMAS, particularly those who engage in sex work, are HIV positive, and/or are at risk of exposure to HIV. Connecting clients with such concrete services may also help strengthen the therapeutic relationship.

Below, we move on from preparation to discuss two of the three phases in our framework for clinical practice with SGMAS; the third phase is described elsewhere.[2] Phases discussed here are Establishing Safety and Stability in Treatment and in the Environment; and, Skills for Managing Asylum Claims. Following elaboration of the second phase, we expand upon it, to incorporate the Testimony Method.

Establishing Safety and Stability in Treatment and in the Environment

The first step in our framework requires clinicians to provide SGMAS with avenues for internal and external safety. Establishing safety is contingent upon creating a holding environment, which consists of a relationship with the clinician that is secure and trusting (Winnicott, 1965). For SGMAS, past relationships with those in authority may have been defined by discrimination and maltreatment; therefore, it can be difficult initially for the SGMAS to view the clinician as trustworthy (Kahn, Alessi, Kim, Olivieri, & Woolner, 2017).

The clinician welcomed Arman with a phrase from the language of his country of origin. This broke the ice when Arman laughed at her pronunciation and the clinician acknowledged her difficulties learning new languages. By risking vulnerability, the clinician modeled that Arman might be willing to be vulnerable, too. Further, it served to humanize the clinician. After introducing herself and talking a little about her background and experience supporting SGMAS in their proceedings, she asked Arman what he was told about the purpose of the meetings, and what his experiences meeting with mental health professionals, if any, had been in the past. The clinician listened to Arman closely and ensured that she conveyed a nonjudgmental stance. She also informed Arman that, although the meetings would help him write his narrative for the asylum hearing, he could talk about what he liked in their sessions and that she would answer any questions that he had about their work together.

After soliciting the client's understanding of the purpose of the sessions, and clarifying any misperceptions, clinicians may then engage their clients in a discussion about their rights to privacy and confidentiality under the laws of the host country. This may help them to feel more at ease with disclosing personal stories. Clinicians should clearly communicate that the client is in control of what to share and whether or not to share it, and that information shared with the clinician can only be exchanged with their attorney by way of signed consent forms. Once these preliminary matters are settled, clinicians can set the stage for how the sessions will unfold: that is, the first few sessions will focus on (a) assessing and stabilizing any acute psychological symptoms, including suicidality or self-harming behaviors, and (b) linking clients with resources they may need to provide for themselves (e.g. housing, food, clothing, legal representation, medical care, social support).

After doing this, the clinician works to help establish internal safety. More specifically, the clinician helps the client strengthen their capacity to tolerate strong affect.

The clinician asked whether Arman knew they would be working for the next 4 weeks to write his story of persecution for the asylum hearing. After he nodded, she asked whether Arman had told the story before, or any parts of the story; if so, what what the telling like? He responded that he had not told the story to anyone before. In fact, Arman stated, he did everything he could to avoid thinking about his past. The clinician wondered what Arman expected would happen, how he would feel when he began to tell the stories of his experiences in his country of origin. He replied that he was frightened of having a 'nervous breakdown' and 'going crazy', but he believed that it would help him to finally share the truth of what he had been through. The clinician then explored what Arman felt he needed in order to feel safe. He offered that he had a prayer he found calming and empowering. Before any story-telling began, the clinician worked with Arman to notice the earliest signs of 'going crazy' in his body and to stop the story, then to invoke the prayer at those moments to calm himself. After practicing this with relatively low-stress stories from his life, Arman felt ready to gradually discuss more distressing memories.

As described above, the clinician and SGMAS can discuss the likelihood that discussions of traumatic events during the preparation of the asylum statement may evoke disturbing memories and physical sensations, potentially including unwanted images of past events (re-experiencing), as well as negative views of the self as helpless or victimized (cognitive disturbances). The clinician should assess for these, as well as for disturbances in mood, regulation of affect, and the use of avoidance strategies, including dissociation, substance misuse, somatization, or self-harm (Briere & Spinazzola, 2005). Safety plans should be co-created with the SGMAS and, subsequently put in place, including the possibility of psychopharmacological or psychiatric evaluations, and/or the use of meditation, prayer, homeopathic remedies, and traditional healing approaches (Alessi & Kahn, 2017; Berthold et al., 2007; de Jong, 2004). Developing these strategies in partnership with SGMAS clients can help remind them of their existing capacities for coping with challenging situations.

We also note in our framework that psychoeducation and reframing is important for helping SGMAS beginning to prepare their persecution narrative. For example, clinicians may share with SGMAS that strong emotional and somatic reactions are natural responses when exposed to threatening situations, and that these feelings may reappear when remembering past psychological, physical, and sexual violence (see, e.g. Courtois & Ford, 2012). In addition to providing psychoeducation about traumatic stress, the clinician may reframe threats, persecution, and violence based upon sexual or gender non-conformity as violations of their client's human rights. Constructing their trauma story can be couched as an act of resistance, in itself, even as it fulfills the requirements of documentation (Agger et al., 2012). For SGMAS, the narrative may also serve to counter the silencing and shaming that survivors of homophobic and transphobic violence may experience (Alessi & Kahn, 2017; Dworkin & Yi, 2003). It may also be helpful to discuss the concept of minority stress (see Hendricks & Testa, 2012; Meyer, 2003) and its descriptions of internalized homophobia and transphobia. This may be useful to begin a reappraisal of cognitive schemas (Cloitre et al., 2014), wherein they may have held shame about their sexual and gender minority identities.

Arman said that in his culture, one did not exist in isolation from one's family and community. He said he "knew" his homosexuality brought shame upon his family; his older sisters would have difficulty finding a good marriage. Some of his relatives who lived in the countryside wished to kill him, to preserve the family's honor. He told the clinician that he felt he was to blame for being "sick." The clinician gently inquired about what images and words Arman recalled associated with homosexuality in his country, and children tend to believe what adults say about them, about how the world works, and who is acceptable and who is not.

Social Worker: Do you, as an adult, believe that? Do you believe you are 'sick?'

Arman: In my soul, I know that God made me the way I am, so how could I not be loved by God?

Social Worker: So, may I ask: did God tell you you were not loveable, or did people tell you that?

Arman: (deeply breathing) People told me that. Many people. But, deep down, I know that people are told by their political and religious leaders to hate homosexuals. But, he wondered, why shouldn't I have the same human rights as anyone else? What crime have I committed?

The issue of internalized shame is important to address, and may appear throughout the clinical relationship. The clinician should assess with the client the emotions expected to arise when talking about shame, past trauma and current stressors—before asking clients to disclose the details of their trauma stories. This phase of our framework involves continuing to strengthen a sense of internal safety, built through learning and practicing new skills *in vivo* and at home, and mobilizing the asylum seeker's existing positive coping strategies (Alessi & Kahn, 2017). As in the preparation phase, above, spiritual practices should be explored. Some SGMAS may associate religion with persecution, but others will find comfort in their own spiritual beliefs and practices (Kahn, 2015). Otherwise, basic relaxation and grounding techniques should be offered and practiced with the client in order to strengthen the therapeutic bond and the sense that the clinician is accompanying them through all of the steps in this challenging process (Herman, 1997).

Brief Overview of the Testimony Method

Because of its human rights framework, and its focus on bringing a narrative of violence and abuse into fruition with the support of a clinician, the Testimony Method is particularly relevant to individuals seeking asylum, including those identifying as a sexual or gender minority individual. The Testimony Method was first developed by the Chilean psychologists, Ana Julia Cienfuegos and Cristina Monelli, during the 1970s as a brief, empowering therapy designed to treat survivors of torture and politically motivated violence (Agger, Raghuvanshi, Khan, Polatin, & Laursen, 2009; Cienfuegos & Monelli, 1983). Originally seeking to address the impact of, and document, violence perpetrated by the government against political prisoners, Cienfuegos and Monelli discovered that when individuals articulated their life stories—including traumatic experiences—with the support of a clinician, their mental health seemed to improve. In the original model, survivors narrated these stories and clinicians taped and then transcribed them. After this was completed, the survivor decided what they wanted to do with the transcribed report, and whether or not to send it on to a human rights organization and/or share it with family or friends. More recently, in a randomized controlled trial with survivors of the Khmer Rouge in Cambodia, Esala and Taing (2017) found that the Testimony Method, when combined with a Buddhist ceremony and culturally adapted truth-telling event, reduced symptoms of anxiety, depression, and PTSD. The Testimony Method is also the basis of Narrative Exposure Therapy (NET), a manualized treatment protocol for reduction in PTSD and complex PTSD symptoms (Schauer, Neuner, & Elbert, 2011). NET integrates Testimony Method with Cognitive-Behavioral Therapy in order to reduce symptoms of PTSD and complex PTSD (Schauer et al., 2011). In order to help SGMAS prepare their persecution narrative while minimizing psychological distress in doing so, we choose to draw upon the original Testimony Method of Cienfuegos and Monelli (1983), as elaborated by Agger and Jensen (1990). This foundational approach proceeds through the following steps: (1) preparation of the interpreter, who, if used in developing the narrative, is educated about the Method; (2) contact/ alliance/reframe, in which the clinician reframes symptoms and offers the Testimony Method as a means to produce the statement while minimizing distress; (3) giving the testimony, where the client's narrative is audio-recorded and documented in writing by the therapist, and the therapist inquires about present and past emotions related to the story; (4) collaboration on editing and revising, in which more details may be added and further emotional work may unfold; (5) the ritual of delivery, where the client reads the document and signs it, as the therapist bearing witness; (6) the use of the testimony, if the client chooses, for advocacy, asylum claims, or teaching; (7) the potential re-engagement with the testimony at a later time, should the client wish to return to therapy (Agger & Jensen, 1990, p. 120).

The initial steps of the Testimony Method, described above, align with components of our framework that focus on preparation, and the establishment of safety. Below, we illustrate how other elements of the Testimony Method can be adapted and incorporated into our framework to support SGMAS when preparing their persecution narrative. We acknowledge that these components do not necessarily progress in a linear fashion, but are dynamic and cyclical in nature. Nonetheless, they may serve as guideposts for clinicians seeking to support SGMAS in disclosure of sexual abuse and other traumatic experiences.

Constructing the Persecution Narrative

Following from the component of reframing described above, when ready, clients will narrate pieces of the trauma story during each of several sessions until the entire testimony is complete. Here, the asylum seeker should be empowered to choose where to start, to determine what part of the story to tell next, and how to tell it. According the Testimony Method, the clinician takes notes and writes the story. We suggest that this should be discussed in partnership with the client, who may wish to write their own story. If the client agrees, the story might be audio-recorded. The parameters of confidentiality with respect to the testimony must be clarified and reiterated; that is, with the client's approval, the co-created statement will be shared with the attorneys, who will share it with immigration officials and adjudicators. The clinician should adhere to legal and ethical standards to determine what ultimately happens to the recording and the clinician's written notes, with the protocols discussed with the client in advance.

According to the Testimony Method, as the client gives testimony, the clinician periodically pauses and checks in to see how the asylum seeker is feeling emotionally. We suggest that somatic, cognitive reactions be checked as well. Should the asylum seeker become overwhelmed by somatic responses to traumatic memories, the clinician should be prepared to stop the narrative, and help them contain the affect and return to the present.

The subject of sexual abuse disclosure is not specifically addressed in the Testimony Method. Clinicians know that all traumatic memories must be approached with care, and opened only after the asylum seeker and clinician, as discussed above, have developed a good repertoire of grounding, coping, and containment strategies. Moreover, clinicians should be aware that SGMAS may not characterize unwanted or coerced sexual contact as abuse or assault (Alessi et al., 2016; Berg & Millbank, 2009; Kahn & Alessi, 2018), so discussions of sexual violence histories must help clients describe any unwanted sexual contact. Here, too, a trauma-informed approach is critical:

> The clinician acknowledged that Arman had only 6 weeks to put his story together for the attorney. However, within that time frame, she created choices for him, empowering Arman to select the stories to tell, at first. She tried not to assume what Arman considered to be the most

traumatic events, and was surprised when he mentioned that the loss of his father's love caused him the most profound pain. Further, the clinician tried not to assume that experiences she would define as sexual abuse or exploitation would be viewed that way by Arman. She asked questions such as: 'has anyone touched you in ways that you were uncomfortable with or unsure about?' 'How old were you when this touch occurred'? She sought to contextualize the situation by presenting the reality that when people are physically or sexually assaulted by family members, strangers, officials of the church, police, and so on, it can be very difficult to talk about, and difficult to understand. Sometimes people are hurt, and even hurt sexually, because they don't fit society's ideas of what a man or woman should be, or how they should act. She inquired and waited for Arman to answer each question before proceeding to the next:

SOCIAL WORKER: has something like that ever happened to you?
ARMAN: Yes.
SW: Have you ever spoken about it before now?
ARMAN: No, not til now.
SW: What is it like to be asked that question?
ARMAN: I'm afraid.
SW: Hmm. You feel afraid. What sensations are you experiencing, if any, in your body right now?
ARMAN: I feel my heart beating so fast.

The social worker then invited Arman to enlist one of the grounding techniques they had practiced, which they did together to increase the feeling of connection and accompaniment. Then, when Arman indicated he felt calm, she asked a few more questions:

SW: What piece of the story do you think you could tell right now?
ARMAN: I could tell the beginning, until he hurt me.
SW: What would you like to do with the rest of the story?
ARMAN: What do you mean?
SW: Can it be 'put' somewhere until we're ready to look at it together?
ARMAN: Oh, I see. Yes, I'd like to leave it with you in your desk until next time, and then I'll be strong enough to tell it.

Preparation for Public Disclosure

After the testimony document is completed, in the next phase, the asylum interview or hearing becomes the "delivery ritual" (Agger & Jensen, 1990, p. 120). Asylum hearings are, in essence, semi-public, quasi-judicial rituals where the asylum seeker proclaims their testimony. Here, we propose that the clinician work closely with the immigration attorney to help prepare the asylum seeker for the ritual. If successful, the offering of testimony can become an act of empowerment and resistance, or, as Agger and Jensen (1990) suggest, the "private pain has become political dignity" (p. 120). However, it must be acknowledged that the asylum adjudicator may or may not be trauma-informed, and may or may not be trained in the emerging best practices for sexual orientation and gender identity claims. Therefore, it is important that asylum seekers be prepared to have their dignity tested with difficult questions, including challenges to the manner in which they prove their membership in and SGM group (see, for example, Berg & Millbank, 2009).

During Arman's hearing, the asylum judge suggested that he had not been living an 'active' gay life in the host country, so why couldn't he just go home and live 'under the radar' there? Arman had prepared with the social worker and attorney for just such a question. He looked at the judge and said: 'Sir, I live the way I choose here. I live free here. I'm not the kind of person who will be going to the Pride Parade, or who will be saying "I'm gay and proud of it!" No. But in the country where I was born, I had no choice but to hide, from my family, my neighbors, even the police. Because if they discover the truth, I will be hurt or killed. Here, I choose to live a quiet life, a peaceful life, to make a contribution to society. I am gay, yes, but right now, I choose to be private about that. Right now, I wish to say: 'I'm a human being!'

Consolidation of Gains

Agger and Jensen (1990) suggest that the testimony ends at this point, but may be revisited after therapy has terminated. Here, we incorporate the last phase of clinical practice with clients affected by complex PTSD suggested by Courtois and Ford (2012), wherein therapeutic gains are consolidated and the focus becomes more oriented toward the future. In this case, the clinician, together with the attorneys, and their client, can celebrate the achievement of completing the asylum testimony. The entire experience can be reviewed, with areas of growth highlighted, perhaps accompanied by celebratory meal together to mark the occasion. However, this may or may not feel like a cause for celebration for the asylum applicant. While some asylum applicants may learn of the adjudicator's decision immediately following the interview or hearing, others may wait weeks, and sometimes months for an answer (Alessi, 2016). If asylum is denied, the applicant may decide to mount an appeal. Nonetheless, during this phase, the clinician can help the asylum seeker take stock of their gains, continue to practice relaxation and grounding techniques, and connect with supportive, SGM-affirmative and migrant-affirmative networks. Social support is important throughout the process and vital during periods of uncertainty. Even if the claim is successful, grief over the enormity of the losses suffered may loom large.

Arman was overjoyed to hear that his asylum application had been accepted and he was now officially welcomed to live legally in the host country. He began to cry, saying that he wished his father could have seen the day his son did amazing thing, told his story, and because of that, is now free. He realized, he said, that he will never return to the country where he was born. He will not be there when his parents are buried, or when his nieces and nephews are born. This, he told the clinician, he will have to face in the coming days, and maybe for the rest of his life. But today, he wanted to celebrate.

If asylum is granted, the celebration may be tempered not only by grief and mourning and residual mental health symptoms (Kahn, Alessi, Kim, Olivieri, & Woolner, 2018), but also by the realities of resettlement, such as mastering the language, entering training or education programs, finding a job, securing stable housing, adjusting to the culture, and establishing meaningful relationships. We address this phase in more depth in our framework for clinical practice with asylum seekers (Alessi & Kahn, 2017).

Limitations

There are a number of limitations that we must mention. Our framework for clinical practice has not been empirically tested. Thus, we cannot be certain of its effectiveness. Future research would benefit from understanding the feasibility and acceptability of our framework to provide empirical support and to ensure that it will be used by social workers and other mental health professionals to alleviate the burden of the claims process as well as resettlement. In addition, this chapter is limited by the use of a case example that focuses on a gay male. As we and others have discussed (e.g., Lewis, 2014; Millbank, 2002), lesbian women, gay men, and bisexual and transgender individuals have distinct needs that must be addressed during the asylum process. For example, it may be more difficult for a lesbian woman to prove that they were forced to engage in heterosexual marriage and that the interpersonal violence that she encountered in this marriage was related to sexual orientation (Lewis, 2014; McDonald-Norman, 2017; Millbank, 2003). Bisexual individuals also experience difficulties distinct to their identities because immigration adjudicators may believe that they can return to their countries of origin and live as a heterosexual individual or "under the radar" as a bisexual person who passes as heterosexual (Berg & Millbank, 2009). Additionally, although we present our framework as if it progresses in a linear process, we realize that this is not always the case. In real world practice, especially with SGMAS, the situation can change by the moment; thus, the social worker may be forced to engage in psychological stabilization while also attempting to help the client write their persecution story. When this is the case, social workers must still ensure that they pay close attention to the client's mental state to ensure that the process does not precipitate overwhelming anxiety, major depression, suicidality, and psychosis. Finally, while this chapter was focused on micro-level practice, we acknowledged that for structural level changes to occur, social workers and other stakeholders need to advocate so that SGMAS are better protected during the asylum process; that is, they are not forced to engage in behaviors imposed by the dominant culture's notions of how LGBTQ individuals look or act, in order to prove their identities. Recently Canada established guidelines for decision-makers in SGMAS claims to help them avoid stereotypes and biases when adjudicating cases (Immigration and Refugee Board of Canada, 2017). Although it may take time before such principles are fully integrated by decision-makers, it is, nonetheless, an important step in protecting sexual and gender minorities seeking asylum.

Conclusion

In this chapter, we offer social workers practice techniques to best help them assist SGMAS throughout the asylum claims process. In particular, we discuss the importance of preparing SGMAS to share their trauma stories related to persecution in their countries of origin. Being forced to disclose one's history of traumatic events can be difficult in and of itself, but when these stories include sexual abuse it can be quite overwhelming for individuals. As part of the asylum process, SGMAS frequently have little control over when and who to reveal these stories to, which requires that social workers be prepared to help SGMAS share their stories—with lawyers, immigration adjudicators, and other—in ways that will minimize the psychological burden on them. This can be difficult to do since most SGMAS have suffered severe trauma throughout their lives, but we hope that this chapter has provided social workers and other mental health professional with the knowledge and skills needed to alleviate at least some of the burden. Our framework for clinical practice with SGMAS (Alessi & Kahn, 2017) offers foundational knowledge and skills for working with SGM asylum seekers. Addressing their concrete needs and providing a holding environment and other containment functions at a time when SGM asylum seekers may be suffering from stressor-related disorders while also dealing with the exigencies of resettlement cannot be understated, especially in the early stages of treatment. Social workers who do not impart this knowledge and skills in their work with SGMAS may not be able to move ahead to help them formulate their persecution stories so they feel more in control of them. Once SGMAS are equipped with more psychological resources, social workers can use the Testimony Method, which has been used successfully in the past to treat survivors of torture and politically-motivated violence. We believe that incorporating elements of the Testimony Method with trauma-informed principles has the potential to empower SGMAS when they may feel at their most vulnerable. Furthermore, it can also shift feelings of self-blame to societies in which human rights for LGBTQ people do not protect them from victimization and violence that has the potential to cause physical and psychological harm. Using the Testimony Method can also help SGMAS prepare for public disclosure, which can leave them feeling that they must continue to justify why they want to seek refuge, although they have continued to detail their traumatic events and persecution to multiple individuals. Following public disclosure, consolidation of gains can be used to further empower SGMAS for sharing their stories, and this courage must be acknowledged regardless of the outcome of the claims process.

Close Reading Questions

1. Summarize Kahn and Alessi's framework for clinical practice with SGMAS. What is particularly related to the field of social work in their framework? For example, how is client empowerment key to the success of the framework?
2. What types of psychoeducation are most important in work with SGMAS? What would tell a SGMAS client about "reverse covering"?
3. What must SGMAS prove in order to gain asylum? What happens when SGMAS are forced to come out as part of their testimony?

Prompts for Writing

1. In the Testimony Method for SGMAS, the clinician takes notes to develop a story or narrative as means to provide evidence of the necessity for asylum. Collect "testimony" from anyone you know and try to turn their story into a cohesive one; in other words, provide a narrative reconstruction of the events. Then, write about the advantages and disadvantages of writing up someone else's testimony.
2. Imagine being Arman and being denied asylum after working to prove that you are unsafe. How do you imagine it would feel to be forced to return "home"?
3. Look at Jaffe's chapter on queering trauma therapy. How does the framework for working with SGMAS relate to the treatment of Jaffe's undocumented Latina immigrant?

Notes

1 Refugees are vetted for "well-founded fear" of persecution, or fear of future persecution, *prior* to arriving in the host country. Asylees are vetted according to the same standards, but make their case *after* arrival in the host country. Canada calls individuals seeking asylum "refugee claimants" while the US and other countries utilize the term "asylum seeker."

2 For an in-depth presentation of the third phase of the framework, Strategies for Navigating Resettlement, see Alessi, E., & Kahn, S. (2017). A framework for clinical practice with sexual and gender minority asylum seekers. *Psychology of Sexual Orientation and Gender Diversity*. doi.10.1037/sgd0000244

References

Agger, I., Igreja, V., Kiehle, R., & Polatin, P. (2012). Testimony ceremonies in Asia: Integrating spirituality in testimonial therapy for torture survivors in India, Sri Lanka, Cambodia, and the Philippines. *Transcultural psychiatry, 49*(3–4), 568–589. doi:10.1177/1363461512447138

Agger, I., & Jensen, S. B. (1990). Testimony as ritual and evidence in psychotherapy for political refugees. *Journal of Traumatic Stress, 3*(1), 115–130. doi:10.1007/BF00975139

Agger, I., Raghuvanshi, L., Khan, S. S., Polatin, P., & Laursen, L. K. (2009). Testimonial therapy: A pilot project to improve psychological wellbeing among survivors of torture in India. *Torture, 19*, 204–217. doi:10.1177/1363461512447138

Alessi, E. J. (2016). Resilience in sexual and gender minority forced migrants: A qualitative analysis. *Traumatology, 22*, 203–213. doi:10.1037/trm0000077

Alessi, E. J., & Kahn, S. (2017). A framework for clinical practice with sexual and gender minority asylum seekers. *Psychology of Sexual Orientation and Gender Diversity, 4*(4), 383–391. doi:10.1037/sgd0000244

Alessi, E. J., Kahn, S., & Chatterji, S. (2016). The darkest times of my life: Recollections of child abuse among forced migrants persecuted because of their sexual orientation and gender identity. *Child Abuse & Neglect, 51*, 93–105. doi:10.1016/j.chiabu.2015.10.030

Alessi, E. J., Kahn, S., & Van Der Horn, R. (2017). A qualitative exploration of the premigration adult victimization experiences of sexual and gender minority refugees and asylees in the United States and Canada. *The Journal of Sex Research, 54*(7), 936–948. doi:10.1080/00224499.2016.1229738

Alessi, E. J., Kahn, S., Woolner, L., & Van Der Horn, R. (2018). Traumatic stress among sexual and gender minority refugees from the Middle East, North Africa, and Asia who fled to the European Union. *Journal of Traumatic Stress, 31*(6), 805–815.

American Psychiatric Association. (2013). *Diagnostic and statistical manual of mental disorders* (5th ed.). Washington, DC: Author. Retrieved from http://mcgill.worldcat.org/title/diagnostic-and-statistical-manual-of-mental-disorders-dsm 5/oclc/847226928&referer=brief_results

Berg, L., & Millbank, J. (2009). Constructing the personal narratives of lesbian, gay and bisexual asylum claimants. *Journal of Refugee Studies, 22*, 195–223. doi:10.1093/jrs/fep010

Berthold, S. M., Wong, E. C., Schell, T. L., Marshall, G. N., Elliot, M. N., Takeuchi, D., & Hambarsoomians, K. (2007). US Cambodian refugees' use of complementary and alternative medicine for mental health problems. *Psychiatric Services, 58*, 1212–1218. doi:10.1176/ps.2007.58.9.1212

Bögner, D., Herlihy, J., & Brewin, C. R. (2007). Impact of sexual violence on disclosure during Home Office interviews. *The British Journal of Psychiatry, 191*(1), 75–81. doi:10.1192/bjp.bp.106.030262

Briere, J., & Spinazzola, J. (2005). Phenomenology and psychological assessment of complex posttraumatic states. *Journal of Traumatic Stress, 18*, 401–412. doi:10.1002/jts.20048

Carroll, A. (2016). *State-sponsored homophobia: A world survey of laws: Criminalisation, protection and recognition of same-sex love* (11th ed.). Retrieved from The International Lesbian, Gay, Bisexual, Trans and Intersex Association website: http://ilga.org/downloads/02_ILGA_State_Sponsored_Homophobia_2016_ENG_WEB_150516.pdf

Cienfuegos, A. J., & Monelli, C. (1983). The testimony of political repression as a therapeutic instrument. *American Journal of Orthopsychiatry, 53*, 43–51. doi:10.1111/j.1939-0025.1983.tb03348.x

Cloitre, M., Henn-Haase, C., Herman, J., Jackson, C., Kaslow, N., Klein, C., ... Petkova, E. (2014). A multi-site single-blind clinical study to compare the effects of STAIR Narrative Therapy to treatment as usual among women with PTSD in public sector mental health settings: Study protocol for a randomized controlled trial. *Trials, 15*(1), 197. doi:10.1186/1745–6215-15–197

Cloitre, M., Koenen, K. C., Cohen, L. R., & Han, H. (2002). Skills training in affective and interpersonal regulation followed by exposure: A phase-based treatment for PTSD related to childhood abuse. *Journal of Consulting and Clinical Psychology, 70*(5), 1067–1074. doi:10.1037//0022–006X.70.5.1067

Cloitre, M., Stolbach, B. C., Herman, J. L., Kolk, B. V. D., Pynoos, R., Wang, J., & Petkova, E. (2009). A developmental approach to complex PTSD: Childhood and adult cumulative trauma as predictors of symptom complexity. *Journal of Traumatic Stress, 22*(5), 399–408. doi:10.1002/jts.20444

Courtois, C. A., & Ford, J. D. (2012). *Treatment of complex trauma: A sequenced, relationship-based approach*. New York, NY: Guilford Press.

de Jong, J. (2004). Public mental health and culture: Disasters as a challenge to Western mental health care models, the self, and PTSD. In J. P. Wilson & B. Drozdek (Eds.), *Broken spirits: The treatment of traumatized asylum seekers, refugees, war and torture victims* (pp. 159–178). New York, NY: Brunner-Routledge.

Dworkin, S. H., & Yi, H. (2003). LGBT identity, violence and social justice: The psychological is political. *International Journal for the Advancement of Counselling, 25*(4), 269–279. doi:10.1023/B:ADCO.0000005526.87218.9f

Einhorn, B. J., & Berthold, S. M. (2014). Reconstructing Babel: Bridging cultural dissonance between asylum seekers and adjudicators. In B. N. Lawrance & G. Ruffer (Eds.), *Adjudicating refugee and asylum status: The role of witness, expertise, and testimony* (pp. 27–53). Cambridge: Cambridge University Press.

Esala, J. J., & Taing, S. (2017). Testimony therapy with ritual: A pilot randomized controlled trial. *Journal of Traumatic Stress, 30*, 94–98. doi:10.1002/jts.22163

Hendricks, M., & Testa, R. (2012). A conceptual framework for clinical work with transgender and gender nonconforming clients: An adaptation of the minority stress model. *Professional Psychology: Research and Practice, 43*(5), 460–467. doi:10.1037/a0029597

Herman, J. (1997). *Trauma and recovery*. New York, NY: Basic Books.

Hopkinson, R. A., Keatley, E., Glaeser, E., Erickson-Schroth, L., Fattal, O., & Nicholson Sullivan, M. (2017). Persecution experiences and mental health of LGBT asylum seekers. *Journal of Homosexuality, 64*(12), 1650–1666, doi:10.1080/00918369.2016.1253392

Immigration and Refugee Board of Canada. (2017). *Chairperson's guideline 9: Proceedings before the IRB involving sexual orientation and gender identity and expression*. Ottawa, ON: Government of Canada. Retrieved from http://www.irb-cisr.gc.ca/Eng/BoaCom/references/pol/GuiDir/Pages/GuideDir09.aspx#a3

International Commission of Jurists. (2016). *Refugee status claims based on sexual orientation or gender identity – A practitioner's guide*. Geneva: Author. Retrieved from https://www.icj.org/wp-content/uploads/2016/10/Universal-PG-11-Asylum-Claims-SOGI-Publications-Practitioners-Guide-Series-2016-ENG.pdf

Johnston, V., Allotey, P., Mulholland, K., & Markovic, M. (2009). Measuring the health impact of human rights violations related to Australian asylum policies and practices: A mixed methods study. *BMC International Health and Human Rights, 9*(1), 1–12. doi:10.1186/1472–698X-9-1

Kahn, S. (2015). Experiences of faith for gender role non-conforming Muslims in resettlement: Preliminary considerations for social work practitioners. *British Journal of Social Work, 45*(7), 2038–2055. doi:10.1093/bjsw/bcu060

Kahn, S., & Alessi, E. J. (2018). Coming out under the gun: Exploring the psychological dimensions of seeking refugee status for LGBT claimants in Canada. *Journal of Refugee Studies, 31*(1), 22–41. doi:10.1093/jrs/fex019

Kahn, S., Alessi, E., Kim, H., Olivieri, C., & Woolner, L. (2017). Promoting the wellbeing of lesbian, gay, bisexual, and transgender forced migrants in Canada: Providers' perspectives. *Culture, Health & Sexuality, 19*(10), 1165–1179. doi:10.1080/13691058

Kahn, S., Alessi, E. J., Kim, H., Olivieri, C., & Woolner, L. (2018). Facilitating mental health support for LGBT forced migrants in Canada: A qualitative inquiry. *Journal of Counseling & Development, 96*(3), 316–326. doi:10.1002/jcad.12205

LaViolette, N. (2009). Independent human rights documentation and sexual minorities: An ongoing challenge for the Canadian refugee determination process. *The International Journal of Human Rights, 13*, 437–476. doi:10.1080/13642980902758234

Lewis, R. A. (2014). "Gay? Prove it": The politics of queer anti-deportation activism. *Sexualities, 17*(8), 958–975. doi:10.1177/1363460714552253

McCann, I. L., & Pearlman, L. A. (1990). *Psychological trauma and the adult survivor: Theory, therapy, and transformation*. New York, NY: Brunner-Routledge.

McDonald-Norman, D. (2017). No one to bear witness: Country information and LGBTQ asylum seekers. *Refuge, 33*(2), 88–100. Retrieved from https://papers.ssrn.com/sol3/papers.cfm?abstract_id=3065171

Meyer, I. H. (2003). Prejudice, social stress, and mental health in lesbian, gay, and bisexual populations: Conceptual issues and research evidence. *Psychological Bulletin, 129*, 674–697. doi:10.1037/0033-2909.129.5.674

Millbank, J. (2002). Imagining otherness: Refugee claims on the basis of sexuality in Canada and Australia. *Melbourne University Law Review, 26*, 144–177. Retrieved from http://www5.austlii.edu.au/au/journals/MelbULawRw/2002/7.html

Millbank, J. (2003). Gender, sex and visibility in refugee claims on the basis of sexual orientation. *Georgetown Immigration Law Journal, 18*, 71–110. Retrieved from http://digitalcommons.law.seattleu.edu/sjsj/vol1/iss3/61

Musalo, K., Moore, J., & Boswell, R. A. (2011). Persecution based on membership in a particular social group. In K. Musalo, J. Moore, & R. A. Boswell (Eds.), *Refugee law and policy: A comparative and international approach* (4th ed., pp. 615–620). Durham, NC: Carolina Academic Press.

Office of the United Nations High Commissioner for Human Rights. (2015). *Discrimination and violence against individuals based on their sexual orientation and gender identity*. Retrieved from http://www.ohchr.org/Documents/Issues/Discrimination/LGBT/A_HRC_29_23_One_pager_en.pdf

Schauer, M., Neuner, F., & Elbert, T. (2011). *Narrative exposure therapy: A short-term treatment for traumatic stress disorders* (2nd ed.). Cambridge, MA: Hogrefe Publishing.

Shidlo, A., & Ahola, J. (2013). Mental health challenges of LGBT forced migrants. *Forced Migration Review, 42*, 9–11. Retrieved from http://www.fmreview.org/sites/fmr/files/FMRdownloads/en/fmr42full.pdf

Tener, D., & Murphy, S. B. (2015). Adult disclosure of child sexual abuse: A literature review. *Trauma, Violence, & Abuse, 16*(4), 391–400. doi:10.1177/1524838014537906

United Nations. (1951). *Convention relating to the status of refugees*. Retrieved from http://www.refworld.org/docid/3be01b964.html

van der Kolk, B. A., Roth, S., Pelcovitz, D., Sunday, S., & Spinazzola, J. (2005). Disorders of extreme stress: The empirical foundation of a complex adaptation to trauma. *Journal of Traumatic Stress: Official Publication of the International Society for Traumatic Stress Studies, 18*(5), 389–399. doi:10.1002/jts.20047

Winnicott, D. W. (1965). *The maturational processes and the facilitating environment*. New York, NY: International Universities Press.

Yoshino, K. (2007). *Covering: The hidden assault on our civil rights*. New York, NY: Random House.

Interlude

TARA'S STORY

Anonymous; *interview and translation provided by Roxanna Ast*

My name is Tara, and I am a 33-year-old queer woman from Iran. When I tell others who I am and where I come from, a few people think getting a PhD in the USA is the hardest thing I have ever done; some may assume being separated from my family because of the Travel Ban is the most traumatic aspect of my life; others may believe living a life where I have to constantly come out is the hardest part.

While those experiences are all part of my daily life and somewhat stressful, they are pale compared to the hardship I had to tolerate living as a straight woman married to a man. I grew up in Iran in the 1990s during the time of dial up internet, proxies, and basic search engines. Outside of that, any information I had was what I was taught either at school or learned from my parents. While I learned over and over about the importance of education, raising children, being a good mother one day, how to sew a dress, and how to fear God in every aspect of my life, no one ever spoke about identity, who I am, who I want to be, and how to become that person. The only information I was exposed to regarding sexual orientation, gender expression, and gender identity was that everyone is straight, every woman needs a husband, real women are feminine, and if you are not a feminine woman, then maybe you want to be a boy and should have gender reassignment surgery.

In addition to these subtle cultural and societal messages, the State TV often had guest speakers who would talk about evil spirits that "turn" people gay; how gay people are severely sick; they are child abusers; they are the reason bad things happen in the world, and if parents abandon their gay children, then God will forgive them for creating such an evil monster. The most vivid memory I have of one of these "talk shows" was an episode that showed a young gay couple who were arrested when they were 16 because someone had reported them. They were too young to be punished for their "crime," so they were imprisoned for a couple of years, separately. Once they both turned 18, they were brought to trial and executed in public.

I wasn't sure which was the saddest part of this story. Was it how these two teenagers' lives were taken because of the person they loved? How their parents actually supported the court's decision? Or how there were over 100 adults attending the public execution with their young children to teach them a lesson?

It was after that show that I "decided" I was not gay. I started wearing more makeup, learning how to cook all sorts of Persian meals, and even tried going on a few dates with some boys I had met at University. I hated every aspect of it, but hey, I was alive and loved by my parents and family. I lived this life all through university until I met a young man who came from a good family, was well-educated, and had lived in the US for many years. My parents believed this is the person I must marry, so I did! I was married to him for three years and hated every day of it. I did not hate him, for he was not aware of my inner struggles. I did try to talk with him a few times but soon realized despite living in the US, he still viewed queer folk the way people in Iran did.

Over time, I developed a new persona for myself: the perfect wife, good at cooking, good at taking care of her husband, and following all the cultural norms that were expected of me. As the years went on, I'm not sure if it was my low self-esteem, lack of confidence, or just his sense of entitlement that allowed him to start violating all boundaries I ever had, from emotional manipulation to sexual assault. Even though at the time I was working at a Domestic Violence shelter, I was unable to see that what was happening to me was wrong. I was so immersed in my cultural beliefs and expectations that I thought that was just how life is for Iranian women. Things got to a point where I had to get police involved, and I was afraid of who I was becoming.

I was an independent, well-travelled, well-educated strong woman, but somehow it took me a couple of years and the support of my therapist and a great professor to realize I deserve better and what was happening was not right. So, I told my parents and left him. It was not an easy transition but over-time I was able to explore who I was and who I wanted to be. I started going out to gay clubs, parades, meeting queer friends from different cultures, volunteering at Pride centers, and finding a full-time job at an agency that provided services to victims of violent crimes.

I met my wife a year after I got divorced, we dated for a couple of years and got married on an open field where we had our first date. I got my PhD, have a job I love, and have surrounded myself with people who truly love and support me as I am. I have my own chosen family now. I am now living a life I once thought could never be a reality. It took a lot of hard work, resilience, seeking help, and having support and love from people who believed in me. I am happy I was able to find my way, but I know there are many queer people who are not so lucky and need the support, love, and encouragement they deserve.

If I could have one thing I would want people to take away from my story, it is this: despite what many people may think, queer folk who grow up in situations like mine, don't seek empathy, don't seek sympathy, and for the most part don't seek new ways to be resilient. By the time we are at a place to openly express and talk about who we are, we have already escaped execution, survived homophobia, and most likely immigrated at least once. What we are looking for is simply validation. We need to hear that it is okay to be who we are, it is okay to love who we love, and it is okay to be different from others. We need to be reminded of one message we were so desperately deprived of in our lives and that is this:

Everyone deserves to be loved and to love. love is love, no matter how it looks.

Questions for Thinking:

1. As a clinician, how would you respond to Tara's closing point:

   > By the time we are at a place to openly express and talk about who we are, we have already escaped execution, survived homophobia, and most likely immigrated at least once. What we are looking for is simply validation. We need to hear that it is okay to be who we are, it is okay to love who we love, and it is okay to be different from others.

   On a personal level, how would you feel having a client like Tara, who has "escaped execution"? How would help a client like Tara find the validation she seeks?
2. What does it mean to "survive homophobia"?
3. How would you consider the public hanging of a queer couple to be traumatic for a queer individual? Relate Tara's story to Kahn and Alessi's Case of Arman to explore the concept of asylum.
4. How do societal and religious expectations shape Tara's choices? How do her choices connect to Ariel's choices in Jaffe's chapter? And how do their choices relate to Jerrod's choices in Goldblatt Hyatt's chapter?

SAM'S STORY

Anonymous; *interview and translation provided by Roxanna Ast*

My Name is Sam, and I am 28 years old. I grew up in a place that strictly governed against non-normative expressions of gender and sexuality. I am the youngest in a family of five. My family includes me, my two older brothers, my dad, and my mom. My dad has his own business, and my mother is a nurse. Many people would describe my upbringing as middle class and within a well-educated family. I was—and for a long time continued to be—viewed as the only girl in the family: one who needed everything to be pink and glittery, one who required protection, and one who could not decide for herself.

I don't remember much about my childhood. In the place I grew up, we had "only girls" schools and "only boys" schools. I remember during my middle school years, I felt like I was different from the other girls in a way that I couldn't explain. I started feeling some attraction toward girls and developing feelings for them, but I was also a girl. This did not make sense, and I assumed it was due to my lack of sleep, or just a teenager phase everyone would go through. I started writing some of the girls letters; some would respond. I fell in love with some of them. Many broke my heart, and a few bullied me. I remember the names of every one of them.

During my high school years, I felt absolutely no attraction to boys and used to dress like a boy, as much as one could in a place as regulated by tradition as where I lived. As I moved through high school, boys and girls started teasing me and calling me "Lez." Lez is a word that is used in a derogatory way to describe women who are attracted to other women, or women who don't dress in a feminine and delicate manner. Eventually, in the mid-1990s, we got a computer, and I had access to the internet and free information. I searched a lot about what it means to be a lesbian, sexual orientation, and different gender identities. This research took a few years because my only option was dial-up internet; therefore, I had a lot of restrictions on the amount of data I could download daily.

Meanwhile, I continued having relationships with women. I remember one situation where I was madly in love with a girl, and after a year of dating, she unexpectedly got married and told me she was only with me because I was weird, and she wanted to show her friends that she could get close to me. She shared all of my intimate and private details with all of her friends. Soon that information spread around town where I was living, in a town where everyone knew of me and would point me out when walking down the road.

I looked like a girl but thought, behaved, and dressed like a boy. Everyone thought I was strange. No one wanted me the way I was. No one could love me the way I was. This was too confusing for people, and they did not want me like this. Due to the restrictions of my region, men and women are often separated at gyms, pools, bathrooms, weddings. But because of how I was forced to present myself, I was always around women in different settings. I think if the women knew deep down I was not a woman, they would have been very uncomfortable. I often think about all the women I saw get changed, be naked, talk about their private stories in front of me, and wonder how much they would hate me if they knew the truth. But I couldn't tell them the truth.

I was a good athlete. I played football, basketball, softball, and track and field. My parents were against my love of sports and blamed sports for my manly behaviors and manly presentation. I used to have to save up my money to secretly enter tournaments and championships. I won so many titles and awards that my family didn't know about. But sports helped me a lot. When I was competing, it was the only time I felt detached from all my worries and could be me for a short time.

After many years of researching, I realized that they call people like me transgender.

The high school years were like a living nightmare. People constantly called me "Lez" and avoided me. People didn't want to be friends with me. My only friends were my teammates from the many sports teams I was involved with. When you are competing for a title, no one cares who you are, who you love, or who you wish to be. Everyone just wants to win. As long as you are a good team player and put all you have into the game, they love you.

Once I knew I was transgender, I started having real nightmares at night, too. Worries about what will happen to me, to my family, to my future constantly haunted me at night. At night, I woke up screaming from my dreams and hid under my blanket. During the day, I hid from society, family, and friends. People continued to bully me. Police arrested me because I was not dressed like a "proper lady," and I was beaten up by the police for telling them I was a boy. My parents were at war with me, my friends were at war with me, my body was at war with me, society was at war with me. One time, my parents got so angry at me for bringing shame to their family name, they beat me up so severely I was hospitalized.

I decided that if I was able to live and get discharged from hospital, I would leave my country. I thought about killing myself many times, but something always stopped me. Maybe it was what people call God? Some higher power? It always helped me get through the worst parts and promised better days. Finally, I decided to leave everything behind and seek asylum. Right now, I live abroad. I lost my family, lost the only place I knew as home, have nothing to my name. Even though I have a master's degree, I have to start from the bottom again because I don't know the language here.

My life is a parallel reflection of myself. I can't go back home and am not a citizen here. I am not a full man, nor a full woman. I am not whole and never will be; I will never be able to truly be who I am, live in my own country, and be surrounded by family and friends. I live in limbo, but for now, I am free.

Questions for Thinking:

1. Sam says,

   > My only friends were my teammates from the many sports teams I was involved with. When you are competing for a title, no one cares who you are, who you love, or who you wish to be. Everyone just wants to win. As long as you are a good team player and put all you have into the game, they love you.

   Is this a hopeful thought? A sad thought? What more does it say about Sam's split self?
2. Sam was beaten up by police for not dressing in a feminine man. In Healy's chapter, Hal was set up as a sex offender. One might argue that both of these "legal" inventions happened to people who had served as pawns for others' insecurities. How could you make that connection?
3. Consider McGuire's point that sexual development is stifled by LGBTQ sexual trauma. How is that point true for Sam?

Section Two

4

STRAIGHT ON THE STREETS AND GAY FOR THE STAY

The Emerging Bisexuality of a Trafficked Female

Karie McGuire

Pre-Reading Questions

1. How would you define "bisexuality"? Are there other terms, like sexually fluid or pansexual, that mean something similar? Why do these labels matter?
2. What do you know about CPTSD: Complex Post Traumatic Stress Disorder?
3. What are your assumptions about what "gay for the stay" might mean as the phrase pertains to this chapter?

Sex trafficking is defined by the Trafficking Victims Protection Act (TVPA) of 2000 as a situation "in which a commercial sex act is induced by force, fraud, or coercion, or in which the person induced to perform such an act has not attained 18 years of age" (Reid & Jones, 2011, p. 209). Research from the National Incidence Studies of Missing, Abducted, Runaway, and Throwaway Children stated that a large percentage of youth who leave home do so due to physical, sexual, and psychological abuse (Jordan, Patel, & Rapp, 2013). Many researchers have attempted to publicize the number of children being trafficked in the United States; however, at this time there are no concrete numbers to capture the size of the problem (Stransky & Finkelhor, 2012). Yet even if we somehow collected big data statistics with accuracy, we would miss the opportunity to tend to the individual stories that can illuminate for clinicians the lived experience of trafficked children.

Here, I write about my clinical work with Angela, an "n of one," so to speak, in order to explore how Angela's relative safety away from the streets during her periods of incarceration allowed her to explore her sexuality. During these periods of incarceration, Angela explored what she called "gay for the stay." She found great personal and sexual fulfillment in relationships with women and emerged from jail with a bisexual identity. This case will explore how Angela's early childhood sexual traumas, including being trafficked as a minor, impacted her developing sexuality. I will explore how complex trauma impacts the developing self and provide an examination into how trauma might impact or change the course of one's developing sexuality. I will also review my clinical work with Angela as we navigated our therapeutic relationship.

★ ★ ★ ★ ★

Angela's first exposure to a male role-model was her father, who cheated-on and left her mother early on in Angela's life. Angela's father exposed her to alcohol and pornography at age 13. In our earliest work together, Angela described her father as a "creepy guy" around whom she always felt "uneasy." She told me that when she was 16, her father had sex with one of her friends. That was around the same time that she found herself forced to engage in sex work, which came as a result of the drug addiction and developmentally inappropriate sexual activity that her father initiated. She fell prey to her pimps—she called them "boyfriends"—as she sought other male attachment figures. With a demeanor of nonchalance and an effect of calm detachment, she discussed these events and feelings as if they were part of a normal father-daughter relationship. Even after she had turned to the streets at 16—intermittently living with her mother when she was sober—she still visited her father because he lived close by. It had not been long, about two months into our relationship, until she texted me the words I will never forget: "Can you come get me? I just had sex with my father." I had never dealt with incest before, and I felt sick to my stomach for my client. Yet, a key practice in treating survivors of complex trauma is that the therapist must meet the client with empathy—not the everyday kind of empathy—but empathy that is unflinching, as their stories have to be heard without any judgment; bearing witness to victims of sex trafficking requires that one take in the stories in a way that gives the victims an unwavering feeling of safety and support (Courtois & Ford, 2013; Marotta, 2003). I had to hide my bodily response to what Angela had endured, and it was not easy. I barely remember the car ride through the very streets where she regularly was forced to sell her body.

When I picked her up, she immediately began placing the blame onto herself—even though he had drugged and coerced her. Part of her inner conflict came from the religious upbringing her mother had instilled. Angela had found comfort in the youth groups and functions at her church. But the messages that came to Angela from her religion clashed with her reality, especially when it came to her sexuality. She was receiving messages from her religion that were heteronormative, gender normative, and that encouraged submission by the female to her male counterpart. Meanwhile, all of the abuse that she encountered was perpetrated by men. As a therapist in this situation, I could only let her know that I was not judging her and that I would support in whatever steps she wanted to take next. At this moment, it would not serve the client for me to try to purge the demons from her head or stand in the way of her autonomy. Courtois (2008) expanded on a past treatment model by Courtois and Jay (1998), called "trauma responsive therapy," when she analyzed the need for highly individualized care when treating those who endure Complex Post Traumatic Stress Disorder (CPTSD). She stated that "this meta-model does not prescribe or mandate particular interventions for particular clients, it does serve as a general guideline for the therapist that emphasizes safety, security, and affect regulation as core foundations of treatment" (Courtois, 2008, p. 92).

When I first met Angela at the age of 18, she had already been diagnosed with PTSD and was used to running from a warrant. Angela knew how to navigate the streets, but she was often trapped by dark forces in her search for safety. She did whatever she had to do to survive, such as attaching herself to "boyfriends" who only served to feed off the resources her body offered. Still, the streets soon came to feel more like home than her physical childhood one. She was so compelled to return "home" to the streets, that she abruptly left a drug treatment program in Florida. She not only left the program before she had completed the treatment, she had also left with an ankle bracelet that was given to her by court. After she left the program, she removed the ankle bracelet and did what she needed to in order to get back to New Jersey. At 18, she had been to about ten different programs. Some programs were for her recovery as a human trafficking victim, while others were for drug treatment.

Angela's Trafficking History

Angela met her first trafficker at age 16, a runaway on the streets of an impoverished and crime ridden city in New Jersey. She met her trafficker while in search of drugs; Angela's drugs of choice were heroin and cocaine, and she would regularly leave her rural town and go to the city to get drugs, as many people in did in her town. Angela explained that the man lured her into trafficking by offering her drugs, and then, she said, "he wanted something in return." Research further tell us that homeless, runaway, and disconnected youth are often targeted by individuals wishing to exploit them in a number of different ways for financial gain (Bennett-Murphy, 2012). This relationship quickly turned into a coercive one as the drug dealer forced her to have sex with men for his own personal financial gain. He provided her with drugs and a roof over her head in exchange for all the money that she earned from the forced sexual encounters. The trafficker knew that she had run away from home, so he knew she had a place to go back to if she left him; therefore, he would not let her out of his sight, and she could not escape. He would drive her himself to a "date" and wait for her outside. Following the date, he would take her back to the hotel room where he kept her until the next call. After a week or two, he started to become violent, and she was worried for her safety. She didn't know what to do or who to reach out to for help. She often blamed herself for the situation she was in because she was using drugs and, therefore, felt stuck. One of the buyers, known as a "John," who was a friendly customer compared to the others, offered her a way out. He took her to another city where he turned into her next trafficker. Although she was still being forced to have sex with multiple men, it was a better scenario, from her perspective, than the previous trafficker, who was violent. It was not long after she was taken to the new city that the police got involved, and she was rescued. After she was recovered by law enforcement, she was sent to a program across the country for domestic minor sex trafficking (DMST) victims. However, she ran away from the program, went to Florida, succumbed to her addiction, and met her third pimp. This time, when she was picked up by police, she was caught with drugs and faced her own charges for the first time. After that, she was in and out of jail over the next couple of years for different charges, mostly relating to drugs, either her own or drugs she muled for her traffickers.

Incarceration

Though I had been meeting with Angela for a few years on and off the streets, it was during the times that she was incarcerated that we were able to work toward consistent treatment. It wasn't until Angela was removed from imminent danger in the streets, forced to detox as a result of being in jail, and separated from her pimp that she was stable enough to be productive in therapy. Even with the best intentions as a trauma-informed therapist, if the client is in a constant state of crisis or emotional stress, progress is unrealistic in therapy. According to Courtois and Ford (2013), in order to increase functioning in therapy, the client needs to be thinking clearly, which can only occur if life circumstances that are causing emotional distress are removed and the client is stable. As much as my colleagues and I balk at the criminalization of trafficked individuals, at this time in jail, Angela felt that it was the safest available home.

Her mother had reached out to me and asked if I could see her for therapy while she was serving out her warrant in the jail. With the permission of my management, and by the jail administration, I was able to meet her weekly in the jail in a private and confidential room for therapy. When I met with her in the jail, it was the first time since I met her that she had consistent clean time and was stable in one location over many weeks. We were able to start consistent weekly therapy sessions, and she told me about her relationships with all the men in her life, including a prison guard to whom Angela revealed her body in exchange for reduced disciplinary measures. She was attracted to men, she said.

Yet simultaneously, she had started to pursue multiple relationships with the women she was incarcerated with. She had really bonded with one woman who wanted to be in a romantic relationship with her, both in jail and after. Through our relationship, built on safety and trust, Angela started to reveal new feelings she was having while incarcerated. She shared that she had been forced to engage with a girl in a sexual experience while she was trafficked but never had on her own free will. She didn't recall if she enjoyed it. But she did feel that she enjoyed the intimate experiences she was having with them women currently.

Despite all of the abuse she had suffered while on the streets (she was beaten during sex or if she hadn't met her quota and forced to have sex with multiple partners at once; she had no choices about what other people could do to her body), Angela didn't speak ill of her experiences of sex while incarcerated. If anything, at this time she was more interested in sex than ever before. She explained that she and one woman inmate would quietly touch each other's genitals after the lights had been turned off in bed together. She stated that she felt pleasure with these women and, more profoundly, she stated she felt safe. It was not easy for her admit that she felt safe. Angela felt dirty talking about the sexual trauma that occurred in her past and also about the feelings that she was having around sex with women; she felt that it was against her religious beliefs.

While I am mostly experienced in complex trauma related to human trafficking, both in practice and research, sexuality studies are not part of my expertise. Of course, sex was a major part of Angela's life and development, and sex is what she mainly wanted to talk about in session. She wanted approval from me that it was okay to want sex, and it was okay to want it from both men and women. O'Callaghan, Shepp, Ullman, and Kirkner (2018) stated that therapists should understand when working with survivors of sexual trauma that there is fluidity when engaging in sex and in choosing partners; many survivors have different sexual interests throughout their recovery, and at times survivors choose female partners because it feels like the safer choice.

★ ★ ★ ★ ★

Sexual abuse survivors might find relational problems in adulthood and find issues with sexual functioning that range from sexual compulsivity to sexual aversion (Courtois & Ford, 2013). O'Callaghan et al. (2018) stated that even though sexuality and sexual orientation are not necessarily simple to identify, some clients reported feeling more connected with women and safer with them as a result of having been assaulted at the hands of men. Additionally, female sexual abuse survivors may feel some confusion around sex and sexuality if they had a positive physical response or even orgasm during the abuse(s) they endured with men (Wohl & Kirschen (2018). O'Shaughnessy and Speir (2018) found that

> professional organizations have developed ethical practice guidelines for working with sexual minority populations (American Psychological Association [APA], 2012; Association for Lesbian, Gay, Bisexual, and Transgender Issues in Counseling Competencies [ALGBTIC] Taskforce, 2013), yet we still have limited empirical information about what constitutes effective psychotherapy with these populations.

When I went to the literature to understand the best interventions when working with bisexual individuals, I found that research highlights interventions for both LGBT and heterosexual communities and their experience with sexuality identity formation; however, the specific issues bisexual individuals experience are often underrepresented in literature and in interventions; their needs are invisible (Israel & Mohr, 2004; Li, Dobinson, Scheim, & Ross, 2013). Vencill and Israel (2018) discussed the matter further and found that there are currently no best practice models or specific materials to use when approaching the unique sexual and relational needs with a bisexual client. However, Scherrer (2013) stated that "bisexual clients will benefit from clinicians who are flexible and adaptive in their approaches and who use conceptual frameworks that help their clients to better understand their sexuality" (p. 246). Scherrer (2013) found that clinical social workers should understand the ambiguity around sexual orientation and have openness to the idea that the client may change their labels over time.

Bisexuality has been used as a descriptive term since psychosexual studies were first conceptualized; it has been used as theoretical framework to explain aspects of many fields, such as, psychopathology, masculinity/femininity, evolutionary theory, and psychosexual development (Fox, 1996). Bisexuality has been defined as an attraction or sexual interest with people of both genders and has existed in many cultures throughout history around the world (Fox, 1996). Alfred Kinsey was a major contributor to the field of sexual studies with his research on sexual preference. Kinsey and his colleagues found that sexual preference is a complex phenomenon one experiences in development and into adulthood; they believed that sexual preference should be defined as more than just two categories, homosexuality and heterosexuality, and would better be explained along a continuum (Kinsey, Pomeroy, & Martin, 1948; Rodríguez Rust, 2000; Weinberg, Williams, & Pryor, 1995). In their studies, people were rated on the Kinsey Scale based on both sexual behavior and subjective reactions on a seven-point scale which ranges from exclusive heterosexuality, through levels of bisexuality, to exclusive homosexuality (fantasies and feelings about desired partners) (Rodríguez Rust, 2000; Weinberg et al., 1995).

Many theorists have challenged the central role of gender in defining how sexual orientation is defined (Rodríguez Rust, 2000). Researchers have expanded on Kinsey's idea of a continuum by studying the difference between fixed and fluid sexual orientations. Ross, Daneback, and Mansson (2012) referenced studied fluidity in sexual orientations when they stated a fundamental and defining feature of the female sexual orientation is its fluid, not fixed, nature. Many researchers have found that even in adulthood, sexual orientation is more fluid for some individuals than for others (Diamond, 2008a, 2008b; Dickson, Paul & Herbison, 2003; Dickson, van Roode, Cameron, & Paul, 2013; Katz-Wise, 2015; Katz-Wise & Hyde, 2017; Kinnish, Strassberg, & Turner, 2005; Mock & Eibach, 2012; Ott, Corliss, Wypij, Rosario, & Austin, 2011; Rosario, Schrim-Shaw, Hunter, & Braun, 2006; Savin-Williams, Joyner, & Rieger, 2012). Sexual fluidity has been defined in literature as changes over time in sexual orientation components (attractions, identity, behaviors) and situational, contextual, and interpersonal factors may influence sexuality (Katz-Wise & Hyde, 2017; Ross et al., 2012). Blumstein and Schwartz (1976) believed that the environment, both social and familial, in which one lives in impacts one's sexual behaviors, based on support, or lack thereof. Ross et al. (2012) found that for women, a more cosmopolitan lifestyle with less religion tradition, and for men, high education, were associated with higher levels of sexual fluidity.

An example of situational homosexuality is found in women and men who identify as heterosexual prior to and before incarceration, but engage in homosexual sexual behaviors while in jail. Many researchers have found that inmates in correctional facilities developed homosexual relationships while in jail, and although complex and involved, the relationships were situational (Blumstein & Schwartz, 1977; Giallombardo, 1966, 1974; Velez, 1986; Ward and Kassebaum, 1965) and did not necessarily impact their sexuality. Blumstein and Schwartz (1977) found that

> one major reason institutionalized females were able to return to a completely heterosexual adaptation after release was the existence of a routine and simple set of rationalizations for behavior – e.g. that heterosexual contact were absent in the institution, that the institution was a lonely place, and that all inmates were doing it.

Homosexual experiences in jail may cause issues in heterosexual relationships later in life, after incarceration (Velez, 1896). Additionally, discrimination against LGBT individuals has been well documented (Rodríguez Rust, 2000) and may be a reason why many people to do not self-identify.

Individuals choose to self-identify, or do not, as bisexual for a number of different reasons. Scherrer (2013) found that when working with bisexual clients, it is important to consider clients relationships with family and friends, and other social settings; clients may have selective disclosure strategies which vary on their level of comfortability in being open about their sexual identity. In the study conducted by Blumstein and Schwartz (1976) with women, some respondents stated that they didn't always feel they were determining their own sexuality, but they were choosing heterosexual and homosexual relationships based on their current needs at that time. Rodríguez Rust (2000) found that what merits bisexual identity varies by individual; it can merely be feeling attracted to both men and women. For some, it reflects their attraction or ability to fall in love with both men and women, while for others it means being intimate—either sexually or romantically—with the potential to be in a monogamous relationship with either a man or a woman (Rodríguez Rust, 2000). It is important to keep in mind that bisexual identification in individuals is amazingly diverse and lifestyles vary greatly and how one comes to identify as bisexual is also diverse.

Trauma

Van der Kolk (2014) drew on Freud's theories of trauma concerning "the compulsion to repeat" to describe the actions victims go through such as reenactments of past victimizations as a way to gain control over painful situations that could lead to mastery, and, optimally, resolution. In fact, the adaptive strategies learned through information processing of negative experiences might even lead to highly maladaptive behaviors (Freyd, 1994). Bloom (2013) expanded on Freud when she used the term "traumatic reenactment" to describe the repetitious behavior that is a trauma response. The memories around past traumatic experiences are not integrated, they are dissociated, and cannot be processed and as a result cannot be altered (Bloom, 2013). Individuals find themselves repeating previous traumas with a lack of awareness on how it occurred (Bloom, 2013). Reenactment and repetition is ritualistic and a cry to a social group for attention; the body has responded with dissociation and disintegration and traumatized people seek attention outside the body with others to try to heal and mend their wounds (Bloom, 2013).

Some survivors of trauma may engage in more sexual activity as a way to gain control of their recovery and participating in sexual behavior is a way to cope and take control of their own body's autonomy (O'Callaghan et al., 2018). In studying the phenomenology of trauma, we learn that trauma changes the way the body experiences the world, and traumatized people feel distant from their bodies (Van der Kolk, 2014). After trauma, the body is always on guard, and victims cannot heal until they become reconnected with their bodies (Van der Kolk, 2014). Basic safety is critical to an individual's personal development and also social behavior; individuals who do not feel safe may not be able to access certain brain structures and lack creativity or generativity (Porges, 2017). Trauma survivors need to be validated in therapy that their former bodily response strategies were defense mechanisms and what protected them (Porges, 2017).

Complex trauma refers to

> ongoing physical, sexual, emotional abuse and neglect, and other forms of maltreatment in the nuclear or extended family (or quasi-family); domestic violence; community danger and violence; cultural, gender political,

> ethnic, illness and religion-based oppression, violence, and physical and geographic displacement; refugee status; terrorism; torture; war; and genocide.
>
> *(Courtois & Ford, 2013, p. 11)*

After prolonged periods of trauma people will do whatever it takes to decrease emotional exposure, usually in the form of numbing or dissociation (Bloom, 2013). An important framework to use when working with survivors of trauma is trauma-informed care. Trauma-informed care is defined as care "in which service delivery is influenced by an understanding of the impact of interpersonal violence and victimization on an individual's life and development" (Elliot, Bjelajac, Fallot, Markoff, & Reed, 2005, p. 462; McGuire, 2018).

★ ★ ★ ★ ★

Key parts in post-traumatic therapy are that there has to be an assumption of psychological health, the victim is not to blame for the victimization (even when it is repetitive or chronic), and there has to be a working relationship between the victim and the therapist around parity in respect and power (Courtois & Ford, 2013). This intersection of trauma and self-discovery around sexuality with this client required me as the therapist to be open, non-judgemental, and supportive as the client explored her past feelings around trauma and how they influenced her identity. Matteson (1996) found that in therapeutic relationship "persons who are just beginning to face their bisexuality often enter counseling because of their confusion; they may simply need confirmation that it is okay to accept the self that they are discovering" (p. 185). The therapeutic relationship may also assist clients by developing strengths-based narratives to highlight their commitment to self-discovery and individual resiliency in the face of negative messages they receive about being bisexual (Scherrer, 2013).

When working with Angela in her exploration or her bisexual identity, I drew on research around affirmative therapy. Similar with the support and safety trauma-informed treatment provides to a client, a gay-affirmative practitioner validates and advocates for the client as a positive experience in their development (Craig, Austin, & Alessi, 2013; Davies, 1996). LGBT affirmative therapy is culturally relevant and responsive to LGBT clients and their multiple social identities and communities; it addresses the influence of social inequities on the lives of LGBT clients, fosters autonomy, enhances resilience, coping, and community building, advocates to reduce systemic barriers to mental, physical, and sexual flourishing, and leverages LGBT client strengths (O'Shaughnessy & Speir, 2018).

I felt lucky as the practitioner to be able to support Angela in her developing sexual identity while at the same time working through her trauma. Over time, the client explored her past trauma, her relationships throughout her life that have impacted her identify, and her desires to explore her sexuality with both men and women. We processed together what it would be like to disclose to her family and friends and who she felt would be the most supportive and an ally in the community if she were to disclose. However, regardless of her pleasurable experiences while incarcerated she was unsure if she would feel the same when she was back home. While she felt safety with the women she was intimate with, she didn't feel she could be openly involved with women on the outside, and that she felt that she truly could be only "gay for the stay," at least at this juncture in her life. She wasn't closed off to these types of relationships outside of jail but did feel a disconnect between her religion and her sexual identity, and she didn't feel she could integrate both into her life at the same time. In the past, her religion had been a major strength and protective factor for her and she had a hard time imaging them work together. So, we were able to talk through some of those challenges and maybe some ways it could be possible in the future. Before she was released back to her home with her mother, her questions around how her future reality would look, weren't answered. However, she did feel as though she found comfort exploring her evolving sexual identity with me in our sessions, and voiced it was the first time she could truly explore her thoughts, both around past trauma and sexuality, without judgement. As a result of our progress in jail, she wanted to continue to pursue therapy after reintegration back into the community and the exploration will continue.

The case study has many limitations that should be mentioned, as the initial purpose of the therapy was not intended to be an intervention around sexual identity formation. However, as the theme emerged in the clients' life, it was too important to ignore. The intersection of human trafficking, trauma, and bisexuality formation has yet to be researched and is complex. In social work that is culturally sensitive, clinicals must pay attention to the intersectionality of the clients' experiences and address them with the client (Scherrer, 2013). It is important to also highlight this was a single case analysis with a 21-year-old white female; race, class, age, and gender were not explored as factors impacting this client's specific experienced.

Findings indicate that there is a need for future research around the intersection of trauma and sexuality formation, particularly with victims of complex trauma, such as human trafficking, who have experienced many forms of abuse and experienced immense suffering. This research also highlights the need for more education in the social work field around LGBT education and methods to use when working with clients and their developing sexuality. This research should encourage social workers to integrate sexuality research and models into the therapeutic setting if it becomes an important aspect of the client's life and experience. The relationship between the client and the therapist is critical to helping trauma victims towards recovery (Courtois, 2008; Courtois & Ford, 2013; Pearlman & Courtois, 2005). The client's need to feel safe, in order to be open to sharing, created an exploration between the therapist and client in this case, that wouldn't have been possible without the trust created in the therapeutic relationship.

Close Reading Questions

1. Why was jail the safest place for Angela, and how did it keep her from her "compulsion to repeat" and "traumatic reenactment," symptoms of her Complex Post Traumatic Stress Disorder? Define the key terms in this question as you answer.
2. What components of Trauma Responsive Therapy does McGuire apply during Angela's treatment?
3. What did you feel when you read that Angela's emerging bisexuality could be explained by the theory that females feel like a safer choice after a lifetime of sexual abuse by men?

Prompts for Writing

1. Develop a treatment model for cases of incest. Refer to Van Nest's chapter on Lila, who lived in rural Appalachia, and think about how your plan might work differently based on region.
2. How does bearing witness to Angela's trauma produce compassion fatigue for the therapist?
3. How does a child's sense of safety impact their sexual development?

References

Bennett-Murphy, L. M. (2012). Haunted: Treatment of a child survivor of human trafficking. *Journal of Infant, Child, and Adolescent Psychotherapy, 11*(2), 133–148.

Bloom, S. L. (2013). *Creating sanctuary: Toward the evolution of sane societies.* Abington: Routledge.

Blumstein, P. W., & Schwartz, P. (1976). Bisexuality in women. *Archives of Sexual Behavior, 5*(2), 171–181.

Blumstein, P. W., & Schwartz, P. (1977). Bisexuality: Some social psychological issues. *Journal of Social Issues*, 33(2), 30–45.

Courtois, C. A. (2008). Complex trauma, complex reactions: Assessment and treatment. *Psychological Trauma: Theory, Research, Practice, and Policy, 1*, 86–100.

Courtois, C. A., & Ford, J. D. (2013). *Treatment of complex trauma: A sequenced, relationship-based approach.* New York, NY: Guilford Press.

Courtois, C. A., & Jay, J. (1998). Trauma responsive therapy: A shift in perspective. *Centering: Newsletter of The Center: Posttraumatic Disorders Program, 3*(5), 1.

Craig, S. L., Austin, A., & Alessi, E. (2013). Gay affirmative cognitive behavioral therapy for sexual minority youth: A clinical adaptation. *Clinical Social Work Journal, 41*(3), 258–266.

Davies, D. (1996). Towards a model of gay-affirmative therapy. In D. Davis & C. Neal (Eds.), *Pink therapy: A guide for counselors and therapists working with lesbian, gay, and bisexual clients* (pp. 51–68). Buckingham: Open University Press.

Diamond, L. M. (2008a). Female bisexuality from adolescence to adulthood: Results from a 10- year longitudinal study. *Developmental Psychology, 44*, 5–14.

Diamond, L. M. (2008b). *Sexual fluidity: Understanding women's love and desire*. Cambridge, MA: Harvard University Press.

Dickson, N., Paul, C., & Herbison, P. (2003). Same-sex attraction in a birth cohort: Prevalence and persistence in early adulthood. *Social Science & Medicine, 56*, 1607–1615.

Dickson, N., van Roode, T., Cameron, C., & Paul, C. (2013). Stability and change in same-sex attraction, experience, and identity by sex and age in a New Zealand birth cohort. *Archives of Sexual Behavior, 42*(5), 753–763.

Elliott, D. E., Bjelajac, P., Fallot, R. D., Markoff, L. S., & Reed, B. G. (2005). Trauma-informed or trauma-denied: principles and implementation of trauma-informed services for women. *Journal of Community Psychology, 33*(4), 461–477.

Fox, R. C. (1996). Bisexuality in perspective: An examination of theory and research. In B. A. Firestein (Ed.), *Bisexuality: The psychology and politics of an invisible minority* (pp. 3–50). Thousand Oaks, CA: Sage.

Freyd, J. (1994). Betrayal trauma: Traumatic amnesia as an adaptive response to childhood abuse. *Ethics & Behavior, 4*(4), 307–329.

Giallombardo, R. (1966). *Society of women: A study of a women's prison*. New York, NY: Wiley.

Giallombardo, R. (1974). *The social world of imprisoned girls: A comparative study of institutions for juvenile delinquents*. New York, NY: Wiley.

Israel, T., & Mohr, J. J. (2004). Attitudes toward bisexual women and men: Current research, future directions. *Journal of Bisexuality, 4*(1–2), 117–134.

Jordan, J., Patel, B., & Rapp, L. (2013). Domestic minor sex trafficking: A social work perspective on misidentification, victims, buyers, traffickers, treatment, and reform of current practice. *Journal of Human Behavior in the Social Environment, 23*(3), 356–369.

Katz-Wise, S. L. (2015). Sexual fluidity in young adult women and men: Associations with sexual orientation and sexual identity development. *Psychology & Sexuality, 6*(2), 189–208.

Katz-Wise, S. L., & Hyde, J. S. (2017). Facilitative environments related to sexual orientation development and sexual fluidity in sexual minority young adults across different gender identities. *Journal of Bisexuality, 17*(2), 141–171.

Kinnish, K. K., Strassberg, D. S., & Turner, C. W. (2005). Sex differences in the flexibility of sexual orientation: A multidimensional retrospective assessment. *Archives of Sexual Behavior, 34*(2), 173–183.

Kinsey, A. C., Pomeroy, W. B., & Martin, C. E. (1948). *Sexual behavior in the human male*. London and Philadelphia, PA: Saunders.

Li, T., Dobinson, C., Scheim, A. I., & Ross, L. E. (2013). Unique issues bisexual people face in intimate relationships: A descriptive exploration of lived experience. *Journal of Gay & Lesbian Mental Health, 17*(1), 21–39.

Matteson, D. (1996). Counseling and psychotherapy with bisexual and exploring clients. In B. A. Firestein (Ed.), *Bisexuality: The psychology and politics of an invisible minority* (pp. 185–213). Thousand Oaks, CA: Sage.

Marotta, S. A. (2003). Unflinching empathy: Counselors and tortured refugees. *Journal of Counseling & Development, 81*(1), 111–114.

McGuire, K. (2018). The embodiment of complex trauma in domestic minor sex trafficking victims and the dangers of misidentification. *Journal of Human Behavior in the Social Environment, 29*(5), 1–13.

Mock, S. E., & Eibach, R. P. (2012). Stability and change in sexual orientation identity over a 10-year period in adulthood. *Archives of Sexual Behavior, 41*(3), 641–648.

O'Callaghan, E., Shepp, V., Ullman, S. E., & Kirkner, A. (2018). Navigating sex and sexuality after sexual assault: A qualitative study of survivors and informal support providers. *The Journal of Sex Research, 56*(8), 1045–1057.

O'Shaughnessy, T., & Speir, Z. (2018). The state of LGBQ affirmative therapy clinical research: A mixed-methods systematic synthesis. *Psychology of Sexual Orientation and Gender Diversity, 5*(1), 82.

Ott, M. Q., Corliss, H. L., Wypij, D., Rosario, M., & Austin, S. B. (2011). Stability and change in self-reported sexual orientation identity in young people: Application of mobility metrics. *Archives of Sexual Behavior, 40*(3), 519–532.

Pearlman, L. A., & Courtois, C. A. (2005). Clinical applications of the attachment framework: Relational treatment of complex trauma. *Journal of Traumatic Stress: Official Publication of The International Society for Traumatic Stress Studies, 18*(5), 449–459.

Porges, S. W. (2017). *The pocket guide to the polyvagal theory: The transformative power of feeling safe.* New York, NY: WW Norton & Co.

Reid, J., & Jones, S. (2011). Exploited vulnerability: Legal and psychological perspectives on child sex trafficking victims. *Victims and Offenders, 6*(2), 207–231.

Rosario, M., Schrimshaw, E. W., Hunter, J., & Braun, L. (2006). Sexual identity development among lesbian, gay, and bisexual youths: Consistency and change over time. *Journal of Sex Research, 43*(1), 46–58.

Ross, M. W., Daneback, K., & Månsson, S. A. (2012). Fluid versus fixed: A new perspective on bisexuality as a fluid sexual orientation beyond gender. *Journal of Bisexuality, 12*(4), 449–460.

Rodríguez Rust, P. C. (2000). Bisexuality: A contemporary paradox for women. *Journal of Social Issues, 56*(2), 205–221.

Savin-Williams, R. C., Joyner, K., & Rieger, G. (2012). Prevalence and stability of self-reported sexual orientation identity during young adulthood. *Archives of Sexual Behavior, 41*(1), 103–110.

Scherrer, K. (2013). Culturally competent practice with bisexual individuals. *Clinical Social Work Journal, 41*(3), 238–248.

Stransky, M. L., & Finkelhor, D. (2012). Sex trafficking of minors: How many juveniles are being prostituted in the US? Durham: Crimes against Children Research Center, University of New Hampshire.

Van der Kolk, B. (2014). *The body keeps the score.* New York, NY: Viking.

Velez, D. (1986). A study of the effects of situational homosexual experiences on the heterosexual experiences on the heterosexual relationships among previously incarcerated Cubans. *ETD Collection for AUC Robert W. Woodruff Library*, Paper 1631.

Vencill, J. A., & Israel, T. (2018). Shining a light into the darkness: Bisexuality and relationships. *Sexual and Relationship Therapy, 33*, 1–2, 1–5.

Ward, D. A., & Kassebaum, G. G. (1965). *Women's prison: Sex and social structure.* Chicago, IL: Adeline.

Weinberg, M. S., Williams, C. J., & Pryor, D. W. (1995). *Dual attraction: Understanding bisexuality.* Oxford: Oxford University Press.

Wohl, A., & Kirschen, G. W. (2018). Betrayal of the body: Group approaches to hyposexuality for adult female sufferers of childhood sexual abuse. *Journal of Child Sexual Abuse, 27*(2), 154–160.

5

TRAUMA, FANTASY, AND IDENTITY DEVELOPMENT IN A TRANSGENDER CLIENT

The Case Study of Alex

Megan Conti

Pre-Reading Questions

1. How might one's assigned gender influence human development? How would you define gender dysphoria?
2. What does it mean to perform gender? How might the performance of gender impact one's mental health, particularly when one has to perform a false gender identity?
3. What is your thinking on the issues of pronoun usage for transgender individuals? If a transgender person switches their assigned gender pronouns to chosen gender pronouns, how does that impact him/her/them and his/her/their relationship to others?

Introduction

Everyday life as experienced by transgender individuals calls for unique consideration and a nuanced understanding of the ways in which transsexual/transgender people interface with their own bodies in a gendered, binary society during some of the most influential developmental years of their life. The impact of this experience, living on what Hansbury (2017) calls the "transgender edge" (p. 1009), can lead some transgender individuals to experience trauma, a "massive gender trauma" (Saketopoulou, 2014, p. 773), that is intimately linked to embodiment; their person-in-environment circumstance is one that is characterized by living through a daily trauma that is at once social and sexual, bodily and fantasy. As such, we are called to examine the experiences of transgender individuals to understand better how these experiences influence their mental health, their development, and their engagement with the world.

Clinicians and analysts working with the transgender population have noted the connection between the embodied experience of incongruity (Lemma, 2013) and the dysphoria experienced by transgender individuals. Notably, writers have begun to flesh out how work with trans individuals requires a revised way of thinking about being trans, the causes of dysphoria or mental illness in the trans population, and new ways to approach treatment. In doing so, contemporary research and clinical case studies have pushed the discussion about transsexual/transgender identity away from one of pathology towards one that recognizes being trans as a legitimate gender identity rather than the expression of an underlying neurosis, narcissism, or problem (Ehrensaft, 2016; Hansbury, 2011, 2017; Harris, 2005, 2016; Lemma, 2012; Saketopoulou, 2011). As such, clinical questions have focused more on the various etiologies of transsexual/transgender identity as well as the complex questions that arise when treating trans clients. Specifically, much discussion has focused on how trans clients negotiate their relationships with their body and their body-in-society, as well as analytic questions about how trans individuals negotiate their world prior to, during, and after transitioning (or not).

Part of this negotiation involves the ways in which transsexual/transgender individuals express their experiences of their bodies and their worlds and the context within which they come out as transsexual/transgender. For instance, some transsexual/transgender individuals seek to deny their pre-transition bodies as a way to distance themselves from the pain they experienced in a misgendered body (Hansbury, 2017). Or, transgender individuals might split between their "good" gendered selves and their "bad" gendered selves, resulting in the experience of battling between good objects and bad or persecutory objects (Klein, 1952; Winnicott, 1956). Still others express their experiences through complex fantasies and dreams that reflect their embodiment, some of which might be traumatic in nature or organized around a theme of sexual trauma (Hansbury, 2005). Regardless of the form it takes, embracing the complexity of this journey is key to working with individuals who identify as trans, as it gives us as clinicians a window into their worlds, which are complicated, nuanced, and ever-changing.

When considering the role of sexual trauma in the experiences of trans individuals, this aforementioned journey becomes a linchpin for grasping the multiplicity of etiology, scope, relevance, and complexity of trauma and identity development. In questioning how (or not) sexual trauma can be defined specifically in terms of work with transgender individuals, one must be open to examining how (or not) transgender individuals experience trauma on various levels and intersections, such as the gendered body one is assigned at birth versus the gendered (or fluid) body one experiences internally, the body in relation to others, the body in a family system, and the body in a larger, gendered, binary society.

There is a potential for traumatic experience (or not) at every level of a transgender individual's life, and the expression this trauma takes may be as varied as the form the trauma itself takes.

When I first began working with Alex,[1] he was pre-transition and went by she/her/hers pronouns. At the time, Alex seemed like your average 19-year-old Caucasian female grappling with some depression and anxiety. Over time, however, as we explored the extent of Alex's unhappiness and eventual self-harm, what emerged was a series of dreams/fantasies organized around a sexual trauma that belied a deep gender dysphoria, a dysphoria that informed most of Alex's interactions with the world. What Alex ultimately revealed to me was an experience of embodiment and engagement with the world that was characterized by living as a false-self, one whose identity was determined largely by dominant social conceptions of gender and hindered by Alex's family's cultural and religious identity from exploring any further Alex's relationship with his gender or his body. Alex's experiences and the expression of his dysphoria in the form of rape dreams/fantasies called into question for me the nature of sexual trauma, especially when working with transgender youth who mature in a world that is aggressively binary and results in an experience of sexual trauma.

In the following case study, I seek to use the case of a female-to-male transgender identified client, Alex, to examine how a dream/fantasy organized around a sexual trauma was used to make sense of the complicated experience of being in the wrong gendered body and being misgendered by society. Using the case study method, we are able to think in a complicated and layered way about the intersections between gender, society, individual development, and embodiment that can amount to a new definition or understanding of what it means to be traumatized sexually. Ultimately, this exploration calls us to push back against mainstream definitions of sexual trauma in the interest of one that is more flexible and in tune with an individual's experience—particularly individuals who are forced to live on the margins and who are pushed to express themselves within the confines of a society that has been developed largely without consideration of their experiences.

Case Material

Alex initially struggled with his depression because he had been raised by what he described as a "good family"—both of his parents were hard working people, and his family would be classified as middle class in NYC. Both parents were professionals, although his mother was in a white collar profession whereas Alex's father worked up to a management position through manual labor. Alex's father, John, was a supervisor for a shipping company. Alex's mother, however, was an administrator in a city agency; she had her master's degree and was esteemed in her field. Per Alex's report, his father was the "soft touch" in the home; he was kind hearted, easygoing, and comforting to his children when they needed him. Alex's mother, Eleanor, however, was the disciplinarian, the authority figure in the household. According to Alex, his mother was the one who managed the family's budget, who organized the children's education, and who made sure all the bills were paid. By Alex's own admission, Eleanor did this very well. She managed to send all three of her children to private school and to pay off the family's mortgage in one of the most expensive cities in the country.

Related to this dynamic, Alex would often share that he felt like he should be grateful to his parents for the life they afforded him. He was, after all, able to attend an excellent private school, and he never had to worry about the bills being paid or the lights shutting off. Alex and his siblings lived a largely insulated life that was cushioned by middle-class comforts. Underneath their middle-class comforts, however, was a family dynamic that was fraught with tension and that contributed to Alex's gender dysphoria in ways that were not immediately available to Alex's conscious awareness. For example, a theme of Alex's narrative was related to his early object relationships—his inability to link and feel congruence with his early objects. This lack of connection was driven by a deep division between Alex and Eleanor, Alex's primary caregiver, which led to a lifelong pattern of interrupted connections and an overall feeling of never quite being seen by his family and friends, an initial experience that contributed to his deep sense of being traumatized (Harris, 2016). This lack of early connection was only reified as Alex began experiencing dysphoria related to his female body (heightened by puberty) while his family demanded that he fulfill gender norms and stereotypes that were otherwise missing from his home.

Another element of Alex's complex family dynamic was related to their ethnicity. Alex's family was devoutly Catholic and culturally tied to their Polish heritage. At a young age, Alex was enrolled in a Polish cultural club to learn Polish traditions and dances. Alex's parents were active in their community and their church, and Alex remembers that his family was very proud to be a part of Polish-American groups. As such, being Polish and being Catholic were intimate parts of Alex's young identity formation, serving as a framework for his thinking about family life, morals, and traditions. While Alex's culture and religious traditions served, at times, as protective factors (when Alex struggled making friends in elementary school, he felt welcomed and loved by his Polish club friends, and he often relied on his cultural identity for a sense of self in latency years), they also served as harmful elements in the progression of his understanding of his gender identity. Alex was surrounded by traditional representations of gender and family life—couples were to be heterosexual, women were to be mothers, and men were expected to be providers. As such, Alex internalized a rigid binary, suppressed any feelings of identification with men or maleness, and denied any unhappiness with his female body.

Although, in reality, Alex's family subverted many of these paradigms (Eleanor being the breadwinner and disciplinarian, for example), their own perception of their family was one that strengthened these messages. Eleanor would regularly tell Alex about the importance of being the woman of the family, and there were clearly defined gender roles in the home (Eleanor providing most of the childcare and cooking all of the meals despite her work schedule). Additionally, Eleanor would insist upon Alex being feminine and presenting herself in a way that was deemed appropriate for a woman, a key element contributing to their disconnection. Later on in our treatment together (after coming out as trans), Alex would often recall how his mother was rigidly binary, an experience that left him feeling confused and angry when he did not want to fulfill the roles ascribed to him. As a child, Alex reported, he resisted Eleanor's attempts to make him more feminine, only to be met with Eleanor's shame and rage, thusly resulting in the suppression of these urges later in life.

Later in our work together, this same theme emerged when we dealt with Alex changing his gender pronouns to he/him/his. After coming out as trans, Eleanor initially refused to call Alex by male pronouns, insisting that this was just a phase and refusing to accept Alex's right to express his gender as he saw fit. Eleanor would regularly harp back on the fact that Alex would wear makeup and dress up when he was younger (a bone of contention for Alex, as he would often note that he only did these things because Eleanor would force him to do them upon unspoken threat of rage and shame). Immediately prior to coming out as trans, Alex would argue with Eleanor about his desired clothing choices (baggier, more androgynous clothes), and Eleanor would fly into rages over the fact that Alex did not want to wear overtly feminine clothing. In this very important way, Alex was constantly battling with Eleanor to be seen, and to be identified as the right gender. It is worth noting that I have referred to Alex as he/him/his throughout this paper to reflect how important his gender pronouns were to him, and to respect his identity as a male. Alex had to continuously fight back against the rigid binary of both society writ large and his micro-level interactions with family and members of his community.

Both before and after coming out as transgender, Alex would regularly describe his mother as very demanding and punishing, characteristics that totally eviscerated Alex's ability to assert himself in any meaningful way (making the issue surrounding his pronouns even more remarkable and profound). As a child, Alex would recall regularly feeling like Eleanor hated him and belittled him for failing to live up to impossible standards (both academically and socially). Additionally, Eleanor would fly into intense rages, aimed particularly at Alex and his sister, Maggie, for seemingly trivial things, causing a tremendous amount of anxiety and hostility in the girls. In comparison, Alex noted, Alex's brother, Tim, enjoyed a life of relative ease, free of criticism and largely insulated from family conflict. According to Alex, Tim was the baby of the family and, as the only male child, was not required to complete chores, was not expected to help around the house, and was generally afforded a privileged position in the family system. The gendered nature of the treatment was frustrating to Alex for many reasons, as it reinforced his anger at his mother, his resentment towards his brother, and, ultimately, his complicated experience of his embodied gendered self.

John's laid-back demeanor amounted to a depiction from Alex of a father who was impotent; he was completely unable to stand up to Eleanor in any meaningful way, a pattern that was mirrored in Eleanor and John's relationships with their children. John became more of a fourth child than a meaningful parental figure in the family dynamic. This resulted in a lopsided parenting system and what Alex described as an emotionally confusing and at times frightening dynamic of Eleanor's dominance and the essential emasculation of John. That being said, Alex was arguably over-identified with his father, and Alex almost singularly attributed the discord in the home to the actions of Eleanor and never to John's inability or unwillingness to parent or assert himself. After coming out as transgender and beginning the female-to-male transition, Alex would articulate a deep desire to be a father and to be a father like John, a theme that would repeat itself throughout the later part of our work together. As such, Alex presented to treatment with a powerful archetype—maleness as good and femaleness as bad—that was repeated in his family but also powerfully experienced internally, although not yet articulated.

As Alex became increasingly comfortable in session, he began opening up about how the discomfort he felt when he would go on dates with boys. Being pre-transition and still gendered as female, friends frequently set up Alex on dates with boys in the Polish club. Alex would recall how uncomfortable he felt, especially when he felt like he was expected to kiss his date at the end of the night. Alex shared that he had feelings that approached repulsion and severe anxiety when dates would come, feeling compelled to go by his mom but feeling incredibly anxious as the evening progressed. We began discussing boundaries, how to say no, and we began exploring his discomfort as it related to being in situations that were perceived as intimate with a male companion.

During this time, Alex also began to express that he was having intense dreams and fantasies that "felt like rape." When asked to describe these dreams, Alex would explain that he had a deep sense of being raped some time in his past by an unknown assailant. Alex shared that he had dreams of running away from an amorphous male figure, always just out of his grasp, as he tried to sexually assault Alex. It was unclear to Alex whether or not he had, actually, been raped as a child. However, he reported feeling like this dream/fantasy was deeply significant in some way, and often noted that he wanted to figure out what it meant and if it was, in fact, a recollection of a childhood abuse. Through our time together, we worked on getting a sense of when this might have happened, if Alex was ever alone with male friends of the family, if there was ever a period time in his life that he could not recall, or if he had any reason to believe that this dream was a repressed memory. We engaged in psychodynamic psychotherapy for several months, exploring the significance of the dreams/fantasies, and no more details or information emerged.

Our work exploring Alex's dreams and fantasies was punctuated by Alex's developing self-disclosures regarding his sexuality and eventually his gender identity. Alex began to test out the safety of our dyad in expressing how his identified sexuality was shifting. Alex first expressed that he might be bisexual; he noted his comfort level with women in comparison to his intense discomfort on dates with men. Alex shared that he might feel attracted to women as more than friends, but still held that he was also attracted to men. We discussed what it means to be bisexual, and how he might begin to explore his sexuality by talking about it with friends, in therapy, and perhaps seeking out some LGBTQ information online and in support groups. Alex seemed excited at the prospect of feeling connected to a community and exploring his identity.

As a seemingly natural part of Alex's progression, he eventually began to explore the possibility of being a lesbian. As Alex began timidly discussing his preference for women, the influence of Alex's family and culture on his sexuality and gender identity began to come into sharp focus. Despite what appeared to be an obvious attraction to women only, Alex struggled with abandoning the pretense that he was attracted to men. Alex seemed fearful of his increasing openness with me about his attraction to women, and identifying as a lesbian or as queer seemed to be overwhelming. Alex regularly noted that, although his family would struggle with his identity as a bisexual, he felt they would still accept him because he was still interested in men and would "most likely end up with a husband, anyway." Exploring this dynamic with Alex, he would harken back to his family's traditional Polish and Catholic values, stating that his family expected him to be a traditional woman in many ways, all of which involved being in a relationship with a man.

Alex's discomfort grew as he remained stuck in this bind of pleasing his family rather than himself. Although denying his singular desire for women in session, Alex began exploring avenues online where he could express his sexuality more openly. As his two worlds came into increasingly intense contrast over time, Alex reached an impasse characterized by deep depression and self-harm. Alex began cutting himself and expressing suicidal ideation on a regular basis. His rape dreams occurred more frequently, and Alex appeared significantly more dysphoric in our sessions together. At one point during session, I felt the tension and sensed that we might be reaching a breaking point. I looked over at Alex, as he seemed to be holding back, and said, "Alex, are you sure you're not just a lesbian? Because if you are, that's okay, and you don't have to cling to being bisexual to please your family or anyone else, for that matter." Although looking back this seems to be a very blunt way of addressing the situation, at the time our connection was one that enabled us to speak frankly to one another, and it felt like the right thing to do—demonstrate to Alex that our therapeutic space was a safe one, and that he could feel free to be exactly who he was with me. This also was not to discredit the fact that plenty of people are bisexual and are attracted to both men and women, it just sincerely did not seem like that was the case for Alex. As it turned out, I was right.

Alex seemed relieved by my question. He finally disclosed in our session that he was a lesbian, not bisexual, and that he felt like he had to begin accepting himself more fully in order to get better. Affirming and validating him, it was essential that our therapeutic relationship remain one that was open to his self-exploration and shifting identity. Additionally, it was crucial that we did not conflate Alex's experience of being a lesbian (and eventually coming out as trans) as the cause of his mental health problems. Rather, we worked on identifying how the struggle between his family and his internal experiences have historically been fraught with tension (Alex's relationship with his mother was always contentious) and must have resulted in him feeling more and more dysphoric over time. Being gay was not the cause of his dysphoria, his dysphoria was related to his inability to live as his true self.

As time progressed and Alex became more comfortable in disclosing his attractions to women and his fluid identity, Alex also began to explore the fact that he identified himself as a man. Alex had already begun experimenting with looking more androgynous—he cut his hair and began wearing baggier clothes. On one occasion, Alex appeared to my office beaming from ear to ear waiting to share with me how excited he was that he had ordered a binder on the internet and how thrilled he was to finally feel like he understood what had been bothering him for so long: he identified as a man and wanted to begin the transition to becoming a man. Almost immediately Alex's mood improved and his outlook on life became more positive. Although we still had work to do, Alex was able to begin thinking about the future again, and he was full of hope that he would someday feel comfortable in his own skin. Alex began to reflect on the fact that his unhappiness really heightened after he hit puberty and developed large breasts, and noted that his discomfort with himself never fully recovered. As he began to wear a binder and "pass" as a male, Alex grew in his confidence. Alex's family struggled with his identification as a male, and our work began to center on his ability to live in a family that continued to call him by his given name and use she/her/hers pronouns. However, Alex seemed happier, more engaged, and more able to handle his daily stressors.

Most notably, Alex's rape dreams completely abated after coming out as trans. A few months into his transition, I reflected to Alex that we had not discussed his rape dream in quite some time, an interesting departure from something that weighed prevalently in our previous work together. Alex took a moment to think about it and then said, "huh. I didn't even realize but I haven't had that dream in a while. I wonder if it had to do with me being so miserable as a woman." I was wondering the exact same thing.

Literature Review

Melanie Klein's (1952) concepts of the "paranoid-schizoid" and "depressive" positions influence greatly analytic thinking about the development of the child. For Klein, the child's early organization of their world involves experiencing objects and urges as either good or bad, malevolent or benevolent. Klein (1952) organized this concept around the good breast and the bad breast, in which the child feels either fully loved (the good breast) or the child feels hate or pain (the bad breast). Klein categorized this early organization as one of a "paranoid-schizoid" position. Generally speaking, the paranoid piece of the child's organization refers to an anxiety that is persecutory in nature, in which the child fears the bad object. The schizoid piece of the organization is the defense mechanism whereby the child is able to "split" the good from the bad, thusly protecting the good object from annihilation. The child gradually moves towards the depressive position in which the child is able to integrate the good/idealized and the bad/persecutory objects: the mother is neither all good nor all bad, but rather an integrated, complex whole (Mitchell & Black, 1995). This integration, however, symbolizes the beginning of the infant's experience of destruction and restoration of the object, a pattern which continues throughout the development of the self and which reemerges throughout the course of our lives (Hansbury, 2005; Mitchell & Black, 1995). The concepts of splitting, persecutory and idealized objects, and destruction and restoration are key for understanding how all individuals (and in this case transgender individuals) experience the world, their drives, and their objects.

In an application of the Kleinian concepts of splitting, persecutory/idealized objects, and object loss, Hansbury (2005) noted that the trans individual has a need to go through a mourning process by which they are able to shed the persecutory or idealized parts of their identity and move towards a more integrated transsexual/transgender identity. In a later work, Hansbury (2017) further developed our understanding of the transsexual/transgender experience when he argued that transsexual/transgender clients often present to treatment having "split-off" parts of themself, and noted that these "split-off parts have a tendency to haunt both psyche and soma, where they rattle their chains and seek troubling means of expression" (Hansbury, 2017, p. 1013). Consistent with Klein's developmental progression from paranoid-schizoid to depressive positions, Hansbury argues that some transgender clients present to treatment seeking to integrate the split-off parts of themselves, despite intense feelings of guilt and shame they experience, so as to experience their embodiment in a truer way. As such, analysis with a transsexual/transgender client involves a particular understanding of how these clients negotiate their early object relations, their relationship to their embodiment, and their experience of themselves in the world.

Heavily influenced by Klein, D.W. Winnicott (1956) further developed the idea of the impact of the relationship between the object (in this case the mother) and the child's urges on the child's development of the self. One of Winnicott's most important contributions to psychoanalytic thinking, and one that is particularly helpful here, was the concept of the false self. Winnicott (1956) notes that the false self emerges when there are inconsistencies between the person and their primary object during the psychosexual stages of development. The environment in which the infant develops is somehow deficient, and the ego is therefore not established. In other words, the infant's early needs are not sufficiently met (for a myriad of possible reasons) leaving the child unsatisfied and frustrated. What emerges instead is what Winnicott refers to as the "pseudo-self" or the false self (Winnicott, 1956, p. 387). This false self is developed as a means of adjustment to the unfulfilling environment, and serves as a protective factor in the infant's development. Winnicott postulated a true self does indeed develop, but that this true self is hidden due to the failures of the infant's early environmental experiences and lack of ego development. The false self therefore protects the true self and what results is a hollow existence, one that can exist in the world but one that lacks authenticity. The false self survives, but the true self yearns to emerge.

As such, Winnicott (1956) argued, false self disorders are those that emerge when the individual experiences a disordered subjective reality. The infant's early object relations are unsatisfying and their early experience of themself is frustrated and lacks integration with their outside world (i.e. their disordered intersubjectivity). Clinically, the person ultimately "doesn't *feel to himself* like a person" (Mitchell & Black, 1995, p. 124, emphasis theirs). In application to transgender or gender non-conforming clients, Ehrensaft (2016) used this Winnicottian concept and identified what she calls the "True Gender Self" and the "False Gender Self" (p. 36). When applied to gender, Ehrensaft argues, the true self is present from birth in some form as it exists in the psyche and body. The true gender self interfaces with society and is influenced by this intersection, but ultimately remains a deeply personal identity. The false self, therefore, is the shroud the individual must put on in order to exist in the world; it is informed by what the child understands as expected gender behaviors (Ehrensaft, 2016). As early as young childhood, some individuals who experience a disconnect between their gender identity and their biological gender learn to present a gender that is congruent with the expectations of the external environment.

Sociologists have noted that the gendered expectations of the external environment are fundamental to our being in society. According to research, identifying individuals as either male or female is a "primary cultural-category [system]," and is one that is highly influenced by cultural definitions and stereotypes about gender roles and behaviors (Ridgeway, 2009, p. 148). As such, cultural frameworks heavily influence gendered behavior, and individuals perform (or "do") their gender according to social norms and values (West & Zimmerman, 1987). Not only is gender culturally constructed, it is also constructed in opposition to the other gender category, forming a rigid binary in which things are one or the other and from which stems inequality and power differentials (Ridgeway, 2009). This framing of gender influences our expectations for ourselves and for others, and can delimit what we see as possible as far as gender fluidity and expression is concerned. As such, the experience of being born the wrong sex or being misgendered is increasingly difficult as one is socialized to identify sex and gender as rigidly binary and as one navigates various social interactions as well as cultural, familial, and internalized expectations about how one performs their assigned gender.

Lemma (2012) described this difficult experience or disconnect as that of "incongruity," noting that a common theme in her clinical work with transsexual/transgender clients was a feeling of disjointedness in their sense of self, much like that of the Winnicottian false self, not feeling like themselves in their own body (267). According to Lemma, the experience of incongruity is paired with the experience of being seen by others in a body that is not consistent with their internal gender identity. Gender is a lived, embodied experience, and transgender clients are often dealing with a sense of bodily incoherence and a complex, nuanced, and phenomenological negotiation of their gender identity. For Lemma (2012), and importantly for this case study, the etiology of transsexuality is not reducible to a single pathway, it requires room for multiple pathways, and the conundrum facing transsexual/transgender individuals cannot be essentialized as a purely biological or purely social or purely pathological issue (p. 264). Instead, the transsexual/transgender experience is one that requires an appreciation of the subjective nature of embodiment and therefore requires an appreciation of the range and variability in the types of experiences transsexual/transgender clients have.

In his seminal work on the phenomenological nature of the transsexual/transgender experience, Rubin (1998) articulated more extensively what Lemma referred to in her later work. Rubin argued that transsexuals' relationship to their embodiment largely informs their relationships with the world. A phenomenological approach to conceptualizing the transgender experience, therefore, enables us to understand how one's lived experience in a body might be at odds or might cause conflict with one's understanding of oneself. A Rubin (1998) argued, phenomenology allows for an embodiment that is split, and provides for the fact that "...some transsexual men have a body consciousness, a body image, that is at odds with their second-level body, their psychic body" (p. 271). Adequately exploring the transgender experience, therefore, requires that we remain experience-near and identify how each transgender individual came to their particular journey, allowing for the importance of the lived-experience and the embodied expression of gender identity that is to be uniquely found in each individual.

Hansbury (2005) reflected this point when he argued that the process of mourning, the splitting between the persecutory and the idealized objects, and the destructive fantasies that accompany the experience of being transsexual/transgender are not to be considered pathological, but rather seen as adaptive coping mechanisms whereby transsexual/transgender individuals make sense of their world. As such, it is important to note a shift in analytic writing from the etiological approach to the transgender experience towards a more teleological understanding of gender and sex (Hansbury, 2005; Harris, 2005; Saketopoulou, 2014). Rather than reducing the pathways to transgender or transsexual/transgender identity to a singular phenomenon or stemming from a single cause, analysts have argued that gender should rather be considered "softly assembled" (Harris, 2016, p. 362), emerging from a complex matrix of experiences, including one's gendered (or mis-gendered) body and one's internal experience of gender dysphoria (Saketopoulou, 2014). As such, the conceptualization of transgender development must be flexible, understood as multivariate, and recognized as an end to, rather than a cause of, psychological disturbance or traumatic experiences.

An additional layer to understanding etiology of mental health concerns amongst the transgender/transsexual population can be explained by considering the impact of minority stress on clients who present as trans (Leibowitz & Janssen, 2018; Tebbe & Moradi, 2016). Minority stress theory posits that negative mental health outcomes amongst minority populations can be ascribed to the experience of being a member of a stigmatized group. For transgender clients, this includes (but is not limited to) family rejection, trauma, complex vulnerability, discrimination, and interpersonal violence (Leibowitz & Janssen, 2018; Tebbe & Moradi, 2016). Children and adolescents come of age as a transgender/transsexual individual often have internalized messages that their gender identity is one that must be hidden, repressed, or denied, resulting in internalized transphobia and what is sometimes a very complicated relationship with their true selves (Leibowitz & Janssen, 2018). Socially-based discrimination coupled with the internalization of negative messages often combine to leave transgender individuals feeling depressed, anxious, and traumatized, an etiology that is not due to being trans per se, but rather due to being trans in a strictly binary society.

Saketopoulou (2014) argues that transsexual/transgender individuals actually experience what he calls a "massive gender trauma" that *results from* their internal experience of being transsexual/transgender and their embodied experience in the world rather than being the *cause of* their transsexual/transgender identity. According to Saketopoulou (2014), massive gender trauma occurs as these two events (being misgendered and gender dysphoria) occur and interact in the psyche of a transsexual/transgender individual (pp. 779–780). For Saketopoulou, this traumatic experience results in what should be understood as the requisite symptomatology of a traumatic experience (depression, anxiety, dissociation, etc.), which abates once the client is able to express more genuinely their gender identity (both medically and socially). In the process, however, the client must work through the significant impact of the trauma they have experienced and the clinician must be open to identifying the various, unique expressions of said trauma for each client.

For transsexual/transgender clients, the experience of massive gender trauma or the process of coming out as trans may invoke fantasies or defensive posturing that protect their ego from shame or fear associated with the coming out process, from early, fractured internal objects, and from the anxiety surrounding abandoning the protection of the false self in order for the true self to emerge. Part of this complicated process can include the means whereby transsexual/transgender clients seek to integrate the previously mentioned "split-off" parts of the self (Hansbury, 2017). In so doing, treatment must address the ways in which these parts have, as Hansbury puts it, "haunt[ed] both psyche and soma," which might include complicated destructive fantasies (p. 1013). For transsexual/transgender clients, the destructive fantasies might be aimed at what is perceived as the persecutory object. For Hansbury (2005), the persecutory object is the pre-transition body, and the fantasies include the destruction of the bad/incorrectly gendered object, but the fantasy might also involve the unconscious fantasy of being born the wrong gender (Saketopoulou, 2014), making the understanding of fantasy an integral part of understanding some transsexual/transgender clients' journeys towards coming out.

Ultimately, shifting our understanding of the transgender experience away from pathology and towards empathy and recognition of transgender identity as a legitimate gender expression is key to better and more empathic treatment of transgender clients. As Saketopoulou (2014) argues, there is a wealth of analytic information to be gleaned from approaching a transgender individual's experience as a "viable subjective reality" rather than illegitimate or symptomatic of "presumptive pathology" (Saketopoulou, 2014, p. 776). The key difference, here, is identifying how transgender clients present with psychic and emotional pain (and even trauma) that result from their intersectional experiences in a misgendered body and their experience of gender dysphoria (or massive gender trauma, as Saketopoulou terms it) rather than these traumas being the cause of their trans identity or gender dysphoria (Harris, 2016; Saketopoulou, 2014, p. 773). By inverting the traditional approach to transgender identity development, we are freed to consider the complicated and knotty clinical material to be found at the intersection of a client's symptom expression and the experience of their body and their world.

Discussion

When considering the breadth of Alex's experiences vis-à-vis his gender, sexuality, family, and culture (to name a few), it is not surprising that he presented to my office feeling depressed, disconnected, and ultimately really enraged about his embodied experiences. From his earliest memories, Alex characterized his experiences as incongruent—Eleanor was aggressively feminine and intensely binary in her expectations of Alex's behaviors (he was not allowed to play with male toys, he was not allowed to roughhouse with his brother, he was assigned more traditional roles in the home even at a young age). The incongruence grew over time and eventually eroded any sense of connection at all between Alex and Eleanor (however limited it was). Alex ultimately felt unable to meet Eleanor's female gaze—he felt inadequate in his ability to connect with his mother time and time again, despite his best efforts. This was especially true during arguments around gendered behavior (as previously noted, Eleanor would insist upon feminine behaviors from Alex and then later cited these same behaviors as rationale for refusing to accept Alex's gender identification) during which Eleanor would become increasingly agitated and eventually vicious in her verbal attacks on Alex and his sister.

Upon reflection, this disconnection, rage, and abuse might be attributed to Eleanor's own trauma. It is possible that Eleanor was reenacting her own struggles with the roles imposed on her, and, rather than having clarity about the destructive nature of these rigid constructs on herself, she recreated the rigid constructs with her children (Alex's sister had her own issues with Eleanor, organized around a lot of rage and hostility). The intergenerational transmission of trauma impacted every relationship in Alex's family, and characterized their familial system with ruptures and disrupted relationships devoid of any connectivity or emotional fulfillment for those involved (Harris, 2016). This theme carried through almost every relationship in the family, and caused a tremendous amount of tension and unhappiness in the family system.

The result of these ruptures in their relationships was a general failure to connect, which had long-term implications for Alex. The inability to link adequately with his primary caregiver was replayed throughout the course of Alex's young life, and he continued to feel disconnected from people throughout his childhood. Additionally, these ruptures resulted in a rigid paradigm for Alex wherein women, femininity, and femaleness were conflated with negative, bad, and persecutory objects while masculinity, men, and maleness were cherished as good, loving objects. As such, Alex began to over-identify with John and his underlying desire to sever from his female body grew more and more intense. From this paradigm developed Alex's relationship to femininity as oriented towards destruction—Alex had a deep desire to destroy his female body, albeit subconsciously, that was informed by a complex intersection of his rage towards his mother, his dysphoria at being misgendered, and his deep desire to be closer to his father (Hansbury, 2005). Alex did not only desire to be male, he desired to destroy any semblance of connection to Eleanor, a dynamic that was deeply disturbing to Alex prior to coming out as trans. As such, Alex had a hard time recognizing how he could be so unhappy when his parents had provided him for in every way. The fact was that his real needs had never been met, and, at the time, he was not even clear about what his real needs were.

Alex's lack of clarity regarding his complicated relationship with his gender identity, his sexuality, and his place in his family was further complicated by his cultural and religious identity. It can be argued that Alex was a child who experienced a false gender self as a result of the expectations placed on him by those around him (mainly Eleanor and his immediate family, but also by his larger group of friends and associates) (Ehrensaft, 2014). The gender dynamics and social mores present in Alex's Catholic, Polish family and background contributed greatly to his repression of his burgeoning true gender self, as he was increasingly expected to fulfill traditional roles. Although the space here is inadequate to discuss the intricacies and nuances of the ways in which culture and religion influence one's identity, it is important to note the ways in which the aggressively gendered spaces in society impact one's experience of themselves (Butler, 2004; Ridgeway, 2009; Rubin, 1998). For Alex, his interaction with a social system that was rigidly binary delimited his ability to think creatively about his gender identity and forced him to repress any awareness he might have had about his gender dysphoria in the early years of his development. After coming out, Alex reported that he was acutely aware of how unhappy he was about his post-pubescent body, but he lacked the language to describe what he was feeling, which led him to internalize the discomfort and force himself to embrace the feminine qualities of his developing body. Had Alex experienced this dissatisfaction in a society that was open to the fluidity of gender or even just less aggressive in its reification of gender norms, Alex's experience might have been very different.

Instead, Alex's feelings buttressed against a mother who was cruel and punishing, a religion that does not embrace LGBTQ relationships, and a community of people who reinforced the same norms as his family. Alex began to experience his true gender self (his desire to return to his pre-pubescent figure, for example) as an urge that was wrong and needed to be repressed. As such, Alex's relationship with his embodiment took on a falsehood that would take years to expose and even longer to begin to overcome. The more Alex developed, the deeper the repression went. Alex's desire to please those around him brought us to those junctures in my office where he was grappling with his deep discomfort around men yet refusing to identify as a lesbian, or dealing with his burgeoning interesting in being androgynous yet allowing his mother to pick out a prom dress for him to wear. The conflicts he felt which stemmed from his false gendered self resulted in the deep unhappiness and self harm that we dealt with week after week in our work together. As Elliot (2001) argues, "the acquisition of sexed embodiment [is] crucial to human well being," and Alex was struggling to survive (p. 301).

Alex was struggling with the fact that he was deeply unhappy with the disconnect between his physical self and his psychic self, and he was increasingly unhappy with the way he was being gendered by others (although his awareness of this did not reach consciousness until later in his treatment) with nowhere to turn. This juncture reflects what Saketopoulou (2014) identifies as massive gender trauma, and squarely places Alex's experiences in the realm of the traumatic. Although not necessarily considered an experience that is linked to complex trauma, Alex's experience of gender dysphoria and his daily encounters with being misgendered constituted for him a pervasively traumatic experience (Herman, 1992a). Complex trauma is characterized by traumatic experiences that are chronic and repetitive, and often involve close caregivers and attachment figures, the type to which Alex was regularly exposed (Conti, 2018; Ford & Courtois, 2009; Herman, 1992b). Alex had to navigate family relationships that forced him to deny his most genuine self, and had to regularly suffer messages that were painful and stigmatizing, causing him pain, confusion, dissociation, and resulted in the development of dreams related to rape and sexual trauma as expressions of his dysphoria. Characteristic of individuals who have been traumatized in a pervasive and chronic way, Alex presented with mood issues, inconsistent interpersonal relationships, and a fractured sense of self.

Additionally, complex trauma can also be ascribed to those things experienced as a result of larger systems of oppression, including structural violence and transnational forces (Conti, 2018; Hardy, Compton, & McPhatter, 2013). In Alex's case, he was caught in a web of structural violence that is gendered and binary in nature. The forced gendering and the rigid binary of Alex's daily life were experienced as a regular attack on his most basic sense of self, and resulted in the deep repression of his true gender identity. This, in turn, contributed significantly to Alex's mood disorder, his eventual self-harm, and the initial impoverished sense of self with which he presented to treatment. The aggressively gendered nature of society forced Alex into the closet where he suffered for many years without any hope of relief because he was too fearful and too inhibited to explore and understand his true self in any meaningful way. Thankfully, he was able to utilize technology and other forms of new media as well as our therapeutic relationship to explore the true self that was inside, but his fear, guilt, and shame, thrust upon him by his family and society writ large were significant and difficult to work through.

Due to the complex nature of Alex's experience of his gendered self, his physical body, his gender identity, and his person-in-environment, Alex's trauma is uniquely sexual in nature. Although it never emerged that Alex had, in fact, been sexually assaulted, the sexual nature of his trauma remains an important element to his understanding his treatment. If we are to work effectively with individuals who experience the world at the margins of the binary gender social construct, we must understand how this experience can be both bodily and psychological, both physical and emotional. Additionally, the unique experience of what Lemma (2013) calls incongruence, of feeling like one's sex organs are wrong, of feel like one's body is a betrayal, sexual trauma becomes an important frame. In discussing his rape dreams, Alex would regularly note feeling an out of body experience, where the male was coming for his female form, and he would share that this was a scary experience. Ultimately, this came to represent in our treatment as a useful metaphor for Alex's experience of living as a male trapped in a female body. Alex truly was fearful of what it meant to have a male come after him, both sexually and psychically. The fear was informed by both his attraction to women and repulsion to sex with men as well as his fear of living his true self in male form. Alex was frequently filled with anxiety, fear, depression, and even rage when grappling with his evolving sense of self and thinking about the ways in which his sense of self might impact his family, his friends, and his world. His metaphorical rape symbolized so much of the pain that characterized Alex's embodiment in a world, in a family, in a religion, and even in a frame of mind that pushed him to the margins and forced him to hide his most essential self.

Conclusion

This case study is not meant to serve as an epistle for treating trans clients. Not all trans individuals will experience their gender identity or their journey towards coming out as a sexually traumatic experience. Instead, this chapter is meant to expand our understanding of how individuals might find their journey traumatic, and that this trauma might be cast in the category of a sexual trauma in order to make room for a fruitful exploration of their experiences. Allowing for the complexity of Alex's story, we begin to see the ways in which an embodied experience can push us to rethink the ways in which we define disorder, how we approach treatment, and ultimately expand the room we make for narrative to push our understanding rather than having our understanding guide the clinical narrative. Only in doing so can work be truly transformative and liberative.

Alex ultimately decided to terminate treatment in order to work with someone who was familiar with the process of signing forms to begin a physical transition. Alex's depressive symptoms had largely dissipated by the time we ended treatment, and he had stopped self-harming altogether. The reduction in his symptoms and his progress in treatment increased towards the end, particularly in light of the fact that he was about to commence hormone replacement therapy.

Working with Alex expanded my understanding of the various etiologies of gender identity, and pushed me to consider how all of our identities are complicated negotiations of our embodied selves, the ways in which we interface with the world, and the ways that we navigate our families, our cultures, and larger society. Each individual experience requires acute attention to the unique forms that one's experience of themselves and themselves in the world combine and result in one's privilege (or lack thereof), one's power (or lack thereof), and one's safety (or lack thereof). Creating a safe place for the exploration of these intersections is a skill that is required for working with individuals who have been pushed to the margin, so as to open up our clinical dialogue regarding best practice and social justice-oriented clinical work.

Close Reading Questions

1. How does Conti's exploration of sexual trauma shift our understanding of what can be considered sexually traumatic?
2. What evidence of the mind-body connection do you see in Alex's clinical presentation?
3. Work to understand the concepts of "false self disorder," "true gender self," and "false gender self." How does a "rigidly binary" world promote splitting and how might your answer serve to complicate early theories about transgender individuals?

Prompts for Writing

1. Consider the "middle-class" world of Alex in relation to the "middle-class" world in "Sam's Story," translated by Roxanna Ast. What factors beyond their "middle-class status" do they share? What factors make one an asylum seeker and one living a life of relative safety?
2. Look further into Saketopoulu's theory of "massive gender trauma." How does that theory affect your working definition of LGBTQ Sexual Trauma?
3. Conti writes, "we did not conflate Alex's experience of being a lesbian (and eventually coming out as trans) as the cause of his mental health problems. Rather, we worked on identifying how the struggle between his family and his internal experiences have historically been fraught with tension." Why is this clinical approach important to Conti? Would you take the same approach?

Note

1 Alex is an alias, but it is meant to represent the client's chosen name.

References

Butler, J. (2004). *Undoing gender.* New York, NY: Routledge.

Conti, M. M. (2018). Thinking critically about sexual trauma in the 21st century. In M. Jaffe, J. Floersch, J. Longhofer, & M. M. Conti (Eds.), *The social work and sexual trauma casebook: Phenomenological perspectives* (pp. 11–34). New York, NY: Routledge Press.

Elliot, P. (2001). A psychoanalytic reading of transsexual embodiment. *Studies in Gender and Sexuality, 2*(4), 295–325.

Ehrensaft, D. (2014). Listening and learning from gender-nonconforming children. *The Psychoanalytic Study of the Child, 68*(1), 28–56.

Ehrensaft, D. (2016) *The gender creative child: Pathways for nurturing and supporting children who live outside gender boxes.* New York, NY: Experiment.

Ford, J. D., & Courtois, C. A. (2009). Defining and understanding complex trauma and complex traumatic stress disorders. In J. D. Ford & C. A. Courtois (Eds.), *Treating complex traumatic stress disorders: An evidence-based guide* (pp. 13–30). New York, NY: Guilford Press.

Hansbury, G. (2005). Mourning the loss of the idealized self. *Psychoanalytic Social Work, 12*(1), 19–35.

Hansbury, G. (2011). King Kong & Goldilocks: Imagining transmasculinities through the trans–trans dyad. *Psychoanalytic Dialogues, 21*(2), 210–220.

Hansbury, G. (2017). The masculine vaginal: Working with queer men's embodiment at the transgender edge. *Journal of the American Psychoanalytic Association, 65*(6), 1009–1031.

Hardy, V. L., Compton, K. D., & McPhatter, V. S. (2013). Domestic minor sex trafficking: Practice implications for mental health professionals. *Journal of Women and Social Work, 28*(1), 8–18.

Harris, A. (2005). *Gender as soft assembly.* New York, NY: Routledge.

Harris, A. (2016). Winnicott and gender madness. *British Journal of Psychotherapy, 32*(3), 359–375.

Herman, J. L. (1992a). Complex PTSD: A syndrome in survivors of prolonged and repeated trauma. *Journal of Traumatic Stress, 5*(3), 377–391.

Herman, J. L. (1992b). *Trauma and recovery: The aftermath of violence – from domestic abuse to political terror.* New York, NY: Basic Books.

Klein, M. (1952). Some theoretical conclusions regarding the emotional life of the infant. In P. Heimann, S. Isaacs, M. Klein, & J. Riviere (Eds.), *Developments in psycho-analysis* (pp. 198–236). London: Routledge.

Leibowitz, S., & Janssen, A. (2018). Affirming and gender-informed assessment of gender diverse and/or transgender youth across development. In S. Leibowitz & A. Janssen (Eds.), *Affirmative mental health care for transgender and gender diverse youth: A clinical guide* (pp. 1–30). Cham: Springer Books.

Lemma, A. (2012). Research off the couch: Re-visiting the transsexual conundrum. *Psychoanalytic Psychotherapy, 26*(4), 263–281.

Lemma, A. (2013). The body one has and the body one is: Understanding the transsexual's need to be seen. *The International Journal of Psychoanalysis, 94*(2), 277–292.

Mitchell, S. A., & Black, M. J. (1995). *Freud and beyond: A history of modern psychoanalytic thought.* New York, NY: Basic Books.

Ridgeway, C. L. (2009). Framed before we know it: How gender shapes social relations. *Gender and Society, 23*(2), 145–160.

Rubin, H. S. (1998). Phenomenology as method in trans studies. *GLQ: A Journal of Lesbian and Gay Studies, 4*(2), 263–281.

Saketopoulou, A. (2011). Minding the gap: Intersections between gender, race, and class in work with gender variant children. *Psychoanalytic Dialogues, 21*(2), 192–209.

Saketopoulou, A. (2014). Mourning the body as bedrock: Developmental considerations in treating transsexual patients analytically. *Journal of the American Psychoanalytic Association, 62*(5), 773–806.

Tebbe, E. A., & Moradi, B. (2016). Suicide risk in trans populations: An application of minority stress theory. *Journal of Counseling Psychology, 63*(5), 520–533.

West, C., & Zimmerman, D. (1987). Doing gender. *Gender & Society, 1*, 125–151.

Winnicott, D. W. (1956). On transference. *International Journal of Psychoanalysis, 37*, 386–388.

6

ON LOSING AND FINDING MY SISSY BODY

A Psychoanalytic-Phenomenological Perspective on the Trauma of Growing Up Gay

Eric Hartman

Pre-Reading Questions

1. Would you say that, to your cultural knowledge, heteronormative children are more desired than gay or transgender children?
2. The scope of heteronormativity is large, encompassing what Hartman calls "cultural understandings of the body," which impact the legality and legitimacy of gay sex and regulate gender behavior. How does being gay and born into a heteronormative society affect human development?
3. How does an anti-gay insult define the body? What anti-gay insults have you heard, and how do they define the gay body? How might a child embody these insults? How do you define embodiment?

Introduction

In this chapter of a book that focuses on lesbian, gay, bisexual, transgender, and queer (LGBTQ) sexual trauma, I ask the reader to first take time to consider the bodies of people who live as sexual minorities. That is, if the body is the primary site of sexual experience, we should think about the nature of how those bodies as they are lived. To do so, I propose that we consider the living, breathing, feeling bodies of LGBTQ people born into a world in which heteronormativity defines our cultural understandings of the body and the boundaries of what constitutes legitimate sex, desire, and gender behavior. By doing so, we can appreciate what precarity exists in the development of embodied self-awareness when a child's body unwittingly bears the sexual desires and gendered movements of a stigmatized class of people, in the case of this chapter, the class of people colloquially referred to as "sissies." Focusing on effeminate boys who grow up to identify as gay men, I explore the phenomenology of boyhood same-sex desire and gender nonconformity through the lens of embodiment. I posit the sissy body as an embattled site of desire and shame in the context of homophobic bullying and the pressure to defeminize and use the lens of developmental trauma to explore the ways that fear, shame, and dissociation shape the defeminized gay body. Finally, I reflect on how I re-encountered my own sissy body in the working through of a clinical enactment in my training analysis as a psychoanalytic candidate.

My methodology for exploring the embodied development of gay men who were effeminate boys utilizes three primary analytic frameworks: psychoanalysis, phenomenology, and queer theory. Psychoanalysis provides a structure for understanding personality development and the sequelae of childhood trauma, phenomenology helps to dig into concrete bodily experience as it is lived, and queer theory challenges normative cultural assumptions about sexuality, gender, and the body. In addition, I utilize first-person accounts, including my own, from gay male writers who lived the experience of having an effeminate boyhood. I chose this method to honor the first-person perspective of phenomenology and to counteract the sense of detached otherness that can occur when presenting clinical case material.

What Do We Do with the Sissy?

Twenty-seven years ago, queer theorist Eve Sedgwick (1991) made the critique that the only healthy homosexual male in even the most progressive psychoanalytic literature at the time seemed to be one who "(a) is already grown up, and (b) acts masculine" (p. 19). She goes on to make the following claim about the institutionalized silence about gay male development:

> There are many people in the worlds we inhabit, and these psychiatrists are unmistakably among them, who have a strong interest in the dignified treatment of any gay people who may happen already to exist. But the number of persons or institutions by whom the existence of gay people is treated as a precious desideratum, a needed condition of life, is small. The presiding asymmetry of value assignment between hetero and homo goes unchallenged everywhere: advice on how to help your kids turn out gay, not to mention your students, your parishioners, your therapy clients, or your military subordinates, is less ubiquitous than you might think.
>
> *(p. 23)*

Sedgwick's observation about the contested status—the desirability—of the gay child is keen and still relevant today. She is not disputing that gay men have cultural allies, but the extent to which such allies acknowledge, let alone value, the existence of gay children is a very different picture. Imagine, as Sedgwick is asking, if every parent and teacher had an optimistic expectation that some of their children and pupils would be gay and that these children would be deemed not just variants of normal human sexuality but as necessary and valuable members of society. Imagine if such an expectation included cherishing boys who behaved in some manner like that which we typically expect of girls. What would gay male development look like then?

Of course, not all effeminate boys will grow up to identify as gay men. Some will become transgender adults, and others may follow a traditional heterosexual male developmental trajectory and grow up to identify as straight men. So, while childhood gender nonconformity should not be conflated with homosexuality, the two phenomena have considerable overlap and seem to be meaningfully correlated according to a number of large research studies (Bailey & Zucker, 1995; Harry, 1983; Taywaditep, 2001). Thus, it is useful to consider the interconnections of gender and sexuality when thinking about gay boyhoods, while being careful not to collapse gender nonconformity with homosexuality or hegemonic masculinity with heterosexuality. Therefore, I want to think about what psychoanalyst Ken Corbett (1996) calls "protogay" boys, that is, the yet-to-know-themselves-to-be-gay boys who will eventually identify as adult gay men. Even more specifically, I want to narrow in on those particular protogay boys who are considered effeminate, whose interests include conventionally feminine things, and whose girlish behavior results in being labeled a sissy by others. Thus, for the purposes of this discussion, I will also deploy the term sissy in a compassionately re-appropriated form to refer to these protogay boys and the ways their behaviors signify culturally recognizable forms of femininity.

Corbett (2009) considers the developmental needs of non-heteronormative boys in his book, *Boyhoods: Rethinking Masculinities.* Corbett's project explores the diverse ways that boys develop into particular kinds of gendered adults by way of their psychosocial experiences within and outside of the family. Using case examples from his clinical practice with children and parents, he demonstrates how traditional theories of masculine development are insufficient for understanding the needs and conflicts of boys, whether or not they develop into heterosexual men or otherwise. He critiques the socio-cultural norms that restrict boys from freely and fully developing as emotional and creative beings. He pays special attention to the plight of effeminate boys and to children who suffer from gender dysphoria. His rendering of these children is complex and compassionate and speaks to the need to rethink how we expect boys (and all children for that matter) to play, interact, and grow in the world. Indeed, Corbett's keen observations and clinical insight about effeminate boys challenge the pathologizing nature of theories about the etiology of adult male homosexuality developed by psychoanalysts in the past (for examples, see: McDougall, 1972; Schilder, 1929; Socarides, 1970).

While there is work still to be done to revise developmental theories with more inclusive and complex understandings of gender and sexuality, Corbett's thoughts on embodiment in particular invite an ongoing dialogue about the role of the body in male development. In the final chapter, Corbett writes,

> Male embodiment, boys' bodies, men's and boys' states of desire–what they seek, what they carry, what they bury – has, if anything, stalled with original Freudian formulations, or even regressed. It is almost as though the male body cannot be thought.
>
> *(2009, p. 218)*

Here, Corbett sheds light on the lack of updated thinking about the male body in general, but his comments also help to situate one of primary problems in gay male childhood development as the one that necessarily involves the body. That is, if we are thinking about how gay boys develop into gay men, we must consider how that body desires, whether, as Corbett suggests, such experiences are carried or buried, and how that impacts development overtime.

I do not doubt that Corbett's ideas about embodiment are meant to include the felt bodily experience of being male, but his choice of framing his subtitle as *rethinking* masculinities and his comment that the male body cannot be thought represents a liability within the psychoanalytic enterprise such that it privileges analytic thinking and metaphor over sensorimotor perception and concrete lived bodily experience. Yet despite this apparent bias in his writing, we learn something about Corbett's embodied self-awareness in a discussion about his clinical work with a six-year-old boy who called Corbett a faggot during a session of play therapy (2009, p. 180). The passage is Corbett's first-person account of how he, as a gay man, relates to the word faggot. He writes,

> Faggot, therefore, carries a particular and embodied history for me. Faggot not only was a formative dimension of my identity; it continues to sustain that identity. Paraphrasing Judith Butler, the word entered my limbs, crafted my gestures, bent my spine, and shaped my mind.
>
> *(p. 183)*

This short passage reveals Corbett's complex understanding of how culture, identity, and body are intertwined, partially obtained through the concrete lived experience of his own childhood. Yet, it is just a fleeting moment for the reader, who must wonder, how is this true? How did it happen? How does the word *faggot* enter Corbett's limbs, as he says?

Corbett's nod to Judith Butler (1990, 1993) signals an affinity for her critique of heteronormativity and the cultural regulation of gender expression.

He asserts that the "spectrum of masculine bodies and minds is underestimated; how they evolve or how they come to matter is patrolled, and the margins are deemed pathological" (2009, p. 9). The margins that Corbett refers to are the lived experiences of boys who violate the normative expectations of heterosexual development. Indeed, despite the contemporary promulgation of anti-bullying programs in US schools, a study by the Gay, Lesbian, and Straight Education Network (GLSEN) in 2011 reveals how common it is for gay and gender nonconforming kids to be verbally attacked at school with nearly 82% reporting some form of verbal harassment (Kosciw, Greytak, Bartkiewicz, Boesen, & Palmer, 2012). In *Excitable Speech,* Butler (1997) describes how insults—words like faggot and sissy—impact the body. She writes,

> When we say that an insult strikes like a blow, we imply that our bodies are injured by such speech. And they surely are, but not in the same way as a purely physical injury takes place. Just as physical injury implicates the psyche, so psychic injury effects the bodily doxa, that lived and corporeally registered set of beliefs that constitute social reality. The "constructive" power of the tacit performative is precisely its ability to establish a practical sense for the body, not only a sense of what the body is, but how it can or cannot negotiate space, its "location" in terms of prevailing cultural coordinates.
>
> *(pp. 159–160)*

Butler provides a way to understand how the anti-gay insult can have a limiting effect on what a gay body can or cannot do. The lasting stigma of being labeled a sissy/faggot interferes with the freedom to negotiate spaces (e.g., where is it safe to go?) and to do things with their bodies that other non-sissies are authorized to do. Protogay boys may thus feel constrained in their identity practices, such that their very physical presence risks evoking mockery, shunning, or even violence from others, especially other boys.

Writing about violence against queer people, Doug Meyer (2015) describes the overlap of non-normative gender expression and anti-gay bullying. He describes the painful experiences protogay boys face when they are exposed publicly as being gay because of their non-conforming gender before they understand for themselves what their same-sex attraction means. Meyer also points to how race and social class may determine the kinds of violence that protogay boys face. For instance, given that black males are more frequently the targets of police harassment and brutality, the antigay violence a protogay black child experiences may begin as an instance of racial profiling that may evolve to include anti-gay bias.

Schools are predictable sites in which protogay boys are particularly vulnerable to violence, according to GLSEN's 2011 nationwide survey of the conditions of LGBT youth in US schools. They surveyed 8,584 students between the ages of 13 and 20 from 3,224 school districts across all 50 states and found that in the past year, 81.9% reported that they were verbally harassed, 38.3% reported being physically harassed, and 18.3% reported being physically assaulted due to their sexual orientation (Kosciw et al., 2012, pp. xiv–xv). These figures reveal that the threat of physical violence against gay young people is real, but statistics do not show how such threats and violence are lived through the body. I argue that an intellectual understanding that gay identities are embedded in homophobic culture does not account how the embattled protogay body feels and develops over time. To grasp how protogay boys and adult gay men feel in their bodies, we must utilize different tools. The following discussion utilizes a phenomenological framework to explore what it is like to have a sissy body.

Phenomenology of the Sissy

For protogay boys who are teased and bullied by their peers for being sissies, the body may be self-perceived as both a cause of external persecution and a source internal mystery. So how do we go about understanding how these experiences affect the protogay boy's development of embodied self-awareness over time? One approach is to explore the first-person subjective accounts of the body of gay men who were effeminate boys. In other words, we could think about what phenomenology refers to as the lived body of these men (Gallagher & Zahavi, 2015). The lived body refers to pre-reflective bodily experience that is a structural part of all conscious experience and is distinct from the reflective ways in which we can think about and observe our physical bodies as objects. (i) Phenomenologist Maurice Merleau-Ponty (1962), expanding Edmund Husserl's (ii) seminal ideas about the lived body, writes "our body is not an object for an 'I think', it is a grouping of lived-through meanings which moves towards its equilibrium" (p. 177). Thus, our moment-to-moment perception is embodied in the sense that what we experience is always constituted in part by how our bodies are involved in a situation and by the meanings we have accumulated as bodily habits through past experience (Merleau-Ponty gives the example of the ability to distinguish colors as such a sensory habit on pp. 176–177). Merleau-Ponty (1962) emphasized both the generality and ambiguity of embodied perception, stating, "ambiguity is of the essence of human existence, and everything we live or think has always several meanings" (p. 196). Thus, the complexity of the body is lived as a generalized whole which yields a plurality of unarticulated meanings in pre-reflective experience. The ambiguity of embodied experience is important in the exploration of protogay sissy boys, because the lack of transparency creates both refuge from and obfuscation for the spelling out of meanings contained in their same-sex desire and feminine body movements.

Psychoanalysts Blum and Pfetzing (1997) conceptualized the confounding self-experiences of growing up gay as a form of trauma due to the ways protogay children are tasked with discovering their stigmatizing sexuality. They write:

> [T]he proto-gay boy often, from an early age, has some beginning awareness of feeling different. He also, to varying degrees, begins to connect this differentness with something forbidden, terrible, unthinkable. This may perhaps come in a momentary flash or it may be a continual fear; it may be conscious or it may be primarily unconscious. The hatred, hostility, and vehemence with which people around him manifest when using words like faggot, sissy, queer, whether directed at him or others, coupled with his own undeveloped, distorted understanding of these terms, presents a unique situation.
>
> *(p. 431)*

As part of this unique situation, Blum and Pfetzing point to the isolating aspects of protogay children, which, unlike members of other oppressed groups, include the experience of being an *other* even within their own families. I argue that this isolation is partly constituted by the ambiguous, wordless nature of the child's embodied erotic sensations, such that protogay children must try to make meaning out of experience that is not transparent nor is it actively mirrored and validated by their parents. Unlike the sexual development of heterosexual little girls, who may have their erotic feelings playfully recognized in comments from adults about the girl's desire to grow up to marry daddy, the protogay boy unlikely has such help. For protogay boys who are labeled sissies, the problem extends beyond the passive lack of validation, as Blum and Pfetzing illustrate in their case example of an adult gay man whose sense of being defective was "deeply intertwined with the threats, rejection, and humiliation that had pervaded his childhood" (p. 437).

Should we conclude then that all protogay boyhood experiences are lonely, painful, and scary? Education advocate and gay rights advocate Eric Rofes (2005) asks us to not to do so, but instead to imagine a fuller picture of what growing up gay can be like. Recalling his childhood as an effeminate protogay boy, Rofes writes,

> My boyish effeminate hand gestures can alternately be understood as either genetic errors that required social approbation to correct or rebellious acts committed to undermining the macho values constantly thrust on me. My determination to skip rope, enjoy hopscotch, and play with

> dolls rather than join the boys in kickball or dodge ball might suggest an ambitious intent to create an alternative social world for myself outside the bruising sites of boyhood.
>
> *(p. 2)*

Rofes' book project targets how schools relate to queer students, and the above quote about his own childhood experience touches upon the various debates (iii) about the nature of gender identity and sexual orientation. But Rofes' first-person narrative includes an aspect of childhood gender nonconformity that is often missing in the clinical literature about sissy boys, that is, that like most kids, his bodily behavior was driven in part by the determination to play and have fun. Writing about the kinds of pleasure Rofes sought as a child using his body to gesture and play as he chose, he invites us to rethink the narrative about childhood gender nonconformity to include what he calls the ways that "hope, celebration, and respite" (p. 2) are created through the embodied gender practices of these children. His story helps us to remember that there is more than just abuse and rejection in the lived experiences of gay and trans youth. In fact, his story suggests that the pleasures of play and creative self-expression must be so important for some children that it seems worth putting up with the resistance of the world.

Rofes' discussion of his protogay experiences also includes clear memories of homoerotic excitement in which he describes how he was "transfixed" by his father's body hair when they showered together. His narrative of the pleasures of being a childhood sissy thus includes a budding awareness of his same-sex attraction. What did this experience feel like in or on his protogay body and what kind of sense was he able to make of it at the time? Rofes does not address these questions in his narrative, so I reflected on my own similar childhood memories of both cross-gender play and same-sex attraction to examine the possibilities. The following narrative is a first-person account of my own embodied experiences of being a protogay childhood sissy.

I recall being keen on wearing a navy-blue dress during playtime. The dress belonged to my older sister and had tiny white polka dots and a hemline that reached the floor on my four-year old body. I loved how it felt to walk down a flight of stairs while wearing it—in my childhood imagination, the setting was much grander than the orange shag carpeted stairs that led down to our basement playroom. That basement was where I also developed my crush on Kent McCord, the dashing actor who played Officer Jim Reed on the television series Adam-12 (see http://kentmccord.com/). As early as age 5, I remember lying on my stomach on that shag carpet to watch reruns of the show, mesmerized by Officer Reed's handsome face and well-fitting uniform. I remember that it felt so good to watch him—that is, it felt good in my body, warm and tingling—however, I have no recollection of having any explicit sexual ideas about him. I knew that watching Officer Reed felt good, but I did not understand why, nor did I feel that I should ask anyone about it. In fact, it felt like something I should not even try to understand.

Knowing, yet not knowing, of the pleasure experienced in seeing attractive men is a phenomenon I have come to recognize as common within the childhood histories of the gay men I have worked with in my clinical practice. The bodily excitement is tacitly registered, but the reflective understanding of it does not occur. I believe this lack of articulation of the specific erotic meanings in these experiences is facilitated by the ambiguity Merleau-Ponty (1962) describes as an essential feature of the lived body. As a phenomenon, I did not have the explicit thought that my pleasure at viewing Kent McCord was erotic in nature or that it meant that I was homosexual. Pre-reflective experiences of excitement do not announce themselves with such concise meanings; rather, they exist as tingling, as heat, and as an accelerated heart rate. As a five-year old, I did not have the knowledge to make sense of what I now know those feelings meant. Yet, sensing that it was somehow wrong—as Blum and Pfetzing (1997) posit is typical in protogay experiences—I knew not to talk about it with others. Despite efforts to remain ignorant to the meaning of my erotic feelings, I was eventually forced to face the truth through the anti-gay taunts from my peers at school. In the following discussion, I consider the impact of such social interactions on the developing sissy body.

Defeminizing the Sissy Body

According to a number of statistical studies, the prevalence of childhood gender nonconformity in the reported histories of adult gay men has been found to be in large majorities of the research populations, but that many gay men who were once effeminate boys learn to "pass" as conventionally masculine over time (Bailey & Zucker, 1995; Harry, 1983; Taywaditep, 2001). Joseph Harry confirmed earlier research by Whitam (1977, 1980) that gay men are three to six times more likely to have exhibited cross-gender behavior in childhood than non-gay men and that most effeminate boys who grow up to be gay undergo a process of *defeminization* at some point before adulthood (Harry, 1983, p. 8). Although Harry's study did not measure for reported histories of childhood abuse or harassment based on gender nonconformity, he concludes, "it seems that defeminization, to the extent that it occurs, may be imposed on the boy predisposed to effeminacy, rather than being a spontaneous development" (p. 2). So, what does it mean to defeminize? According to the binary system of gender in conventional cultural discourse, the only possible outcome of defeminization would be that protogay sissy boys become masculine. Hence, the term defeminization is somewhat misleading. It is not simply shedding feminine behaviors, but a process in which feminine behaviors are restrained and masculine behaviors are learned in their place.

What happens to the embodied memories of having been a sissy for the protogay boy who defeminizes? If he loses his childhood effeminacy altogether, what happens to the feelings associated with his former sissy body? To answer these questions, we have to include in our inquiry not only the felt bodily experiences associated with male effeminate gender expression as discussed above, but also the experience of being defeminized. What is crucial here is to recognize the social interactive aspect of transitioning from sissy boy to conventional masculinity. That is, the ways that gender is patrolled and regulated by others in the environment. Thus, as Harry suggests, defeminization is primarily an imposed interpersonal process, and one that can be marked by brutality as evidenced by the high rate of harassment and violence against LGBTQ young people who display gender nonconforming behavior (Kosciw et al., 2012, p. 16).

Kittiwut Jod Taywaditep (2001) proposes that one of the consequences of defeminization is the development of *masculinity consciousness*, characterized as persistent self-monitoring of gender expression and a pre-occupation with "fitting-in" (p. 18). Taywaditep attributes this phenomenon to the negative social conditioning of defeminization experiences that engender the association of shame with one's effeminate behaviors. Since all consciousness includes a pre-reflective awareness of the body, what kind of embodied experience is shame in the context of masculinity consciousness? In his phenomenological investigation of the bodily experience of shame, Thomas Fuchs (2002) writes that "shame is the incorporated gaze of the other" (p. 228) that alters the lived experience of the body. He describes the lived-experience of shame as, being painfully affected by centripetal directions, i.e., by piercing gazes or pointing fingers from all sides; lowering one's eyes in order to escape those gazes; a feeling of shrinking such as one could "sink through the floor with shame," a desperate desire to hide oneself—all this means paralysis and corporealization in the presence of the others. The reddening and warmth of the face, or the "burning shame" corresponds to the painful gazes which are felt like hot rays; the ashamed person is actually the "focus" of attention (pp. 227–228).

Fuchs speaks to the rupture that shame causes when the ongoing-ness of the lived-body ceases in its coherence due to the body becoming the self-conscious object of the subject's attention. The body as object, laden with its physiological reactions, is experienced as disorganizing and clumsy, creating what Fuchs calls "a vicious circle of corporealization and self-consciousness" (p. 228). It is this clumsiness and self-consciousness about the body, paired with the tensing of the body in preparation for a physical attack that may characterize the sissy boy's lived bodily experience of being defeminized. This is the state in which he must also learn new gender practices as he develops masculinity consciousness and attempts to control his feminine bodily movements. As a novice to the skills of hegemonic masculinity, the boy may feel clumsy in trying to move his body according to the new, perhaps unclear, set of rules for gender practice. At the same time, he may feel the ongoing self-consciousness that he may slip into sissiness, as if masculinity consciousness is the permanent incorporation of the gaze of the bully. I have observed what might be the long-term effects of this fearful and awkward state in my adult gay male patients in which a bodily rigidity is perpetually present in what seems to be a habituated effort to control the body's movement. While it is true that persistent gender nonconformity might result in escalating harassment and violence for the protogay boy, from the perspective of the rigidified body of masculinity consciousness, both outcomes of defeminizing or not defeminizing come with costs.

If I think about my own experience of defeminization, I recall an agonizing process of learning to stop certain sissy behaviors and replace them with masculine ones. This process occurred over more than a decade and required the instruction of my family and peers. I remember at age 4, while taking a "potty" break during playtime, I was standing in front of the toilet, straining to hold up the skirt of my favorite dress while trying to aim my stream of urine into the toilet as I was taught. With the bathroom door ajar, my mother noticed and said something like, "Look at you! You look ridiculous! If you have to hold your dress up to pee like a boy, it means that you shouldn't be wearing a dress." I know my mother was struggling to understand what was happening with her son in our conservative corner of 1970s rural America, but I remember being devastated by her words. That was the last time I put on a dress for playtime.

I recall a difficult scene in a fourth-grade classroom in that same small Iowa town in 1982. I was only nine-years-old, and this was the moment that the name-calling I had already become accustomed to shifted from references to being a sissy to explicit anti-gay insults. I recall being stunned by the speed at which my attacker lunged across my desk and stabbed me with his pencil. Putting his face up close to mine he said, "You fag, if I had more time, I'd kill you." He quickly returned to his seat only moments before the teacher entered the room to start class. I remained at my desk in silence, absorbing what had happened and worrying I might die of lead poisoning. Despite my (unwarranted) fears about dying, it seemed impossible to face the shame of telling an adult that I had been discovered to be a fag.

One of the confusing aspects of this experience was the physical experience of being so close to my attacker and feeling his body against my own. I can recall how, for a moment, I was titillated when I felt the tense muscles of his arm was against my neck as held me down in my seat, pushing his forearm up against my chin as he used his free arm to stab my shoulder. "How was his body so wonderfully muscular?" I silently thought to myself. As a reluctant participant in rough and tumble play, I had never reflected on the sensation of someone else's flexed muscles against my own. Corbett (2009) describes the "body-to-body, embrace-to-embrace, strong-arm-to-strong-arm push and pull or muscular eroticism" (p. 233) in his exploration of the embodied experiences of male bonding in boyhood. But this was not a typical scene of male bonding. The realization of how pleasurable it felt to have him on top of me was lovely and then mortifying. I knew he was attractive, but that knowledge seemed objective, somehow, not in any way connected to my own desire. It was the same reasoning I had been relying on to organize my feelings about Kent McCord since the age of 5. Some men were handsome, that had simply been a fact. I did not articulate that knowledge in a way that implicated my sexuality. I then wondered if my attacker had noticed me looking at him lustfully? Was I even aware of possessing a lustful gaze? Was it my gaze that provoked his response? These puzzling, shame-filled thoughts thrust me into the question of whether or not I was a homosexual, and I dreaded the conclusion that my body seemed to have already revealed. While I could not deny what my body felt, the best strategy seemed to be to try to conceal what I knew. This was the moment that I consciously joined in my own defeminization process.

By adolescence, my effeminacy had become policed more aggressively by my peers and upper classmen, and I became much more self-conscious of how I behaved. I remember a moment in 6th grade when I was told by another boy that I carried my books like a girl. I was dumbfounded that there was a way that boys were supposed to do it that differed from girls. It was a moment where the unconscious interpersonal aspects of my self-representation met with the conscious interpersonal enforcement of the defeminization process. While I had unconsciously learned to practice cradling my books close to my chest like most girls, it took being mocked by my male peers to show me that I was doing it wrong; I learned that guys carry their books grasped in one hand and down to their sides. Lessons like these peaked in my late adolescence and subsided in my early twenties. In high school, my defeminized identity was clumsy and inconsistent, but by age 25, despite being out of the closet for 7 years, the ongoing self-monitoring and restraint of my sissy body had become habituated. While still self-conscious at times about making the wrong move and appearing feminine, I found myself embodying the identity of a normatively masculine adult male in all its regimented and emotionally-stifled splendor. So, what remained of my sissy body past? In the final section, I consider this question through the lens of developmental trauma and the role that dissociation may play in the embodied experience of growing up gay.

The Dissociated Sissy

Psychoanalyst Philip Bromberg conceives of a kind of trauma resulting from the refusal by parents to acknowledge the subjectivity of a child, writing, "the often undramatic but equally impactful trauma of living day in and day out in a family that systematically disavows the existence of a child's subjective experience and discredits the validity of that child's emotional states" (2003, p. 572). If we apply this concept to the protogay sissy boy whose attempts to express himself through his body are continuously discredited, ignored, or thwarted by both family and peers, we can imagine a developmental trajectory in which some of the boy's deepest bodily desires must be disavowed without adequate means of making sense of them—perhaps leaving in suspension a vague question about the nature of his difference. Indeed, Blum and Pfetzing's (1997) case formulation demonstrates just how such a traumatic upbringing can impact the adult gay man's personality in the form of persistent dissociative process. They wrote of their patient's "dissociated cravings for love, tenderness, attachment, and physical contact," which they attributed to his "terrible fear of punishment and annihilation" for being different (p. 438).

Writing about the consequences of developmental trauma, Bromberg (1998) describes how dissociation is a means of coping for traumatized children. He writes,

> To the extent that a traumatized child has the capacity and opportunity to use dissociation as a means of coping, he will typically do so, but the cost of shaping the personality in this direction is for some people, an enduring experience of something being 'wrong' – something the adult patient cannot put into words – and a consuming determination to put it right.
>
> *(p. 133)*

Bromberg speaks of dissociation shaping the personality, but how might dissociation also affect how a person experiences, or does not experience, the body? Perhaps a better way to frame this question is to wonder in what ways dissociation interferes with the protogay boy's capacity to reflect on his bodily experience? If we imagine that the most dissociated aspect of the protogay boy's life are his unspeakable bodily desires—his desire to move his body in feminine ways, his desires to feel his body in sensual contact with another male—then we see how the anti-gay words and actions of the bully threaten the boy's precarious existence in which he needs to not know the nature of his shameful, dangerous desire. Such an existence might even seem solid, so long as sexuality is avoided. Dissociation thus allows the body to be the lone knower of the aspects of the boy's desire that he cannot spell out to himself let alone speak to another.

The ongoing dissociative organization of the gay body may leave protogay boys habitually detached from certain bodily experiences, and I propose that this can have lasting effects on how adult gay man experience their bodies. This may include chronic experiences of feeling disconnected from the body or the experience of having to enter a sequestered state that is detached from the adult gay man's ongoing sense of self in order to access his sexual desire or the archaic joy he once experienced as a sissy boy. The sequestration of erotic or feminine-gendered self-states, in which such states are felt to be discontinuous with the rest of one's identity, may be another way that dissociation leaves a lasting impression on how gay men experience their embodiment. Instead of fluid shifts from context-to-context, sexual encounters and "sissy states" may be experienced as jarring temporally-disjointed moments that cannot be reconciled with the ongoing sense of who he feels himself to be.

Finding My Sissy Body

Bromberg (2003) writes of the hope in therapeutic work for making formerly dissociated aspects of the patient accessible for reflection by creating a safe-enough space that allows the patient to speak his or her truth. Bromberg is concerned with how shame can interfere with this process, and his words speak to the precarity in what I have described above about the protogay boy's dissociative structure. He writes,

> Shame is, of course, the affect that signals a loss of personal identity—"I don't know who I am"—but in the context of retelling, the word fails to capture the full magnitude of the experience when one was threatened with traumatic loss of selfhood. It is only through its reliving (the last thing that a patient wants to face) that it can be known by an "other"—hopefully this time an "other" who will have the courage to participate in the reliving while simultaneously holding the patient's psychological safety as a matter of prime concern.
>
> *(p. 567)*

Bromberg's hopeful outlook on the therapeutic relationship resonates with my own experience of having found a courageous "other" in my training analyst, who helped me recognize and tell the story of my embodied sissy past. So, I end this discussion with reflections on my own experiences of having lost and then found my sissy body.

For many years, I arrived to my analyst's office with my workout bag in hand. I would sit on his couch for session after session, week after week, with that bag at my feet. After joining a boxing gym just two blocks from his office, I even started wearing my workout clothes to our sessions. I would go to analysis and afterwards head to the gym to workout. Acknowledging my fit body and my investment in some traditionally masculine activities (e.g. kickboxing and weightlifting), he periodically tried to elicit how I felt about our differences in body shape and gender expression. My analyst, a gay white man twelve or so years my senior, was unabashed about his own effeminacy and not having a gym-trained body. His candid acknowledgment of these features of his bodily appearance always disoriented me. It made me uncomfortable, and I did not want to think about it, much less talk about it. It seemed to me that there was nothing to say about his body, and that is what I would tell him whenever he asked.

Eventually, after many repetitions over a period of several years, I became irritated by my analyst's questions to me about his body. Agitated, I told him that it was an entirely empty pursuit. In response, he shared with me the source of his persistent curiosity about it. He disclosed a sense of shame he noticed feeling about his body and gender expression at times when we were together. He acknowledged that this shame was his own, but that he was not aware of experiencing it while working with other patients, even other men who shared my physical characteristics. It made him curious about the potential that something was being enacted during our sessions.

Donnel Stern (1997, 2010, 2015) writes extensively on the concept of clinical enactment, that is, the tendency for patients and analysts to create circumstances that evoke material that cannot be reflected upon due to mutual dissociative processes in the interpersonal field. Stern writes of this relational aspect of dissociation, stating "[o]ne's own involvement with the other—that is, one's motivation to create and maintain the very state of affairs that is later revealed to have been problematic—is invisible" (2015, p. 7). What this means is that my analyst had an idea that something was being enacting between us, and that some dissociated aspect of own my experience that related to his body may have something to do with it.

Prompted by my analyst's careful disclosure, I noticed myself indeed feeling something, not about his body at first, but my own. I recognized that uncomfortable feeling that came up each time he asked me about his body. Instead of passing over it as usual, I reflected on it and recognized a sad familiar feeling of being shamefully effeminate and alone. Hence, what was discovered through the enactment was my dissociated shame about being a sissy boy, unavailable for my own self-reflection, but left to be experienced by my analyst through intercorporeal structure of our interactions. That structure, sissy body and not-a-sissy-body—or sissy body and disavowed sissy body—was charged with my indifferent attitude and avoidant involvement, which elicited feelings of shame in my analyst. Left out of these enacted interactions were our explicit demands on each other, such that I did not want to be the sissy, and he did not want to be invisible. My initial constriction of the ability to reflect on these interactions—that is, my dissociative involvement—projected a relational void that left him feeling both locked-down and erased. I locked him into the position as being the one who is the sissy, while I simultaneously shamed him and refused to acknowledge it. For him, this meant that not only would I not recognize his sissiness, but that he was left to feel that he could not be anything more than his sissiness to me. Unable to reflect on that meaning prior to this confrontation, he found himself enacting behaviors to get me to notice him in other ways, such as suggesting books for me to read or being aggressive and provocative in his interpretations. These behaviors left me feeling bullied and shamed by him, and I withdrew in a variety of physical and psychological ways. In working through the enactment, I became able to reflect on his bodily presence as well as the shame and archaic fear that the rigidity of my own body was supposed to shield me from feeling but had only cloaked. I became aware of the defensive quality of my gender practices and how they stemmed from a hypervigilance about revealing myself as the sissy.

Through our subsequent work I realized how controlled my bodily movements were when interacting with others, especially in the presence of heterosexual men. In this intercorporeal arrangement, I noticed myself reflexively stiffening my posture and reducing my hand gestures to somehow constrain myself. These uncomfortable self-realizations drew my attention to how much shame I experienced about having been a sissy boy. I realized that this history was almost always left out of my self-narrative when speaking with others and that somewhere along the way I had lost contact with my sissy body. So where did it go?

Defeminization experiences like those I discussed throughout this chapter occurred on a daily basis throughout my childhood and adolescence. Yet these hostile interactions with my family and peers were not the sole cause of my disconnection from my sissy past. By carefully retracing the transitions in my identity from childhood to adulthood, my analyst and I located a late-stage disavowal of my sissiness that occurred when I entered the adult domain of gay dating. In line with Taywaditep's (2001) research on the marginalization of effeminate gay men, I encountered significant anti-effeminate attitudes in the gay communities of San Francisco and New York, where I had lived starting from age 19. Such attitudes are exemplified and reinforced through the discourse of "no fems" in gay dating and hookup scenes (Taywaditep, 2001, p. 12). Thus, my final move to defeminize was motivated by the desire to find a mate. What intrigues me about this process is how effectively I was able to learn to signify hegemonic masculinity once I had the capacity to accept my sexual desire as a gay man. I was no longer hampered by the dissociative need to remain blind to my body's movements and erotic sensations. Instead, I was able to know them, but I actively chose to turn my back on the specific feelings of joy once embodied by that little sissy boy in the navy-blue dress. I may have gained the capacity to reflect on my body, but my shame about the joy I once felt in being a sissy became detached from my ongoing experience of being a gay man.

My self-narrative should not be read as an epiphanic break-through that resulted in the joyful recovery of my sissy body. My prior defeminizing experiences made reconnecting to my sissy past more complicated than that. On the one hand, learning to signify hegemonic masculinity rewarded me with social privileges that I am still too invested in to give up easily. Not only that, my defeminized gender practices are now habituated in a way that would be difficult to stop, even if I fully wanted to do so. As the enactment with my analyst unfolded, I grieved for abandoning my little sissy self, yet I can still feel contempt for his effeminate ways in moments of mindless childhood remembrance. Thus, the work for me has been to attend to the self-consciousness and shame that occurs when I think of my sissy past or notice fearing that my sissiness might show in the present. When I do notice such things, I now try to make contact with the little boy I was who, for at least some of the time, felt unconstrained by the rules of heteronormative masculinity. I take a deep breath, relax my shoulders, and try to sooth the remnants of pain, fear, and shame that became associated with being a sissy.

Through the therapeutic process of remembering my sissy past, there are now times when I find my boyhood sissiness in my adult bodily experience. It is a particular kind of memory in which I feel the kinetic, postural, and even physiological sensations that belong to that childhood version of me. Perhaps the best example of such a moment is when I catch myself feeling my sissy body as I descend a staircase. That is, there are times in the present that this activity triggers the joyful memory of pretending to walk down a grand staircase in my elegant gown, I can feel it through my body—in my torso, shoulders, and legs—the poise and sophistication I used to imagine through my little sissy body. The freedom I once felt is revisited for the briefest of moments in the lived through meaning of this bodily experience. Remembering a childhood sissy experience like this would have resulted in shame in the past—and sometimes it still can—but more often now it tickles me. It puts me in touch with the fantastical aspects of my sissy boyhood and gives me a renewed sense of continuity between who I was then and who I am now.

In my best moments, I feel admiration for my former sissy self and vow to honor his place in my history and my body. No doubt, this admiration was facilitated by my relationship with my training analyst, whose sissy body led to the rediscovery of my own. And from that place of mutual recognition, I had the good fortune to experience him not only as a fellow sissy but also *more* than a sissy. I grew to see him as courageous and loving, sharp-witted and compassionate, strong and tender, and my feelings of admiration deepened into a sincere form of love. Because of him, I can now to speak of my sissy boyhood with a similar kind of affection, and I am freer in my disclosing my sissy past. Thus, in the spirit of such openness, I have chosen to share this aspect of my lived experience with you, the reader. I hope that it opens your heart to your own nonconforming practices and those of your clients, whatever those may be, and provokes a sense of curiosity about the joyful, embattled, contested, and sometimes unruly ways our bodies exist in the normative structures of our culture and our concrete involvement with the social world.

Close Reading Questions

1. Hartman begins, "it is useful to consider the **interconnections** of **gender** and **sexuality** when thinking about gay boyhoods, while being careful **not to collapse gender nonconformity** with **homosexuality** or **hegemonic masculinity** with **heterosexuality**." Take a look at the bold keywords here. How do you define gender and sexuality? What is the difference between gender non-conformity and homosexuality? What is hegemonic masculinity and how does it relate to heterosexuality?
2. Does Hartman suggest that coming out is in and of itself a trauma? Either way you answer, consider how coming out is different than passing and covering in ways such as defeminization and dissociation.
3. What are Hartman's points about the clinical enactment he experienced?

Prompts for Writing

1. How do schools relate to gay male students? How have they been portrayed in school contexts in current media, like television shows or youtube? How do these portrayals connect to Hartman's discussion of the sissy body?
2. How does Hartman's description of bullying connect to the one in Sam's story, in which Sam was hospitalized after his parents beat him and arrested?
3. What does it mean to feel that no one can love you as you are? Write about a time that you felt that way yourself.

References

Bailey, J. M., & Zucker, K. J. (1995). Childhood sex-typed behavior and sexual orientation: A conceptual analysis and quantitative review. *Developmental Psychology, 31*(1), 43.

Blum, A., & Pfetzing, V. (1997). Assaults to the self: The trauma of growing up gay. *Gender and Psychoanalysis, 2*(4), 427–442.

Bromberg, P. (1998). *Standing in spaces: Essays on dissociation, trauma and clinical process.* New York, NY: Routledge.

Bromberg, P. M. (2003). Something wicked this way comes: Trauma, dissociation, and conflict: The space where psychoanalysis, cognitive science, and neuroscience overlap. *Psychoanalytic Psychology, 20*(3), 558.

Butler, J. (1990). *Gender trouble: Feminism and the subversion of gender.* New York, NY: Routledge.
Butler, J. (1993). *Bodies that matter: On the discursive limits of sex.* New York, NY & London: Routledge.
Butler, J. (1997). *Excitable speech: A politics of the performative.* New York, NY: Routledge.
Corbett, K. (1996). Homosexual boyhood: Notes on girlyboys. *Gender and Psychoanalysis, 1*, 429–461.
Corbett, K. (2009). *Boyhoods: Rethinking masculinities.* New Haven, CT & London: Yale University Press.
Fuchs, T. (2002). The phenomenology of shame, guilt and the body in body dysmorphic disorder and depression. *Journal of Phenomenological Psychology, 33*(2), 223–243.
Gallagher, S., & Zahavi, D. (2012). *The phenomenological mind* (2nd ed.). New York, NY: Routledge.
Gallagher, S., & Zahavi, D. (Spring 2015). Phenomenological approaches to self-consciousness. In E. N. Zalta (Ed.), *The Stanford encyclopedia of philosophy.* Retrieved from http://plato.stanford.edu/archives/spr2015/entries/self-consciousness-phenomenological/
Harry, J. (1983). Defeminization and adult psychological well-being among male homosexuals. *Archives of Sexual Behavior, 12*(1), 1–19.
Kosciw, J. G., Greytak, E. A., Bartkiewicz, M. J., Boesen, M. J., & Palmer, N. A. (2012). *The 2011 national school climate survey: The experiences of lesbian, gay, bisexual and transgender youth in our nation's schools.* New York, NY: Gay, Lesbian and Straight Education Network (GLSEN).
McDougall, J. (1972). Primal scene and sexual perversion. *The International Journal of Psycho-Analysis, 53*, 371–384.
Meyer, D. (2015). *Violence against queer people: Race, class, gender, and the persistence of anti-LGBT discrimination.* New Brunswick: Rutgers University Press.
Ponty, M. M. (1962). *Phenomenology of perception* (C. Smith Trans.). London: Routledge.
Rofes, E. E. (2005). *A radical rethinking of sexuality and schooling: Status quo or status queer?* New York, NY: Rowman & Littlefield.
Russon, J. (2003). *Human experience: Philosophy, neurosis, and the elements of everyday life.* Albany, NY: SUNY Press.
Schilder, P. (1929). On homosexuality. *The Psychoanalytic Review (1913–1957), 16*, 377–389.
Sedgwick, E. K. (1991). How to bring your kids up gay. *Social Text, 29*, 18–27.
Socarides, C. W. (1970). Homosexuality and medicine. *Jama, 212*(7), 1199–1202.
Stern, D. B. (1997). *Unformulated experience: From imagination to dissociation in psychoanalysis.* Hillsdale, MI: The Analytic Press.
Stern, D. B. (2010). *Partners in thought: Working with unformulated experience, dissociation, and enactment.* New York, NY: Routledge.
Stern, D. B. (2015). *Relational freedom: Emergent properties of the interpersonal field.* New York, NY: Routledge.
Taywaditep, K. J. (2001). Marginalization among the marginalized. *Journal of Homosexuality, 42*(1), 1–28.
Whitam, F. (1977). Childhood indicators of male homosexuality. *Archives of Sexual Behavior, 6*, 89–96.
Whitam, F. (1980). The pre-homosexual male child in three societies: The United States, Guatemala, Brazil. *Archives of Sexual Behavior, 9*, 87–99.

Interlude

APPLIED INTERSECTIONALITY IN THE CASE OF A BLACK LESBIAN

An Example of Clinical Supervision

Tracy M. Norris

The following is a transcription of an actual supervision session, led by Dr. Tracy M. Norris.

SUPERVISOR: The case we will discuss today is about a Caribbean woman, 40 years old, who emigrated to the US not long ago. She is married with preteen kids. She was raised in a very religious Christian family. The family was one where homosexuality or any kind of sexual deviance from heteronormative behavior was considered an "abomination to the Lord." Moreover, in her island culture, one could get killed for homosexuality.

When the woman came to the US, she fell in love with another woman, and her whole identity was shaken to the core. Her undeniable lesbian sexual identity went against her belief system. Even though she was in love with another woman, engaging in lesbian sex brought on intolerable guilt and shame. She questioned whether or not she could be loved in the eyes of God. She questioned how she could fit into her island culture. She felt that could not tell anyone—not family members, not her husband. She was very afraid. You see, a sexual trauma does not have to occur because of some physical assault. For my client, this was an inner psychological trauma. A chasm within. An inner conflict.

She presented with symptoms of depression and anxiety, but another aspect of the case is this: my client felt it was taboo for her to go to a therapist. She couldn't tell anyone about coming to therapy, but she wanted to work on managing her symptoms. I wanted to help her negotiate the space between "I'm bad; I'm going to Hell" and her desire for happiness.

STUDENT: What was the main focus in treatment? You said she came in with anxiety and depression, so as you're going through all these details, my mind is just focused on all of these identities that are in conflict. Were you treating anxiety and depression or were you doing something else?

SUPERVISOR: The reason I used those terms is because in the clinic, there is a whole admission process. You get the psych evaluation from the psychiatrist, who is the lead person to put in the diagnosis for the patient. It doesn't always coincide with what people would say about themselves as patients because clinic culture is a very prescribed way of operating. However, once that process is done, then the patient just uses that diagnosis for billing. It's tied to insurance. It's a categorization. That's how it works. She had symptoms like withdrawing from people, overeating, undereating, oversleeping, fearfulness. She'd had a couple of panic attacks, rapid heartbeat, sweaty palms.

STUDENT: But then you heard her story, and what was your first instinct? What was the first thing that you did? It just sounds impossible to reduce it all to depression and anxiety. It sounds really complicated.

SUPERVISOR: The first thing I always do is to listen. I offer empathy. I tried to engage her by checking what her body language was saying because she was very reticent about sharing. She was embarrassed. She reluctantly came into treatment even though she was self-referred. So, I tried not to be judgmental and not to come across as judgmental. I was creating a safe space. That's the first thing I do. I ask questions. But really, it worked with me because I'm a non-white person, and she's a non-white person. That was the hook.

STUDENT: Does that non-whiteness serve as a hook to this population because sometimes people of color kind of lumped into "Queer" categories?

SUPERVISOR: That's how I'm thinking about it: I love my own people. I rely on my familiarity with being marginalized. That may be good and that may be bad. There is something that exists between people of color that does not exist in a cross-racial interaction. Being a person of color with another person of color removes that barrier. There are still other barriers, but it sort of removes that barrier.

She was happy that I was a non-white clinician. She was relieved. We shared a non-white culture even though we're in a diaspora; we have some familiar issues. She was relieved but still cautious.

STUDENT: How much did you self-disclose? There's so much that is not on the surface, not about skin.

SUPERVISOR: My style of treatment, no matter the case, is to bring concerns about race to the forefront immediately. I made a comment: "Wow, for us non-white people—for black people—being a lesbian, coming to therapy, is really difficult." I just know that it is not accepted in our community. I said to her, that must be really challenging, because in our community being a lesbian is not acceptable. Some of us see homosexuality as a product of slavery, a disease we got from white people. It is common belief, not the only belief, but one of the beliefs.

STUDENT: How could I, as a white therapist, enter this line of conversation without the experience of being non-white?

FELLOW CLINICIAN: I hear this as being so layered. There are layers to identity, her ambivalence, even in going to therapy, and the *parallel process* of the taboo of homosexuality. It is layered and complicated, and the most important thing we're trying to communicate to each other as clinicians and to our clients is that it is so layered and complicated. Cultural identity, race, sex, sexual orientation—however the client identifies these elements of her being—you have to give her the chance to have a genuine *embodied experience* with all of these layers.

SUPERVISOR: She's Caribbean. I'm African American, so there were divides, different geographical locations, but we talked about what we shared. I relied on what we shared early.

I'm not a Christian person like her, but I have Christians in my family, so I could understand that. I grew up in the church. She wanted to know that about me, if I was a Christian. She wanted to know who she was sitting in the room with.

STUDENT: I'm hearing something interesting that I have to level with. If I were in the room with this same client, I'd be having a very different experience. All white clinicians would have a different experience. So, why wouldn't we assume that it would be a better fit for a non-white person to have a non-white therapist? Are we allowed to admit that in mental health practice, a culture of its own, a culture that pretends... I feel like I'm being too risky, but I see that your shared status as non-white really helped.

SUPERVISOR: Historically, non-white people were not permitted to be therapists. A lot of black people feel that they have to be careful as non-white people about what they say to a white person because of trust issues. So there is going to be some holding back. It doesn't allow for a person to really examine themselves on the deepest level if you don't bring in race. You have to bring it into the treatment even if you're not explicit about it initially. Race will come up because everything for a non-white person is tied to the experience of being non-white. Even though my client was so tied to Christianity, I questioned why she trusted it so implicitly. Christianity was imposed on black people throughout the African diaspora. With Christianity, basic relationship configurations were imposed on them.

STUDENT: What I hear from you is that, of course—or even more so—we need to understand that if your client as a person of color, an immigrant, a Christian, it is a whole different kind of negotiating with the world, like automatic marks against you from the start.

SUPERVISOR: Yes. My client was black, a woman, and gay. You have to contextualize. You have to put a person's life in context. One thing psychiatry does that is not good is that it puts everybody in the same box. It does not contextualize. It is something only a seasoned and well-read therapist can do.

FELLOW CLINICIAN: The medical model is white-centered.

SUPERVISOR: And the final layer is that therapy is stigmatized in the black community.

STUDENT: Why is it stigmatized? In this country, a lot of people do go to therapy.

SUPERVISOR: More people of color are starting. But when you start out as a people being enslaved... I'll speak as an African American: one of the things you had to do to survive was to shut up. You had to keep everything secret. That was one of the habits of survival that we created. If you said something, you could be lynched. Your husband, your house, your children—everything could be taken. You could be beaten. We had to learn to be quiet. We had to teach children to be quiet. You could lose your life. That has become part of African American behavior. It is epigenetic. Talking and telling you how you feel—as therapy is conceptualized—goes against that taught silence impacts us. That silence is still part of our culture now. Are we going to go and talk to the enemy? It is something uncomfortable to imagine, to go to a white therapist.

STUDENT: Transgenerational trauma has not been a part of my training. Because we have to talk diverse populations while pretending there is a universality, genetic exploration seems like it might be considered twisted assumption making, racism, rather than something that we are allowed to acknowledge.

FELLOW CLINICIAN: I feel like the voices of non-white clinicians and supervisors are missing. And what the student touches on is that because of white centeredness, we cannot really value certain nuances. We can't make the assumption that we can understand the experience of a non-white person. "Cultural competence" is sometimes limiting and dangerous.

SUPERVISOR: Cultural competence is dangerous because it extends white control in a very sophisticated way. You make the person you are supposed to be competent about remain more subjugated.

FELLOW CLINICIAN: It is a mechanism of privilege to overlook these things.

SUPERVISOR: It is a position of authority that is already a dynamic in the therapeutic dyad. As a non-white person, you are not the authority because you can be gunned down as soon as you leave the office. It is a real possibility. Probably, your white client or white therapist doesn't realize her power or privilege. But all people seeking presence from their clinicians, including a presence regarding the realities of race and culture as a part, in this case, of sexual identity. Being truly present is to be really vulnerable while still having some expertise.

STUDENT: In a case that wasn't a physical trauma, but a psychological trauma, it is interesting how the outside affects the inside. We can't see the inside, and we spend so much time trying to get inside that we miss how what someone looks like on this outside affects the trauma inside.

SUPERVISOR: Yes. My client felt hat she had been traumatized when she had finally been with another woman. The schism within her was too painful to really bear. She was disgusted by act. She was traumatized by her own self-hatred.

Let's say it was you. What would you do? Without my melanin? You have to tap into your own self-loathing in order to treat this kind of inner turmoil, even if it is different. Human to human. Think about transference and countertransference. That's the language of therapy. If you don't know what to get from this case, use those terms to follow through your case conception here.

STUDENT: Thank you for that. I can mine this case a little more with these terms.

FELLOW CLINICIAN: How do therapists tap into their own vulnerability? The takeaway is that we all have to be able sit in the space of not being fully actualized so that we can use that space, and the exploration of that space, in our work as therapists.

SUPERVISOR: There's passing and covering, but often skin color is hard to hide. You can stay in the closet with homosexuality, but subjugation continues when you hate yourself, when you hide yourself. Hatred, in all its layered manifestations, is often at the root of trauma.

Questions for Thinking

1. What does "Cultural Competence of LGBTQ folk" mean if it is informed by white privilege and straight privilege? When white privilege and straight privilege exist in clinical supervision, what assumptions of omission make supervision imbalanced, if not dangerous?
2. How do you define the intersectionality in this case? What is parallel process?
3. What is self-disclosure when something like skin color is already disclosed? Read Dee Watts-Jones' "Location of Self: Opening the Door to Dialogue on Intersectionality in the Therapy Process" for a well informed answer.
4. Does Gay Affirmative Treatment require the inclusion of models that address historical trauma in any other chapter in this book? Where do you see it addresses specifically in Norris's supervision?

STEVE'S STORY

A Case Conceptualization

Jeffrey Longhofer

* *In order to assure confidentiality, I will not provide clinical detail that would otherwise permit more nuanced understanding of important historical and analytic material.*

Steven, age 19, came to see me at age 17, during the spring before his senior year. He'd been a very successful soccer player and was being recruited by several college teams. He was sad and lonely and isolated, he said. He had been an excellent student but found it very difficult to focus during the most recent spring semester. He was well spoken but unable to maintain eye contact. He was worried that he might not manage to finish his senior year, "…or that [he] could be the guy everyone expected [him] to be throughout [his] school years–so active in sports." There was a special affective resonance to "…be the guy." And in saying this, he averted his gaze and blushed, intensely. In the beginning weeks of our twice-weekly work, Steven would repeatedly return to this feeling, rich with affect. And soon after we began to observe and wonder about this, near the end of the second month, Steven reported that he could not get out of bed and was increasingly sad and anxious. I suggested that he might benefit from seeing me with greater frequency. Without hesitation he started to see me three and sometimes four times weekly, a schedule that we maintain to this day, while he attends a local university.

From the first day, he was eager to tell me about his sadness and had his own strong thoughts about the push to follow the pediatrician's (a family friend) advice and begin a course of anti-depressants. His mother, he said, insisted that he "take the drugs." I knew from two meetings with his father (his mother could not attend) that she had long suffered with depression and soon after Steven's birth had been hospitalized and over several months received a course of ECT. By mid-summer, during the first months of our work, Steven became increasingly interested in my interest in his sadness and for the first time he began to talk about his mother and father. He talked at length about his mother's sadness and how he never understood it, how he felt like there were times when he'd wished that she would just go away, that he felt responsible for her sadness. He remembered once telling her "that he had long wished she would just die." He said that it was only his father and two older brothers (two and three years older) that he felt connected to, that it was only his father that gave him a sense of "going on." And in the middle of the hour, he said to me, with urgency, "how do I get an HIV test, without my parents knowing?" I was startled not only with the urgency in his voice but also his coming to life. His tone changed so remarkably that he seemed a quite different person. I ask him about the worry and observed the sudden change. He said that if his parents found out, "his dad would kill him." He then began to report, without hesitation, his use of Craig's list to connect with "jocks," as he said, on the neighboring college campus. Four or five times, he said, he'd connected.

"I am so ashamed to tell you." He continued, with urgency, as if he wanted to get it all out. He offered detailed accounts of the secret rendezvous arranged in the college dorms, as he would repeatedly say, as to confirm his masculinity, "all with jocks, only jocks, mind you." In a continued outpouring of words, laden with urgency and aliveness, he said that he felt a fraud, that soccer had been an excuse to be close to other boys, and that all of this energy to be the best soccer player had been a complete waste of his life, and that now he was no longer interested in soccer. For the first time he cried. Near the end of the hour, he looked at me with a kind of directness and relief, and said, "I guess I've got a lot of work to do, no?"

Over the course of the summer, Steven reported to me his desire to be anally penetrated, his first experience with an older teenager, a college student and athlete, and his lack of pleasure in masturbation. He talked of special longing to be close to one particular high school soccer buddy and of his many but failed attempts arranging for intimacy and of one particularly abortive attempt to arrange a common bed on a fieldtrip and the shame of rejection. I advised that he purchase the new HIV 20 minute test and bring it to my office. He tested negative, and in the fall of his senior year, he talked more about his anal desires and shared in detail his connections, found on Craig's list, with a local group of barebackers (i.e., men not using condoms) and his continuing fears that he might die. We worked to understand this profound urge and desire for penetration, for the pain and pleasure in it, the engulfment. He remembered anally masturbating as a very young child and the pleasure this brought him.

We began to understand that these urges for unprotected penetration came at particularly troubling moments of sadness. Most important, we understood his passive desire to give such pleasure to his barebacking partner as a need to bring, in his words,

> ...total pleasure to someone. I can't put into words what it feels like with the penis inside me, pumping, and waiting, for the final moment when I feel it explode. I say over and over, don't stop. It's so mixed up in my mind. It feels so good but it hurts. It's not the same with a condom.

He for the first time could be angry with me and over many sessions would say that I didn't understand, couldn't understand this pleasure. He often talked of being engulfed and he loved to be "fucked on his back, feeling and smelling sweat, just disappearing under it all." Over many hours we talked about his feeling that with the condom, he could not ultimately please his partner and that so much of his need was to fulfill their desire and how when it was all over, he was left feeling empty, limp, sad, and disappointed; and again, urgently longing. And in the urgent longing and seeking, he would feel alive again. He would often say something like, "I'm almost immediately on Craig's list looking for someone. I feel a kind of overwhelming urgency, like it's biological, deep in my body, like a demon, trying to get out, but I like it, I can't stop myself."

Very recently he brought for the first time a dream and then a torrent of dreams. He brought one of many soccer dreams. In one soccer dream, in a very ornate locker room, with marble floors and steam showers, his mother appeared in a flowing white gown, happy and pleased, yet she seemed far in the distance, in the room but not really in the room. His father appeared in the room, naked, much younger and beautiful. He was close, not distant. He embraced his father and awoke from the dream, disturbed, unable to return to sleep. I wondered with him (something that I'd long had on my mind) about how his mother is there in the distance, beyond his grasp, and that if only he could bring her into the room, give her the pleasure he so wished her to have. He sobbed, deeply, for what remained of this most recent hour. He was now associating to his dreams with greater freedom and reported that he was masturbating with pleasure and enjoying an especially pleasurable and not so secretive rendezvous with a college friend, where he was also enjoying mutual masturbation.

Questions for Thinking

1. Is being gay or realizing he's gay a sexual trauma for Steve? What details of this case inform your answer? In other words, is coming out or having non-heteronormative sexuality always traumatic?
2. In Longhofer's case conceptualization, he says:

> I wondered with him (something that I'd long had on my mind) about how his mother is there in the distance, beyond his grasp, and that if only he could bring her into the room, give her the pleasure he so wished her to have.

How does this point relate to Steve's barebacking? How does this point relate to the previous question?

3. How does the space of Longhofer's office provide safety enough for Steve to take a rapid HIV test? How does Steve's experience relate to the one in Jaffe's podcast featuring a counselor at a free HIV testing clinic?
   i. Readers unfamiliar with phenomenology and its methodology will find Gallagher and Zahavi (2012) to be a helpful introduction to the philosophical study of lived experience. Russon (2003) provides a synthesis of phenomenology and other continental philosophies as frameworks for understanding the nature of everyday experience.

Section Three

7

(MIS)TAKEN JUDGEMENT

The Social Construction of Loyalty and Love for a Lesbian in Rural Appalachia

Sandra Van Nest

Pre-Reading Questions

1. Would you be able to "meet your clients where they are at" and/or "offer unconditional positive regard" if they participate in family systems that perpetuate incest and corrective rape?
2. What is social constructionism? How might it serve as an incubator for transgenerational trauma?
3. How does region affect the practice of social work? In particular, what do you think it would be like to practice clinical case management in a rural region?

Lila, a 16-year-old girl from rural Appalachia, just wanted to "be true" to her girlfriend. Though Lila had always known that she would date girls, this was her first relationship, and she wanted to do it right. However, when she explained this to her father, his ongoing sexual molestation of her escalated. Lila's father forced her to have intercourse with him. To Lila, the desire to be faithful in her new romantic relationship was the impetus to disclose to a teacher that her home life was full of incest and abuse. Lila's father believed that it was his job to show her the ways of men and women, which she obviously did not understand since she said she wanted to be with a girl. As a clinical case manager, my job was to help Lila and her family through the court system and child protective service system. In this rural community, there were few therapeutic options and many barriers to overcome: geography, isolation, and ignorance. To help Lila begin to heal from the trauma of sexual abuse, we had to begin with family psychoeducation, while empowering her to develop as any adolescent should be allowed. Rural social work and the role of the case manager will be examined using a systems perspective with the frame of social construction.

(Re)Cognition

I was a clinical case manager, recently out of school. What is a "clinical" case manager, you may ask? Well, in this situation, it was a nebulous title that meant that the worker had not only some clinical responsibilities but also clinical limitations. I was in a very rural area in the southern Appalachian Mountains. The geographical area that I covered spanned two large counties. The area was rural enough that if asked where they're from, residents would say the county—not the town. Towns mostly consisted of a post office and convenience store. There were two traffic lights in all of the two counties that I covered. Both in the same town. As a sexual violence clinical case manager, my role was to follow child victims of sexual violence through "the process." Usually child protective services or the police department called me in when the child or her family disclosed sexual violence, and this process varied from child to child. From start to finish, it might look something like this: I would accompany the child to the hospital. I would help the family connect with any needed resources for health and safety (i.e. food, gas money, medical care). I would help the family and child understand the child protection service process, the court process, and any other bureaucratic system that might be involved. In other words, my job was to educate, advocate, and alleviate the child through the systems. I was a Jill of all trades, sometimes a voice of reason, sometimes a hand of assistance, always a protector of childhood. This was a lot to ask of a new social worker, but there were few resources for mental health in this rural area, and we all did what we could.

When I think back to that time, now that I have more experience as a clinician and as a wanderer of cultures, I am struck by a few things. This community had many strengths. The land was beautiful with green farms and lots of wildlife. The people who grew up there were close knit with familial connections that went back generations. There was a definite "take care of our own" mentality that lifted people up when they were down. The community was generally working poor, white and protestant, with strong conservative opinions socially and politically. They were polite to all in a "bless your heart" kind of way. As my husband said when we moved there, "Bless your heart sounds nice, but what it means is 'You're just as dumb as a box of rocks.'" He has said this many times over the years when we look back at our time living there, with his unfortunate imitation of a rural southern Appalachian accent.

When I think back to this time in my career, in my ongoing study of humanity, I always go back to one case. One family. One child in a situation. It would be easy to judge the family as backward or ignorant. But that is not where I go. When I look back, I judge my skills and my own ability to be of help to children. From the beginning, I have always seen the world and my clients through a social constructionist lens. Social constructionist theory states that an individual creates his or her own "truth" by sharing it with another. When the other agrees or rejects the "truth," it gains power or is dismissed. Therefore, "truth" is deeply individualized and ever evolving. I did not have words for this until my graduate studies quickly ran through it. As a student, once I was introduced to the concepts, social constructionism became the long lasting overall lens that I look through. It provided the words to what I had always known. Every person has wisdom. Every person looks at the world through their own experiences and sees it differently. In order for me to find the wisdom, in order for me to be of help, I have to join them there.

(De)Position

The family that comes to mind when I look back was a complicated one. Lila was a teenager at the time. She knew from an early age that she was a lesbian, though in this rural community, there were no adult role models for her to look to for the words to explain this. And in this time in history, television's "Murphy Brown" was shocking to many of the adults she knew in real life. American culture as a whole seemed to be in its infancy of acceptance of gay culture. People could make jokes about being a gay man on television and women could kiss on the screen for mostly the sexual titillation of others. It was the early 2000s.

We sat together in my cramped little office with no window. It was hot and muggy outside and worse still inside. My agency didn't have the budget for central air, and I was annoyed that I didn't have a window like most of my colleagues. I was the youngest of all of the clinical case managers, and the most recently hired, so I got the little office. The office that was so hot, I could smell the brimstone seeping out of the overflowing filing cabinets and through constantly running fan of my ancient desktop computer. I had just been chewed out by my supervisor for tardy paperwork, and after completing the intake of the new family waiting for me in the hall, I had to sit with a rather snitty coworker to discuss how to best "plan my work and work my plan." Jerks. This new family would officially make me ten families over what my agency considered a full caseload. But it didn't matter, the work had to get done and we all had to do it together. As an underfunded non-profit, there was no budget for overtime pay or to hire another case manager. Earlier in the month, I had asked for a raise; I explained to my executive director that at my salary, I was eligible for all of the state benefits that we brokered to our clients. I was behind on my bills and my student loans. She basically laughed at me with a "join the club" twinkle in her eye. It was a hard job, and we all knew it. And in the moments before meeting Lila and her family, I knew it too, but I was flustered and scared and pissed.

I showed Lila into my office. At 16 years old, she looked like the all-American girl next door. She was blond haired and blue eyed with a lovely summer tan. She walked in with her head up and met my eyes with a smile. Behind her, came her father and grandmother. While Lila looked modern in her jean shorts and a t-shirt, her father and grandmother had on the typical uniform of farmers and rural church ladies. He wore a white t-shirt with bibbed overalls and a cap featuring his favorite Nascar driver's face and she, a flowered dress loose through the waist, stockings, and sensible low-heeled shoes. Together, they sat squeezed on a loveseat and looked at me expectantly. Just then, I realized that I didn't have the file out. It was somewhere on my messy desk or in the file cabinet, I hoped. I frantically looked through stacks and drawers and in the extra pile of paperwork that I had out of view under my desk. My "to be filed" pile. I couldn't find it. To the outright annoyance of the father and the grandmother's polite smile starting to melt in the heat, I walked out of the office to find the file with the shared administrative assistant. Minutes later, I returned to my office, file in hand, to see the three speaking gently with each other about a litter of puppies that had just been born on the farm. It seemed that they planned to take the litter to Lords Acre Sale that would happen in a month or so to give them away. Someone would take them. Good dogs are hard to come by, and they expressed comfort that the good church people attending the event would take care of them. Lila was trying to talk her father into keeping one, probably not the right moment, as by this time, he was as annoyed as I was flustered. I sat down and opened the file.

"Ma'am, I don't want to be rude. But how old are you?" the father asked.

I hate this question. I am young. Newly out of college. And I look even younger. In an effort to look older, I wore a suit. My favorite college professor told me before I graduated, "You're going to get questioned about your age. I recommend that you cut your hair and wear suits. Polyester suits." While I didn't cut my hair, I totally bought into the idea of a good polyester suit, which made me look professional, feel strong—or so I thought. Mostly, in retrospect, I think it made me warmer than necessary and itchy to boot. Not a good and put together look. While at the time, I thought I had some control of my face, I am after all a good southern girl with good home training, I imagine that I made a cranky face at the question. Luckily, the grandmother saved me.

"She's old enough to eat a bowl of beans and not choke. Let her do her job."

With a wilted smile of my own, I looked down at the file. This time, I am sure that I grimaced. The notes in the file were incongruous with the people sitting in front of me. I looked up and said the only thing that came to mind. The phrase that human service workers use often as an open-ended invitation and a way to get a moment to find our bearings.

"What leads you to my office today?"

Lila looks at me, then at the silent figures beside her and says:

"Daddy and I started fucking. I told my teacher at school about it, because I needed a woman's opinion, and she called the police."

(De)Construction

When I was introduced to social constructionist theory in my MSW program, I was at once mystified by the nuances and enraptured by the truth that I felt within the concepts. Put simply, social constructionist theory contends that each person's truth is different, a sum of all experiences that the person has had, as well as similar in that the perception of these experiences is shaped by social context. Social constructionism states that meaning is made from social interaction and is highly impacted by language (Hoffman, 1991). In other words, there is no "truth" to be discovered, only the truth that is created in stories. As a tool for social work, it means that we see the power of hearing another human being. And that our interactions while hearing the story will impact how meaning is made in the story teller. My school flew through the theory as a unit on "Post Modern and Existential Theories" with an implicit framework of "hard to understand, not practical, philosophical mumbojumbo." But I fell into it with abandon.

I grew up a few counties away from where I now worked and Lila was growing up. Close community. Closed community. Community with deep beliefs in right and wrong. Community that appears homogeneous of socioeconomics, race, religion, and creed. But I knew from my own experiences that while we appeared the "same" on the outside, no one was actually the same on the inside. And reality is not what it seemed. As a student, I clung to the first tangible theory that I'd read that made explicit what I knew to be true. To fully understand a person, to be able to help a person, we had to set down what "appears," let go of what we expect, and join the other person's reality. Add to this are the ever-important social work ideals of "conscious use of self" and "person in environment," and I had a framework to use for most any professional situation that I entered. Enter every situation with humility and the knowledge that this person will see things in a highly individualized way. That the person is the expert on the situation and the lived experience brought into the situation. And finally, perceptions that are framed by the cultures of the systems that surround the person.

In this first meeting with Lila and her family, the social constructionist framework and the skills of conscious use of self allowed for a few ideas to come quickly to my slightly thrown off thought process. I needed to have a boundary with Lila's father; for the purpose of our relationship, my age was not important. However, Lila's father was asking for something that was important to our relationship: do you have enough experience to help us? Will you be able to handle my daughter and my self? Will you accept us or reject us? I didn't need to directly answer his question about my age, and his mother helped me avoid directly not answering it. Presenting to him in my addled cranky state did not help him feel comfortable in the situation. While I felt ill at ease with Lila's words, they were his norm. While I felt in control of my office and myself, he felt vulnerable. As McCarthy and Byrne (1988) wrote in a large scale study of best practices in clinical relationships with families involved in incest "curiosity, moral outrage, impulses to protect, rescue, or abandon family members" must be set aside (p. 181). Social construction allowed me to join this family's truth. The father and child sexual relationship was so normal within the family that the child, Lila, felt quite comfortable saying it out loud. Or at least she seemed to. When discussing our first meeting later, Lila commented that her defiance in the situation revolved around word use. She thought our shock…maybe the shock that you felt when you read it…was related to her use of the word "fuck."

> No matter what he did, how bad it got, the only time Daddy apologized was when he said 'fuck' in front of us kids. I thought I was being big and bad by saying it in your office. I sure got my butt busted afterward for saying it. I still hadn't figured out that what happened at my house was bad.

In order to understand Lila's story, we first have to examine her social construct, we have to build a theoretical scaffold with which to lay down the details of her story. In the book *The Social Construction of Reality* (1966), Berger and Luckmann discussed "reality" as independent of an individual. It cannot be constructed alone. Groups of people embrace certain versions of objective and subjective individual experiences and reject others as "not real." Society on the bigger level is made by an ever moving reciprocal flow between the "me" and the "we" for the purpose of continuously recreating a version of reality. And while this "reality" of the situation seems shared on the outside…common expectations of behavior…it is perceived differently on the inside of each individual. The composite reality of a society is established and maintained through social interactions; who is listened to, who is ignored, who is honored, and who is chastised (Berger & Luckmann, 1966). To effectively join a family and be a true instrument of intervention, we must reflect on our own implicit prejudices and constructs (McCarthy & Byrne, 1988). In Lila's reality, incest is normal, cursing is highly offensive, her father is the leader of the family and not one to be questioned, and her grandmother is a smoother of rough situations like direct questions.

(Dis)Loyalty

Lila's story was complicated and simple all at the same time. She, her father, and her little brother lived on the farm that their family had lived on for four generations. The farm was large and remote, probably about a half of an hour drive from town and my office. Lila told me once that her closest neighbor lived about a mile away, and that neighbor was one of her four aunts and cousins. Lila's grandmother lived in a trailer park at the edge of town, close to another of Lila's aunts. After Lila disclosed that she was sexually active with her father to a teacher, the police and child protective services became involved with the family. Lila was told by authorities to move in with her grandmother. She didn't mind, though, because her girlfriend lived in the same trailer park. And while her grandmother thought of Lila's "girlfriend" as her best girlfriend, she was actually Lila's first romantic relationship, the object of her affection, and the impetus of Lila looking to her teacher at school for a "woman's opinion."

As Lila later explained to me, she always knew that she did not like boys in "that way." She understood what it was to be a lesbian and how much her family and church would be against it. Her father and brother often made "queer jokes" and thought they were very funny, and so did the kids at school, and even her grandmother sometimes. Lila didn't like them, but wasn't offended particularly, just uncomfortable. As the only girl in the house, Lila knew what was expected of her. She made the food and took care of the house. She loved to read and write and hoped to be an architect someday. She also knew that part of her "place" in the family was between mother, wife, and child. She didn't question this. For her entire life, her father moved seamlessly from kissing her forehead to kissing her face, from her sitting on his lap for comfort to him sliding his hands across her chest. Both Lila and her father explained to me on separate occasions that this is the way that fathers and daughters were. If Lila hadn't begun to date her girlfriend, it is hard to know when the family would have disclosed what was happening on the farm. Lila decided to speak with her teacher after an argument with her father escalated into rape and physical assault, but not because she thought it was wrong to be hit and raped, but because she wanted to be faithful to her girlfriend. Lila was overcome with guilt that she had cheated on her girlfriend. She wanted her teacher's opinion on how to make it right.

As a person outside of Lila's family, it would be easy to doubt Lila's stated truths. How could she not know that it is wrong for her father to kiss her in a romantic fashion, much less rape her? But there are many truths here and many layers of socially constructed meaning. We see the first as it is true for many abused children: "The child's task is to accommodate to a family in which exploitation, invasiveness, and the betrayal of trust are normal" (Rieker & Carmen, 1986, p. 364). In order to exist, to survive, in this family, Lila had to find self-value where she could. She was good at caring for her brother and father. She would make a good wife someday because she already knew about keeping a house. She was proud of these skills and felt comfortable with her path. She would marry, have children, run her family farm. It hadn't occurred to her yet that she would be unable to marry another woman in the state that she lived in. It also hadn't occurred to her yet that the patriarchal family and community structure that she lived within was not the only option.

Lila did not conform to the socially constructed love norms of her society. She was a lesbian and being so led her to be raped by her father. She understood and voiced her differences from her culture in that way. But she did not question or actively articulate the differences of power within her family between men and women, boys and girls. Lila's mother was not a part of her life and hadn't been for many years. From the time her mother left, Lila was in charge of cooking a cleaning the family home. She also coordinated life for her little brother. She took care of him and made sure he had what he needed for school and sports activities. Lila's dad worked the farm with the help of her brother. Lila was isolated from life off of the farm except for school. While her brother participated in many after school activities, Lila was not allowed to. Lila hoped to talk her father into letting her have a job at some point before she finished high school. The seeds of a life that was different were there, but not yet cultivated. Lila experienced a vast power differential between herself and the men around her. But she didn't know another option. She did not voice concern or angst around the preferences of the adults around her, the fact that her brother's needs came above her own. She found a sense of accomplishment in taking good care of him.

Feminist theory adds a layer of understanding here. As outsiders, we may question the belief system of incest, but we must also examine who has the power and for how many generations this has happened. Sheinberg and Fraenkel (2000) explained how feminist and social constructionist theory can be combined to create a framework for understanding the family systems that include incest. When multiple loyalties and perspectives exist within a family, the family experiences a "disruption in the sense of trustworthiness...of family relationships" (p. ix). We can see already the layers of relationship and loyalties from Lila's perspective. She finds a sense of self in caring for others. She maintains the status quo in many ways. Yet, as a teenager, she is also fiercely loyal to her peers. In this case, being raped by her father, in her mind, was cheating on her girlfriend. She did not disclose her sexual encounters with her father prior to complete intercourse because she didn't question it as a problem. Through it, she found her father's affection and care. Lila had a grandmother who intervened to help calm uncomfortable situations. Situations that were unseemly. And Lila counted on that as care and protection. Lila loved her brother and enjoyed her pseudo-mother role with him. While so many people told her what to do and where to be, he was the only one who listened to her. Her sense of self was enmeshed with him and his success, as her patriarchal family values taught her it should be. The foundation of Lila's life experiences leaned heavily on the fact that her "truth" was based on the needs of her father and brother. Lila's father tried to coerce her into heterosexuality by inflicting his norm, his truth, on her. His needs took precedence over her own, even in her own mind. Reflecting on these dynamics help us to see how much Lila's life was being turned upside down. Not only was she removed from her home and family, her very value system and sense of her place in the world was being shaken. As I got to know Lila more and more, there was a constant moving between what I knew to be happening developmentally to Lila as a teenager, as well as the person in environment dynamics of the situation, all tied up with the real-life tangible needs of Lila and her family.

Like many rural community members, at least on the outside, Lila was deeply religious. Her church and youth group were an ongoing and consistent creator of her life and viewpoints. As Allport and Ross (1967) explained in a seminal article, intrinsic religiosity is when religion is the central organizing factor in a person's life. Lila and her family went to church twice a week, they attended Bible studies and spaghetti dinners. They were friendly with members of their own small church and antagonistic toward members of the other protestant church varieties in the county. I heard Lila and her family members pray more than once. Lila, herself, spoke to me about her relationship with Jesus and how prayers were answered every day. Intrinsic religiosity is connected to more restrictive sexuality and homophobia (Rowatt & Schmitt, 2003). Accessing and connecting with an LGBTQ community is harder for rural areas where people are more spread out geographically and politically (Bell & Valentine, 1995). As I knew, Lila's religion, her "church family" as she would call it, was both a tremendous source of strength and a potential place for great harm. Finding an LGBTQ community for Lila to connect to was important for her healthy development (Rothblum, 2008). Not in place of her church family, but as another source of support for her enlarging world experiences. Unfortunately, I never found this connection for Lila; my hope is that she did eventually find it. In that moment, I could only do my best to plant the seeds of the need for LGBTQ adult role models and teenaged peers for Lila. This was before extensive social media was easily available to most people, though internet access is still not readily available in many rural areas in the United States.

About a month after our first meeting, Lila and her aunt came to my office to discuss an upcoming court date. Part of my job as case manager was to discuss the court process to the victims of domestic and/or sexual violence. I explained their rights as witnesses or victims, helped them anticipate what might happen, and advocated for them with the county prosecutor's office and state victim/witness office. Lila would soon have her first appearance in court and the prosecutor asked me to help her consider if she wanted to speak in open court or via a closed-circuit camera. Open court meant that she would see her father and the court personnel and a closed circuit meant that she would be in a small room outside of the courtroom and speak only to a camera. The people in the courtroom would see her through a television, but she would not see any of them. Since the last meeting, Lila had moved in with her Aunt Sally. Sally lived in the next county over, about an hour from the rest of the family. Lila lived only a week or two with her grandmother after CPS removed Lila from her father's custody. Lila's grandmother told her that she had to move out after Lila repeatedly snuck out of the trailer to visit her girlfriend, who lived a few doors down. Lila's grandmother did not agree with Lila's "choice to be with girls, like that." She stated that it was sinful and would not happen under her roof. Lila's girlfriend was no longer allowed to visit, so Lila went to her trailer. Lila and her grandmother argued so loudly about the relationship one night that the police were called and CPS supported the move to Aunt Sally's house. Aunt Sally considered herself to be the black sheep of the family. She moved off of the family land and to another county. She worked as an office manager and attended community college in the evenings. She was not married and didn't have children. She was happy to have Lila live with her, but worried about how to pay for the gas needed for Lila to go back and forth to school each day. Lila sat down on the loveseat with a harrumph. She did not want to discuss court and when the subject of her move out of her grandmother's home came up, Lila became livid.

> I am glad she kicked me out! All she wanted me to do was clean up, and sit around the trailer, and go to church. It was fine until she heard that I was dating my girlfriend. Stupid bitch next door told her. Busybody old biddy…

"That's enough Lila." Her aunt cut in.

> I won't have you talking about her that way. She is doing her best. You need to concentrate on your schoolwork and be happy that I am bringing you back and forth so that you don't have to change schools.

"But I hate that I can't call my girlfriend from your house!"

This was in the days before cellphones were common. Because Sally lived in the next county over, it was long distance to call into town, which meant that it cost money to call. Sally did not want Lila to call her girlfriend and waste money since she saw her each day at school. Calling long distance, at this moment, was the biggest tension between Sally and Lila.

I tried to move the conversation back to court proceedings and finding financial assistance for Lila and Sally to have gas for their cars. I asked Lila if she had any questions about the upcoming court date.

"Will my brother be there?" she asked.

"Probably not. I will find out for you. How would you feel if he were there?" I replied.

Immediately, Lila went flat. Her face became pale and her voice lowered. She looked down and picked at the frayed hem of her denim shorts.

"I don't want to see him. He was there the night Daddy and I fought. I can't look at him. I am ashamed that he saw all of that."

"Your grandmother will be there. And your father too. If you choose a closed-circuit testimony, you won't see them. They will see you on a television. You will only see the prosecutor and your Aunt Sally."

"I don't want to see any of them."

Lila moved on then to bring the conversation back to gas money. She had her own car to drive herself to school. She worried that she would have to miss school and seeing her girlfriend if she didn't get money soon. Sally discussed that they'd found a therapist for Lila that accepted Medicaid, but that the therapist was in the other direction from Lila's school. The court mandated individual counseling for Lila and her father, but it had been a struggle to find a therapist with an opening for Lila, and Sally had to cancel the last two appointments because she didn't have enough gas money to get Lila to the therapist's office. Sally and Lila also disclosed that they didn't have enough groceries for the week. Our time together ended at the food pantry located in my office building. They left with a bag of stuffing, cranberry sauce, and canned green beans and tuna. The food pantry always received most of its contents around the holidays, and these items remained from the previous Christmas.

Rural social work requires specific skills and cultural humility. As Reibschleger (2007) wrote, rural communities are both "...isolated and connected; self-reliant and recipients of mutual aid; slow to change, while dynamically changing" (p. 212). In my job as a clinical case manager with Lila and her family, I understood the closed nature of the community and even though I grew up nearby and had the same accent, skin tone, and religion, I was an outsider. A couple of counties away can seem like the other side of the moon in some rural communities. To connect with rural communities as an outsider, a social worker must recognize and accept that local customs and values are important. There is an underlying implicit distrust of outsiders. There are often more traditional gender roles and extended kinship systems within families (Reibschlegar, 2007). Familial ties are long reaching and long remembering. If the social worker is not closely tied into the long warp and weft of the community cloth, the social worker is an outsider. Even beyond the closed nature of rural communities, a rural social worker encounters less funding for a greater geographic area. In times of decreased funding, rural communities tend to not lessen services provided, the needs usually haven't lessened with the funding, and instead, the service area gets bigger. The food pantry that Lila's family had access to once only served one half of the county that she lived in; at the time that Lila used it, the food pantry served two counties.

(Dis)Closure

A few months later, Lila came to my office for a planned check in. She brought her Aunt Sally and Grandmother. The three of them sat closely in my little office and chatted brightly about an upcoming shopping trip at the mall. Lila rarely went to them mall because it was an hour-long drive. Lila was excited to eat the large pretzels that she could only get at the mall. We began our conversation with the updates. They explained to me that Lila attended school regularly.

They'd found a therapist for her as directed by child protective services, but it was still difficult to make it to sessions as gas money was a problem. And I explained to them that there was nothing new happening with the court case, we were at a standstill. Lila began to talk about her brother and father. She had recently begun visits with her father, supervised by a child protection worker. Lila's brother often joined the visits, and Lila reported that things were going well.

"I like visiting with Daddy. And my brother makes me so happy. He's always funny and he's so smart. My daddy says he's going to be an architect someday. Daddy wants him to go to college and get a good job. Then he'll come back here and live on the farm with us…wait…I can move back to the farm with Daddy when I am an adult, can't I?"

That took me by surprise, up until now, Lila ranged from rage to ambivalence to embarrassment when her father and brother were mentioned. I replied, "When you are an adult, it will be up to you where you live. What do you think of living with your dad and brother on the farm again?" Before Lila could answer, her Aunt Sally sprang from the couch.

> You can't possibly want to go back to the farm, Lila! What are you thinking? When you go back there, it'll be just like it was and just like it's always been in this family. Your daddy will just start all over again! And he won't let you see your girlfriend. I've heard from people that still go to that church. They are all sure as fire that you're going to hell for dating her. They don't understand that you're a lesbian.

Lila's grandmother visibly flinches when Sally says "lesbian." Sally doesn't notice and keeps shouting while pointing her finger at Lila's face.

> They 'pray over you' every Sunday. Your daddy walks to the front of the church every Sunday and witnesses his story for the congregation. Do you know what he confesses? He confesses that you are dating a girl!?! He doesn't even admit that he did something wrong! You are not supposed to have sex with you father! Everyone is supposed to know that! But they all go along with him at the church. They pray for guidance for him… to bring you back. And they pray for your soul. They want to pray and change you back. You can't go back to that, Lila. You deserve better. You deserve love and support while you figure this out.

Lila becomes tearful. "But maybe they are right. Maybe I don't like girls. I never had a boyfriend. Maybe I should try."

"Well. I don't know about that, Lila. That's up to you. What do you think, Mama?" Sally replies.

Lila's grandmother sits up a little straighter. She does not look at any of us in the eyes. She stares straight ahead and says flatly, "Sally, that's just the way it is with daddies and daughters. We ain't gonna change that. And talkin' about it ain't gonna change that church. You ain't a member no more. You should mind your business."

This heated conversation really left me in a quandary. Lila, Sally, and Grandmother hinted at a much larger history of abuse and incest within their family. As I sat and digested this and the ramifications played out in my mind, I was stuck. In all honesty, I was shocked by the casual dismissal of Lila's grandmother, that "this is the way it is with daddies and daughters" and I saw Sally in a new light. She'd moved away from the farm to another town, which was unusual. What was her story? I wondered. But ultimately, Lila was my client and I was struck by what this meant for her. How do I advocate for her best interests? What were her best interests? Who was I to decide? Lila did not outright say that she believed that the incest between she and her father was a problem; to all adults involved, she noted the violence as the problem. Lila's grandmother seemed to accept that fathers and daughters had sexual relationships and that the main problem here was that Lila was a lesbian and therefore going to hell. And how do I open the door for Sally to discuss her story without overstepping the boundaries of my role as case manager? These were all issues for a real therapist...not a new case manager. Looking back now, I realized that I leaned on the policies of the agency. I vividly remember not engaging most of these issues with the family in that moment. I went back to the problems that I could solve. Money for gas. Suggesting that Sally join Lila in the next therapy session. Strategizing how to support Lila's social life despite long distance phone calls.

(Dis)Position

Later, once they'd left my office, I reflected on the framework offered by my job description and the theoretical background that informed my work. And it kept at me for days and days. There is an ingrained complexity of working with Lila and her family. I could see that the family loved her. They were embedded in a community and had strengths. When child protective services became involved, Lila had many adults, many women, come forward to shelter her. And her father jumped through every bureaucratic hoop given to him by the agency and the court. And he actively sought the support of his religious community. But these strengths were grotesquely framed with what I now knew was multigenerational incest. How could I manage the needs of the whole system? Or was my place to only look at the interest of Lila, the child? Sheinberg (1992) discussed the balancing of such situations in an article about the use of social constructionist and feminist theories as a tool to navigate such clinical impasses in working with families with incest. There is an inherent difficulty in advocating for the child as well as the parent. Once the child is in a safe environment and the incest has stopped, what's the next step? Sheinberg suggested that in psychotherapy, there is room to understand that the parents in instances of incest are not all bad, that there are other circumstances that lead to the situation. These circumstances can be teased out and examined within psychotherapy. Social constructionist theory depends on the multiple perspectives of any given situation, allowing for a "both-and" instead of an "either-or" within the psychotherapeutic environment (McCarthy & Byrne, 1988). I could apply this framework to help my feelings of judgement, outrage, and confusion around this family. And through this reflection and application, I could best do my job and be of help. There were others in the community sitting in judgement, neighbors, child protective services, the court system; it was not my place to be one of them.

I could stay neutral and compassionate by remembering that Lila's father and grandmother could be both loving and misguided. They could be both strong and weak. They could be both necessary for Lila's overall emotional growth and healthy development and a hindrance to her overall health and development. The trauma that Lila suffered was not only the violence of being hit, as she saw it. It was also the systematic changing of world view. Her innocence was actively being lost as people explained to her that not all families have incest. Not all daddies and daughters had sex. She had been removed from her home and the people that she loved with no expectation that it would happen. She went to a teacher in outward simple need of advice and left with police asking questions. In order to help navigate the on-going trauma, I chose to be a place of predictability and unconditional positive regard for Lila and her family. From then on, I had a purposeful use of self in regards to my interactions with Lila.

I was nonhierarchical to the extreme. I purposefully became a person who was curious about the needs of Lila as she saw them. I helped her find what she identified as her main necessities. Lila and I discussed this change in the form of creating goals of our time together. I explained that I would like to help her find her voice and be comfortable saying what she wanted and needed. She was almost an adult and had spent so much of her childhood being the tool to someone else's happiness that I wanted her to experience support in a different way when she was in my office. Lila agreed.

I discussed this with Sally as a way to help Lila see that there was another way to be in a family. I suggested a caring style that was framed in health and safety (the adult is always in charge of health and safety), but had a definite balance of questions more than statements, and curiosity more than declarations. Lila was what we would call an "old soul." She was not prone to making risky choices as some teenagers do. Generally, she had the responsibilities of an adult for much of her childhood, so her aunt didn't need to control much in the realm of day to day activities. Going back to the conversation that began this revelation, Lila had asked if she could go back to her farm when she was an adult.

If the opportunity arose again, Sally or I could ask questions of Lila. What would it mean to go back to the farm? What were the pros and cons? What parts of farm life and homelife on the farm did she enjoy? While I had started out in this way in the original conversation, it all went sideways with Sally's outburst and Grandma's revelation. I used this idea of ways for Sally to support Lila as a reason to call Sally and discuss the conversation. My hope was to not only engage Sally in new ways at looking at Lila, but also as a way to open the door to her own recovery. While she did not bite in that conversation, she did not disclose that she had been sexually abused by her father in childhood, she was very grateful to hear a tangible way to help Lila. Months later, she called me to ask for help for herself. My agency had a program for adults molested as children. Sally connected with them and eventually became a volunteer peer support group leader. She facilitated a group for non-offending parents of children who had disclosed incest.

A few weeks later, I went to a nearby park to meet Lila, her father, and her brother. The CPS worker could not supervise all of the parent/child visitations on her caseload, so the agency contracted my agency to supervise some of them. This was my first. I was nervous as I had little training in child protection, and really, what was I going to do if the parent became violent in a supervised visit. Although I knew this was not a dangerous situation, I didn't know how to protect myself or Lila. And my cell service was inconsistent in the park...like everywhere out in rural Appalachia.

Lila's father arrived first. We awkwardly said hello. We hadn't met since that first meeting in my office. As the alleged offender, he had a different case manager in a different agency. There was not agency except for CPS that saw the family as a whole. Lila's father took the opportunity to speak to me as a "person with some power," though I had no power, I thought.

> Hello, Miss. It is nice to see you. Let me tell you what's happening. I want my Lila back. Can you help me figure this all out? She's my girl. She belongs on the farm with her brother and me. I love my sister and mama. I'm grateful that they took her. But she needs to come home, to go to church, and to get back to reality.

"Sir, really, I cannot do much for you here. The people who can answer this are your CPS worker and your lawyer and your case manager."

"Yeah. But the CPS lady doesn't answer my calls. My lawyer is too busy. And the case manager can't find me an offender's group like the judge wants me to go to."

This was a common occurrence. Judges gave parents involved in CPS cases mandated therapy. But the therapists for offenders were few and far between. Either they had no availability to new cases or they were so far away that people could not reach them due to finances or work schedules. My agency spoke often about offering offender services, but we could not find funding. Funding for non-profits at the time was specific to registered offenders. Anything for alleged offenders was considered "prevention," and prevention of crimes was not something that grant givers were funding at this time.

"I understand sir. I'd be happy to give the message to your CPS worker and let her know you need to speak with her. I am sure she will get back to you as soon as possible."

> It's just that I want my girl back. I didn't know that what I was doing was wrong. That's how it was in my house growing up. It's up to the daddy to teach a girl how things are. It's up to the daddy to make sure she knows what's expected and how to be right with the church. When she told me she loved that girl, I just knew I'd failed her. I had to make it right. I had to show her how god intended for girls to be. I'm so sorry that this is all happening. I just want my girl home where she should be…

he began to sob.

I didn't know what to do with all of this in that moment. I have thought about it many times over the years. In this moment, did I do right by him? Did I do right by Lila? By my community? By my profession? By my ethics?

> I hear you, sir. We all do what we think is best. We all want our children close to us. We want them to be safe and happy. I will reach out to your CPS worker and case manager to let them know that you need them to call you. Here comes Lila and her brother now. Let's keep calm for a nice visit.

I waved to Aunt Sally across the parking lot. She didn't come over to see her brother. The supervised visit consisted of walking around the park and sitting at a picnic table. It was uneventful.

And that's unfortunately where I left it with Lila and her family at the time. Soon after, the family was finished with the court system. Lila's father went to the county jail, and her brother moved into their grandmother's house. As Lila had all of the court ordered services that she needed, and she would be followed by child protective services until her eighteenth birthday, my work was finished. I had to move on to other situations and families similar to hers, but I heard about her every now and then through her aunt Sally. As a social worker, I am always tuned in to the social justice needs of the people that I interact with. I have never been a stand up and shout kind of person with most anything. I see my role in social justice as more like a stream. I roll along gently, joining those that I come across and seeping my social work knowledge into every crack and crevice that I encounter. My hope is to interrupt social injustices one family at a time; to plant seeds of unconditional positive regard in an effort to show a person that there are many ways to be in the world. With Lila and her family, this meant that I had to accept the interdependence of her truth with those of her family and community. If I hadn't, they would have shut me out as the outsider that I was. Instead, I created a safe space for Aunt Sally and Lila to discuss the many generations of incest that had happened in their family. For this style of intervention to work, one that is based on social constructionism in a socially conservative rural system, one has to hold the same reverence for the intricacies of the family and community belief systems as the community itself (Rosik, Griffith, & Cruz, 2007). At the time, my hope is that Lila would find support for healthy development and healing, Aunt Sally would create a community for herself to heal, and that grandmother, brother, and dad would see that what has always been does not have to always be. As McCarthy and Byrne (1988) stated, "to accept that one has been ruined before one can be restored is a heavy burden" (p. 182). In order to change and heal, Lila and all of her family members would need to carry this burden, a rearranging of the interdependent and socially constructed "family."

In the 1980s, McCarthy and Byrne were asked to do a large-scale study of families being treated for incest in rural Ireland. They were asked for best practices for clinical intervention and tried, in part, to understand why incest happened. As explained by McCarthy and Byrne (1988) there is a concept in Irish mythology called the "Fifth Province." The fifth province is an abstract space where a thing can be neutral. It isn't geographical or political and can be separate from bias. It is a place that everything can be seen as something new. They suggested that families with incest be placed in the theoretical fifth province. In Lila's family, there was a need for this new and non-biased place. There she would find a new way to be…with herself, in herself…and with her family. Rieker and Carmen (1986) wrote that a child involved in incest eventually "gives up the right to assign personal meaning to the abuse experiences and accepts the family's assertions that what was done was non-abusive or was in the child's best interest" (p. 362). In Lila's family, for at least three generations, incest was a part of the family idea of "right" and "normal." Each generation had lost its right to see their bodies as their own, for their own use as they chose. In Lila's family, people, women especially, were a part of the collective without the power to control and enjoy. The power lay in the hands of the "family" and the "community" in service to the farm and the "church." The irony is not lost on me that McCarthy and Byrne (1988) studied a large group of families with incest in Ireland, and I am writing about rural Appalachia where the population is predominantly what we'd call Scotch/Irish. In many ways, I found the structure of this chapter in their article. Both the ability to stand inside and outside of the situation as the social worker. And with the (re)imaginings of words and families.

Close Reading Questions:

1. Van Nest writes that

   > social constructionist theory contends that each person's truth is different, a sum of all experiences that the person has had, as well as similar in that the perception of these experiences is shaped by social context. Social constructionism states that meaning is made from social interaction and is highly impacted by language (Hoffman, 1991). In other words, there is no 'truth' to be discovered, only the truth that is created in stories. As a tool for social work, it means that we see the power of hearing another human being. And that our interactions while hearing the story will impact how meaning is made in the story teller.

   Try to explain social constructionist theory in your own words. Use an example of your own to explain it, if possible.
2. In what ways does Van Nest perform her role with a conscious use of self? In what ways is her "self" limited by her age, agency, and station in the rural United States?
3. Try to explain the meaning of Van Nest's subtitles as she uses them to frame the central issues of this case study.

Prompts for Writing:

1. Compare Lila's testimony experience to that of Arman in Kahn and Alessi's chapter. How do region, religion, and gender shape Lila and Arman's experiences?
2. Compare Lila's loss of her religious community to Jerrod's reclamation of it in Goldblatt Hyatt's chapter. How do region, religion, and gender shape Lila and Jerrod's spiritual experiences?
3. Would you handle this case the same way that Van Nest did? How would you establish unconditional positive regard for your clients?

References

Allport, G. W., & Ross, J. M. (1967). Personal religious orientation and prejudice. *Journal of Personality and Social Psychology, 5*(4), 432.

Bell, D., & Valentine, G. (1995). Queer country: Rural lesbian and gay lives. *Journal of Rural Studies, 11*(2), 113–122.

Berger, P., & Luckmann, T. (1966). *The social construction of reality: A treatise in the sociology of knowledge* (1st ed.). Garden City, NY: Doubleday.

Hoffman, I. (1991). Toward a social constructivist view of the psychoanalytic situation. *Psychoanalytic Dialogues, 1*, 74–105.

Lewis, M. L., Scott, D. L., & Calfee, C. (2013). Rural social service disparities and creative social work solutions for rural families across the life span. *Journal of Family Social Work, 16*(1), 101–115.

McCarthy, I. C., & Byrne, N. O. R. (1988). Mis-taken love: Conversations on the problem of incest in an Irish context. *Family Process, 27*(2), 181–199.

Reibschleger, J. (2007). Social workers' suggestions for effective rural practice. *Families in Society: The Journal of Contemporary Social Services, 88*(2), 203–213.

Rieker, P. P., & Carmen, E. (1986). The victim-to-patient process: The disconfirmation and transformation of abuse. *American Journal of Orthopsychiatry, 56*(3), 360–370.

Rosik, C. H., Griffith, L. K., & Cruz, Z. (2007). Homophobia and conservative religion: Toward a more nuanced understanding. *American Journal of Orthopsychiatry, 77*(1), 10–19.

Rothblum, E. (2008). Finding a large and thriving lesbian and bisexual community: The costs and benefits of caring. *Gay & Lesbian Issues & Psychology Review, 4*(2), 69–79.

Rowatt, W. C., & Schmitt, D. P. (2003). Associations between religious orientation and varieties of sexual experience. *Journal for the Scientific Study of Religion, 42*(3), 455–465.

Sheinberg, M. (1992). Navigating treatment impasses at the disclosure of incest: Combining ideas from feminism and social constructionism. *Family Process, 31*(3), 201–216.

Sheinberg, M., & Fraenkel, P. (2000). *The relational trauma of incest: A family-based approach to treatment*. New York, NY: Guilford Press.

8

ATTACHMENT PATTERNS AND GAY MALE IDENTITY IN A CASE OF COMPLEX TRAUMA

Michael Jarrette-Kenny

Pre-Reading questions

1. How might a therapist's personal attitudes toward gender and sexuality impact the development of the therapeutic alliance?
2. How do the therapist's own attachment dynamics impact the therapeutic relationship?
3. What is the relationship between attachment dynamics in the family of origin and the development of PTSD in later life?

Introduction

"I've decided: I don't do humans anymore."

These words are to become his main catchphrase, as fundamental a mission statement as has ever been issued by a survivor of abuse. As if to hammer this fact home, Richard stands by the door for the entire intake, and for every session thereafter, as if preparing to escape. Often after a particularly emotional statement, he will jokingly shout "Okay, see ya," and reach for the door handle. He cancels appointments, leaving multiple messages on the office voicemail. This occurs mostly in the middle of the night, his voice arguing with and then absolving himself. The sound is almost unintelligible due to the strong medications he would take in order to sleep through the night, haunted by vivid dreams of abuse suffered years earlier at the hands of multiple perpetrators. Richard's anticipation of my response to these calls could be heard in his self-dialogue, an intense childlike pleading before an imaginary, condemning parent, angry and disappointed in him for failing yet again.

As Richard's therapist, I might wonder at this point how I should proceed, perhaps anxiously consulting one of the many treatment manuals available, part of the veritable industry built around the exegesis of psychological trauma. In addition to the materials aimed toward the clinician, a multitude of self-help books and television programs await each survivor seeking relief from the burden of psychological suffering, guiding them into the offices of well meaning therapists, fresh from weekend seminars on the treatment of PTSD. The unspoken intention seems clear: to unlock the secret to trauma's insidious grip by exorcising the phantoms of a remote and often murky past.

Freud, the most influential of the explorers of this landscape, prefaced his *Studies on Hysteria* with the striking description of his method "of clearing away the pathogenic psychical material layer by layer," an enterprise undertaken "with the technique of excavating a buried city" (Breuer & Freud, 1895/2000, p. 139). Over a century later, this metaphor continues to exert an often problematic influence amongst mental health practitioners. I know for myself, as a fledgling clinician, this image of the therapist sifting through the unconscious mind in search of the elusive insight that would solve the puzzle of the patient's pathology was indelibly imprinted within me. Like the rituals of a long lost religious faith, the instinct continues to linger, even as the relevance of this type of intellectual excavation has appeared to diminish in my actual practice. The person, despite the implications of our increasingly manualized approaches to psychotherapy, is not a puzzle to be solved, or a series of irrational core beliefs to be teased out and challenged. Long before I can avail myself of the many interventions available, I have to address the elephant in the room of trauma treatment; within all of these various communications lurks the fundamental question, "I have been hurt before, are you here to help me or harm me?"

Attachment and the resulting capacity to trust others, are arguably the fundamental linchpins of every successful therapeutic endeavor, and often the most severely impaired aspect of a traumatized individual's life. Learning to trust, to attach to another human being, and to tolerate all the ambivalence associated with connection is arguably, beneath all the sophisticated theorizing associated with modern psychotherapy, the central lesson of our work. Attachment theory, as originally conceptualized by John Bowlby and his successors, has moved in recent years toward a theory of emotion regulation and interpersonal neurobiology (Schore & Schore, 2008). When developmental factors impede self-regulation, dissociative states become the central means of self-preservation, but at great cost to the individual, laying the groundwork for the development of later psychopathology (Schore, 2007). In this chapter, I will attempt to explicate how traumatic experiences shape this experience of trust in terms of attachment to treatment providers such as therapists, as well as the ability to form romantic and social attachments to others when this trust has been violated. The case material is used to explore the phenomenological experience of the therapeutic relationship, and the dissociative mechanisms which may be responsible for the apparent contradictions seen in behavior and perceptions of sexual identity.

The Boy Who Fell To Earth

"It is so nice to speak to a real person," he said declining to sit, circling the same area before the door, setting the precedent that was to remain for the duration of our treatment. This inability to sit was attributed to a recurring series of physical complaints; fibromyalgia, osteoarthritis, various fractures and herniations brought on I suspected during his former drinking days, though anyone who has worked with survivors of abuse will note the frequency of these vague and troubling medical issues. Meta analysis of research on health outcomes of individuals with histories of childhood sexual abuse indicates that they experience "higher rates of subsequent physical health symptoms, including general health, GI, gynecologic, pain and cardiopulmonary symptoms, and obesity" (Irish, Kobayashi, & Delahanty, 2010, p. 8). Similar relationships were observed between sexual abuse, substance use, and psychiatric disorders (Ouimette, Kimerling, Shaw, & Moos, 2000).

When we first met, I was struck by his physical appearance. He admitted during the evaluation that he had been diagnosed with alcohol-related liver issues, giving him a flushed, bloated appearance. The physical issues had been frightening enough to inspire his detoxification and sobriety for over a month. Almost immediately, he seemed to have decided, in a pattern that soon became familiar, that he could impart intimate details of his life without fear of judgement, as he had always done with receptionists and checkout clerks, anyone of the innumerable single serve friendships he had cultivated around the businesses he frequented.

He said that his reason for coming into therapy was his attempt to come to terms with returning to his family home after the ending of a long term abusive relationship. He referred to his former boss/partner of 19 years as "the man upstairs," summoning to my mind the image of some specter from a horror movie. They met when he began working at the physician's offices, gradually moving into his apartment building in the upper east side of Manhattan. He was charged with driving him around and performing various tasks in and out of the office. The doctor's odd hours and frequent intoxication gradually resulted in his withdrawing from his practice, eventually moving to the suburbs and descending further and further into his addiction.

> I would pick him up at midnight and we would go to a a diner and he would always, rudely insist that they brew an entire fresh pot of coffee, and he would drink the entire pot after drinking 5 Jack Daniel's manhattans, one after the other.

As the session progressed, it became apparent that the ending of the relationship, far from being the cause of his distress, was actually a great relief. The real source of his discomfort was the nightmares and flashbacks that were keeping him up at night. The act of returning to the house he had grown up in had unexpectedly brought up "all this garbage from my past that I thought I was done with."

I had asked about his previous experiences with treatment, and I expressed my surprise at the ease with which he opened up about the details of his life given his lack of previous therapy.

"Like I said, I'm kind of used to talking about things. In a way, you're just like my video camera, haha."

I asked him what he meant. He admitted that he would talk for hours into his ancient camcorder, discussing his thoughts and feelings, "drama-trauma without a comma," as he would often refer to the more distressing aspects of his life. Afterwards he would stockpile the tapes along the wall in his bedroom. He said that he had looked at one once or twice, but that had been years ago. There were over ten years of tapes, and before that, cassette tapes. His entire history had been recorded and abandoned, disowned but left there as a reminder that it was still taking up this much needed space in his current life. In later sessions, I inquired if he would be willing to revisit some of the tapes. He found the thought of it terrifying.

We discussed his bringing in some of his photography, albums filled with images from his wanderings around his former neighborhood in New York City. Apart from a solitary street vendor or a doorman he had befriended from his building, the scenes were devoid of human life, favoring isolated strips of building and emptied stretches of sidewalk, as he purposefully set out to record the space as he would have preferred to have it, the aftermath of some sinister weapon that erased the people, but left everything else intact. A photo essay of a weekend trip to Boston yielded similar results, almost as if he were the lone figure walking isolated streets, like a wanderer on some abandoned planet, an observer safely hidden behind the lens of his camera. An obsessive movie fan, he often used his favorite films as a way to connect. When we discussed the isolated landscapes from his photos, he told me he felt like David Bowie's performance in "The Man who Fell to Earth," jokingly referring to his arrival at his mother's home as the time when he "landed here," an alien whose spacecraft had crashed on this strange, often hostile world, a world that out of self-perseveration, he held at arm's length.

"This is the first time I really am talking to someone officially...except for when I was 16." He fell silent for an unusual amount of time, a look of discomfort displacing his usually jovial expression.

> I just couldn't take it anymore, and I stupidly took an overdose of sleeping pills. I panicked ten minutes after I took them and called the ambulance. I didn't really want to die, I was just so tired, you know what I mean? I ended up on the kid's ward at........... Medical Center. As soon as I got there, this one orderly started sniffing around me, and one night he came into my room. I was so out of it from the meds they were giving me that I

> was in no shape to fight him off. I can't believe I didn't mention it before. I knew I was gay, or at least I knew I didn't have any feeling for girls. I was only turned on by much older men, pop pop figures. It wasn't the first time something like that happened.

he added cryptically without elaboration.

Life after the hospital seemed an indistinct blur. He fondly recalled enrolling in a prestigious art school and the praise he received from professors regarding his artwork. He continued to draw and paint throughout his life. When he finally felt comfortable enough with me to show me his art (a far more private act he pointed out, than the monologues about the traumas of his past) the majority were intricate drawings of houses, the ideal homes he would like to build or live in in the future, settings which, like his photographs, were empty museums where he could live without the intrusions of his mother's religiosity.

Despite his enjoyment of his professors' attentions, his sheltered existence prior to entering school and his difficulty relating to peers made the experience anxiety provoking. Never confident in his academic performance, the science and English classes proved difficult and boring and he soon left, taking a job as a live in caretaker for a young man with cerebral palsy in Florida. This experience established a precedent that was to follow him throughout his life. Soon after his arrival, he became romantically involved with the boy's father. Tony, a painter who etched out an existence painting landscapes for tourists, subsisted mainly on his teenage son's social security checks, spending the leftover money on cocaine and alcohol. The relationship, despite being the first real consensual sexual relationship of his life, seemed confused in his descriptions, navigating a strange space between employee, family member, and casual sex partner.

> He showed me how to paint and that was okay. I had the feeling he would fuck anything, so he would come home, and I think he would have sex with me because I was there. The next day, he would be all weird and cold. We never really talked about what was going between us. I was just playing the mommy role, taking care of his kid while he went around doing his thing, partying and getting loaded.

At a certain point, things became strained between Richard and the young man whom he was caring for, as if they were each competing for the affection of the disinterested father. Still, the experience of caring for another was empowering, bringing to mind the times in his younger years where he helped take care of his chronically ill parent. The relationship ended abruptly when he returned to New Jersey after his father fell into a diabetic coma.

> He died not that long after. I was glad he was dead. Does that make me a bad person? I don't care. The last time I saw him was right before I left for

> Florida. We were at the dinner table and Mommy was yammering on like usual. He never answered her, he would just grunt. I told her not to talk about that stuff (the church) with me anymore, because it brought up all the stuff that happened at school, and then he was on top of me choking me…Not like fake choking, like I felt like I was going to die. He was strong, even though he was sick all the time and he was just on top of me with all his weight and the room started to go black. Mommy somehow pulled him off of me, but from that moment on he was dead to me.

He spent the summer following the death of his father going down to a small beach house that the family owned down at the Jersey Shore. He gradually became involved with Keith, a drug dealer who lived in one of the crumbling hotels nearby frequented by the local prostitutes. Despite the squalid surroundings, he found some measure of comfort socializing with the denizens of the surrounding neighborhood. It was around this time that he became a regular marijuana smoker, enjoying the relief it gave him from the flashbacks.

"That all changed when I found out he gave me an STD. I totally freaked out, I had to have surgery to remove these growths." Later that year he met the "man upstairs" when he took a job doing office work at his medical practice. Soon afterwards he had moved into his apartment. As with his earlier relationship, the boundary between employee and romantic partner was again blurred to the point where it no longer seemed to exist. At once caretaker, abused partner, and employee, Richard spent the next 19 years in a kind of stasis, shuttling his partner back and forth from his practice and the home they shared, handling the domestic responsibilities, a hostage to his partner's frequent rages. The few brief moments of intimacy in the first few years became less frequent until the final escalation of Richard's own drinking that had ended the relationship.

Family Dynamics

As our sessions progressed, the focus became less about his escape from the "former man upstairs" (as he now referred to him), centering on the power struggles that had resumed with his mother upon his return to the family home, the seat of so much of his emotional pain.

"Mommy's starting in again, talking about the rapture. The whole house is like a church. Sometimes I feel surrounded."

He would often refer to "Mommy's love affair with J.C," as if her religion had taken the place of his father, competing with him for her affection. The ubiquitous presence of religious iconography was a frequent sore spot as it brought up the religious community that he associated with his childhood abuse as well as the church's stance regarding his orientation, problematizing the one stable relationship in his life. The use of theistic triangulation, that is the invocation of religious authority and doctrine in maladaptive ways within the family power structure, is often a source of contention within religious households with gay family members. Etengoff and Daiute (2014) note that "theistic triangulation was reported by gay participants to be the primary source of familial conflict and pain during the post–coming-out process" (p. 40).

"She's getting worse and worse." he would say each week, reporting how she would be constantly moving and rearranging furniture or cleaning out the refrigerator. A particular sore spot was her hiring of a local handyman who would be charged with throwing out things and going through Richard's belongings without his consent. "Psycho Mark" (as he referred to him) would appear as if out of nowhere, banging on the door to the basement where he slept, yelling at him to "get those prostitutes out of there." On more than one occasion he reported how he would appear to walk around the house with a visible erection. The presence of this unwanted presence flooded him with memories of the frequent bullying he experienced in parochial school and the lack of protection he received from the school following the incidences. Almost nightly he would experience vivid nightmares about returning to previous situations related to the abuse. Even in his waking hours there were frequent triggers, particularly since his return to the family home.

Around this time, I received the first of many communications from Richard's elderly mother. From our conversations, I understood that she suffered from her own traumatic circumstances: parents who suffered from episodes of serious mental illness and an older son who was killed while serving in the Army, shortly before Richard's birth. That along with her deceased husband's chronic medical issues would have been enough to explain the challenging relationship with Richard. Compounding this situation was the escalating cognitive decline that, if Richard's accounts were to be believed, indicated that she was suffering from at least some of the symptoms of dementia.

The subject of our discussions, however, was primarily her concern about Richard, in particular his escalating alcohol use. Seeing the differing accounts of the same events provided a strange sort of counterpoint, like the famous film *Rashoman*, in which a crime is told from the point of view of all the participants, none of the facts of their account agreeing with each other. His descriptions of fleeing from his mother's paranoid and repetitive behaviors were interpreted by her as his retreating into isolation to drink. Every conversation was concluded with the request, so familiar to anyone who works with the family of alcoholics, to be sure not to reveal the conversation to Richard, in order to avoid upsetting him. Despite his mother's religious fervor, there seemed to be no judgments on her part regarding Richard's sexual orientation.

> Mommy doesn't care about it. You would think with all the Jesus stuff that she would be ranting about the gays, but she always seemed supportive. At first I didn't think that she noticed, but it would be hard not to, right?

He was alluding to the obvious ambiguities of his appearance, the feminine clothing and glasses which called to mind Jackie Onassis.

I discussed his mother's concerns and he admitted that he continued to drink on occasion, self-medicating after a particularly grueling day with his mother. Discussions regarding the possible benefits of attending an A.A. meeting or group therapy session were met with laughter. Despite his occasional indulgence, he claimed the episode of near liver failure had scared him sufficiently.

"You don't have to worry, I'm never going to put myself through that again."

The irony that the mother who was attempting to rehabilitate him was in essence his excuse for drinking was not lost on him. Later on, this type of cycle was recapitulated at an important point in the therapeutic relationship.

After several months, Richard began to feel well enough physically to retrieve more of his belongings from his former partner's home. An avid collector, he had amassed a considerable amount of vintage video game consoles and games as well as model cars, all of it acquired during his adulthood, as he was not permitted to have toys or watch television when he was a child.

"I mean, daddy would watch the game in his room, but I didn't know anything about television until I was in my twenties."

In our sessions, we discussed how he had been having the childhood he didn't have as an adult. Even in his dreams he was always a child or teenager, younger and smaller, even when the events in the dream reflected his current adult life.

He reported that his sleep schedule was in a constant state of disruption due to the recurrent nightmares of the abuse he had suffered in the school locker room, as well as the physical attacks he had suffered at the hands of his father. The image of the perpetrator dragging him out from beneath the bathroom stall and the jeers of the other boys who had been present returned again and again whenever her attempted to close his eyes. At this point we began to discuss attempting to process some of this traumatic material through the use of EMDR.

Eye Movement Desensitization and Reprocessing (EMDR) therapy is an integrative psychotherapy protocol developed by Francine Shapiro (Shapiro, 2001) which utilizes elements of psychodynamic, cognitive and behavioral approaches in conjunction with some form of bilateral stimulation (typically eye movements). Traumatic material is thought to be somehow unintegrated, causing disturbances in the form of flashbacks and nightmares (2001, pp. 29–56). The adaptive information processing model according to Shapiro is the mechanism by which unintegrated traumatic experience are processed in the "here and now," allowing the reframing of core beliefs underlying the trauma.

This emphasis on information processing in the narrow sense (relying as it does on the metaphor of the mind as computer) fails to capture the essence of what EMDR has represented to my practice. In some sense, it has introduced me to the presence of the body in psychotherapy. Prior to my training, the wider realm of interpersonal communication and its relationship to bodily states were largely invisible to me. Therapy was something you did with language, as if two brains in jars were communicating via satellite. As you sit moving a pen or some other object back and forth before the patient's visual field, encouraging them to go with whatever thoughts have arisen in their mind, or to focus on a tension in their chest while they think of a traumatic incident, something unexpected happens. Again and again the image of the mother calming the child in a moment of activation seems to hover over the whole process, allowing the internal state of the patient to resolve unintegrated aspects of their affective selves.

Current discussions by Allan Schore (2007) and others have reexamined attachment theory (a model essentially at odds with the psychoanalytic frameworks of the time) through a relational psychoanalytic lens, reconceptualizing it in terms of affect regulation. This reconciliation has been enacted thanks to new understandings regarding the neurobiology of child development which have highlighted the importance of right-brain to right-brain communications between mother and child and the impact of these implicit communications on the development of an integrated core self. Of particular interest in Schore's discussion is the notion of interactive regulation, where the mother in the first year of life co-regulates the child's nervous system through the process of attunement and repair. The result of this process is the instillation in the developing brain with the capacity for later self-regulation. Failure of this intersubjective regulatory function can result in the familiar traumatic stress responses of hyperarousal on one hand and pathological dissociation on the other (Schore, 2007).

Schore and Schore (2008) also note the implications of these factors for effective psychotherapy. These right-brain unconscious communications, as they occur within the therapeutic relationship (the moment to moment fluctuations in tone of voice, and non-verbal communications such as facial and postural cues which constitute the phenomena of countertransference), recapitulate and correct the parental regulatory function. This aspect is at odds with prior ideas that emphasized interpretative aspects of psychotherapy, highlighting the importance of interpersonal/relational features such as therapeutic alliance and empathic engagement over strict concentration on cognitive analysis (Schore & Schore, 2008).

Returning to the significance of establishing safety in the therapeutic relationship, the use of techniques such as EMDR in the processing of traumatic memory requires an explicit understanding of attachment concerns. If I had attempted to introduce this type of intervention at an earlier stage in treatment before a sense of emotional safety had been established, the likelihood of a premature termination of therapy would have been almost certain.

To that end, my approach, in accordance with the EMDR protocol, was directed at addressing his feeling of being overwhelmed and identifying and anchoring a safe place/resource that he would be able to return to when closing a session. I asked Richard to select a memory or setting which represented a safe environment, a task which proved difficult for him. He eventually settled upon a hilltop near his home, overlooking a small patch of forest where he used to go to escape the stress of his homelife. We would periodically end sessions with a guided meditation centered around this imagery, until it became second nature for him to use this as a kind of holding environment when he was particularly overwhelmed by the intrusive images.

Slowly, we began to address the specific memories related to the abuse beginning with his assault in the school locker room, and the later indifference of his once adored principal to the abuse.

> It was like nobody cared, and mommy and daddy didn't seem to press the issue. I thought Mr. G. would help, but I remember the look of disgust on his face as I sat across from him, telling him what happened, and I felt like I wanted disappear.

Through these sessions, it became apparent that he still experienced the event from the vantage point of a small child (also evidenced by his continued references toward his mother and father as "mommy" and "daddy"). This vivid connection to one's prior bodily self appears to be a crucial aspect of traumatic memory. By way of illustration, I recall the experiences of an incest survivor who described to me the invisibility she experienced in her obesity, a sense of protection from the unwanted interest from her older brother. After undergoing lap band surgery and losing much of the weight, a traumatized younger self-state continued to act out in various ways (compulsive spending and other addictive behaviors). This younger self-state continued to experience itself as morbidly obese, buying clothes that were objectively too large for her, forcing her to turn sideways when entering subway turnstiles even though she was now slender and able to enter without difficulty. In a similar way, perhaps Richard's regression to a presexual child self-state was reflected in his loss of sexual interest, the shame and confusion of the abused child.

Returning to the subject of his initial trauma, the subsequent abuse (sexual assaults in the hospital and an earlier incident with an adult neighbor while a young teenager) were all experienced through the lens of this primary abandonment. The actual details of the abuse seemed less important than the fact that he was not protected by the adults around him. The similarities between the various relationships he had entered into since leaving home as well as his childhood relationship with his abusive, chronically ill father, became more obvious to him. The caretaking behavior was explicitly linked to his belief that he was flawed in his essential being, a fact that required a continuous and exhausting effort on his part to earn the love and care of his preoccupied if not overtly hostile parental figures. As van der Kolk notes in regards to these relational dynamics,

> Children have a biological instinct to attach; they have no choice. Whether their parents or caregivers are loving and caring or distant, insensitive, rejecting, or abusive, children will develop a coping style based on their attempt to get at least some of their needs met.
>
> *(van der Kolk, 2014)*

This style may encompass a whole constellation of behaviors designed to maintain some connection to the feared but necessary "other" whether they be a parent or romantic partner.

These sessions were frequently draining for Richard, partially due to the fact that he was standing rather than seated for the duration. While we would often have several session breaks, he began to report a shift in his experience, particularly in regard to his dreams.

"I notice that I'm not small anymore. When the thoughts come I feel like I'm a grown up."

The content of his dreams, while still centered around the environment of his childhood was now divested of the sinister character that it had held for him in the past. Like his photo albums, he reported only a series of benign landscapes, as if he had returned to the safety of his own private universe. Soon afterwards he began selling off his collections of video games and toys, artifacts of a childhood he had never actually had. The acute experience of the traumatic past had receded, but the all too real conflicts with his very real parent, as well as his reluctance to engage with others except on the most superficial terms, remained.

Self-States, Identity and Internalized Homophobia

We are perhaps accustomed to viewing sexual identity as a reified structure, leading to a tendency toward absolutist assertions regarding human behavior. Political and legal arguments often hinge upon the ongoing debates between essentialist and social constructionist views of orientation, ignoring the messy and confusing realities that lurk beneath the generalizations. Reviews of the scientific literature regarding the etiology of homosexuality tend to favor biological explanations over social ones, noting the role of unspecified genetic and epigenetic influences, including significantly higher rates of homosexuality in both male and female monozygotic twins than dizygotic twins, and genetic variations in women with gay offspring as compared the general population, amongst other factors (Ngun & Vilain, 2014). Other researchers have noted the strong relationship between gender nonconformity in childhood and later homosexual identity, as well as the emergence of these tendencies in children before there is any awareness of sexual orientation or behavior (Bailey et al., 2016). This is not to suggest that there are not complications to this notion of biological determinism. Diamond (2016) suggested that orientation is much more fluid than was previously thought, noting the frequent discrepancy between identity and actual behavior. That is to say self-identified gay or straight individuals may engage in sexual behavior across the spectrum while maintaining a primary orientation toward a particular sex. She states that cross cultural research has supported the fact that love and desire may function independently of each other noting that "little is known about the precise association between sexual and affectional feelings and how each is influenced by sexual orientation" (2003, p. 173).

There is a complex interplay between our subjective experience of the world and our attempts to examine and measure it objectively. The social sciences efforts to ape the methodology of other disciplines often fails to account for this very human tendency to create categories and in turn be directed by them. Philosopher Ian Hacking (1999) discussed the distinction as it relates to science, introducing the notion of interactive kinds and the "looping effect," "That is, new knowledge about "the criminal" or "the homosexual" becomes known to the people classified, changes the way these individuals behave, and loops back to force changes in the classifications and knowledge about them" (p. 105). While our methods of classification have very real implications for the individuals so categorized (one need not dispute whether their self-identified gender, race, or sexual preferences are real), this tendency inevitably complicates our efforts to "carve nature at the joints" in regards to sexuality, as well as to other aspects of human experience. As Diamond notes, "human sexual and affectional experiences are neither "mainly cultural" nor "mainly biological" but must always be understood as products of powerful interactions between biological and social factors" (2003, p. 174).

Beyond this question of what constitutes sexual identity is the question of this identity's relationship to the self. It is often taken for granted that, like sexual orientation, our sense of self is somehow solid and immutable, though even a casual reflection upon our behavior over time and in various circumstances reveals that this is not (pardon the phrase) a self-evident truth. In the case of trauma, the situation becomes even murkier, particularly as it relates to the subject of dissociation and the fragmentation of the self that occurs in these situations. Most discussions of dissociation, for example van der Hart, Nijenhuis, and Steele's (2006) Structural Dissociation model (building upon the work of Freud's contemporary Pierre Janet), have focused on the pathological nature of dissociation, particularly in the more extreme examples of Dissociative Identity Disorder. Philip Bromberg, whose relational approach relies heavily on the notion of self-states and the multiplicity of self, notes that

> Dissociation, like repression, is a healthy, adaptive function of the human mind. It is a basic process that allows individual self-states to function optimally (not simply defensively) when full immersion in a single reality, a single strong affect, and a suspension of one's self-reflective capacity is exactly what is called for or wished for.
>
> *(Bromberg, 1996)*

While the dysfunctional dimension of dissociation is acknowledged, particularly in cases where these states are unable to function in a cohesive manner, dissociation in and of itself is not seen as inherently pathological, but as part of everyday human experience. The notion of a single, cohesive, unitary self from this perspective is a misapprehension of the true state of affairs: the self considered as object rather than process. We are all in some sense shifting continuously amongst many momentary selves; now a petulant child when scorned by a partner, a moment later, the responsible adult professional when confronted with a work problem. Traumatic experience only complicates what is an already indeterminate and elusive subject.

How do these ideas intersect with sexual identity? If we are to accept the premise that as Bromberg (2006) suggests (citing the work of Whyte (1960) and Whyte's analysis of the writings of Hippolyte Taine), that the mind functions as an ever-shifting theater of self-states, might their attendant bodily/affective components as they relate to sexuality in certain individuals be in a similar state of flux? This idea may help to elucidate this fluidity amongst individual with well-defined orientations, as well as long held observations regarding the fluctuations of sexual identity in individuals within the borderline personality disorder/complex trauma spectrum (Reich & Zanarini, 2008). A broader scope might examine how disorganized attachment strategies that are often the precursor to these disorders intersect with cultural attitudes regarding marginalized identities.

One of the central tenets of gay affirmative therapies is the acknowledgment of internalized self-hatred reflected in the dominant heterosexist culture. In Richard's case, the shame surrounding his sexual preferences for older men is intimately bound to his disorganized attachment strategies. It is not at all evident where his desires for safety and protection from an older male intersect with his identity as a gay man. When one's formative sexual experiences are abusive, the sense of pleasure and desire may be experienced as confusing ("I was hurt, but some part of me was aroused, therefore, I was a party to the abuse, or responsible for it happening"). The object of desire is in a very real sense also the image of the oppressor. A double bind is created, where the need for attachment is complicated by the equally intense need for self-protection from the abuse. Blizard (2001) noted the frequent appearance of this type of dynamic in abused and neglected children, conceiving of these antagonistic self-states or internal working models as alternately sadistic and masochistic representations of abusive and neglectful caretakers. For Richard, the self-shaming instinct may be a general theme that, while not centered around his homosexuality, intersects with his ambivalence regarding sexual feelings in the aftermath of abuse. Disorganized attachment acts as a method of self-protection, a type of appeasement strategy that, at least on some level, allows him to meet the rudimentary needs of attachment while maintaining an optimal level of safety and distance. In practice, however, this is more likely to result in relationship choices which recapitulate the original suffering he received at the hands of his primary attachment figures. This is evident in his long term relationships with older men who, in some sense required his care, like his chronically ill father, but whose actions were, as with the father, overtly rejecting or abusive. While identifying as gay, his experience as the alien and outsider is aligned more generally against anyone who might be a possible attachment figure.

A reenactment of the family triangle between Richard, myself, and his psychiatrist serves to illustrate some of these dynamics. A frequent subject of Richard's joking (and at other times the source of shame and self-disgust) was his attraction to "pop pop" figures (men whom he viewed as father or grandfather figures). Fantasies had developed toward the various physicians who treated him, particularly his psychiatrist. He would recount walking down the hallway to his office at his appointments, playfully imagining a wedding march playing in the background. This psychiatrist, while initially supportive, became understandably irritated by his frequent missed appointments, a violation of the office's strict cancellation policies. Often, I would find myself attempting to intercede on his behalf in order to prevent the inevitable break from occurring, probably in the same fashion as his mother in dealing with his enraged father. This would result in a pattern of self-defeat, anxious phone calls expressing concerns about being cut off from his psychiatric medications and pronouncements of how he would not be coming back. A similar pattern had developed with Frank, a shop owner with whom he had developed a friendship over the years of his adolescence. Frank, whose son was also gay, showed him acceptance and provided him with a safe haven from the harassment of his peers and the tyranny of his family.

As he became older, he agonized about contacting him, fantasizing about the old days at the shop, but consoling himself that he was better off never seeing him again. He eventually went to visit him and, despite the warm reception he received, formed the intention of cutting off all further ties in order to avoid the inevitable pain of his passing.

All of these instances served to highlight just how precarious it was for him to be in therapy at all. In addition to his fearfulness about my anger and the anger of his psychiatrist, there was also this fear of my fragility. At the end of sessions, he would invariably pause at the door and admonish me to be safe. The statement struck me as beyond the usual ritualized statements one makes when arriving and departing from another person. Now that he had entrusted me with these aspects of his inner life, I was as exposed and vulnerable as he perhaps felt himself to be, almost like a child for whom object permanence has yet to develop, imagining that his mother disappears forever whenever she leaves the room. In such situations, the drive to remove this vulnerability by breaking off contact continued to reassert itself.

Therapist Attachment Considerations

In the moment, it can be difficult to evaluate one's therapeutic successes and failures. With 20/20 hindsight, our missteps seem so glaringly obvious. In reviewing Richard's attachment struggles, his various solutions to the problem of engagement with others, I began to perceive the mirror image of the therapist's situation, and my ambivalence regarding attachment as it relates to my patients. Perhaps my eagerness to make therapy a safe space for him allowed me to collude with his attempts at entertaining me, as he often entertained other transient individuals with whom he interacted over the course of his day, failing to acknowledge often enough how he might use his comedic persona as a means of distancing and avoiding connection. Am I, after all the smoke clears, simply another one of Richard's single serve friendships, a video camera recording his experiences, only to be placed on the shelf afterwards to collect dust? Perhaps this fear motivated my efforts to rescue him from the inevitable clash with his psychiatrist and my failure to acknowledge his need for self-protection through avoidance. A more troubling thought than this occurred in one of our sessions; that perhaps my patients are performing the same function to me as Richard's cashiers and receptionists, people with whom I interact in this brief and intense forum, a social relationship without the risks of actual connection. What makes one choose to enter the helping professions in the first place? Let us admit the relational weirdness involved in the provider/patient relationship. Nowhere else (save perhaps in the confessional booth) is one placed in a situation where one discloses intimate details of one's life to relative strangers. At times, does the treatment situation itself not act as a form of ambivalent attachment for the caregiver, where one repeatedly forms relationships with others that are in some sense unreal, driven at times by the need to fix or undo our own problematic relationships? To the extent that we disavow these feelings we risk acting them out unconsciously with our patients. While this is not to suggest that therapists and other treatment professionals as a whole suffer from traumatic attachment, it does suggest that one must possess or develop certain personality traits to allow this paradoxical engagement with another human being; at once intimately connected and fundamentally detached. Perhaps the frequent existence of dual relationships in Richard's history (functioning as both romantic partner and employee/caretaker) served as this kind of relational buffer against the vulnerability of attachment.

In regard to psychotherapists, this sense of detachment may be a crucial feature of many therapists' choice of vocation. McWilliams (2006) in her discussion of schizoid dynamics cited an ongoing Australian study regarding the personality types of therapists noting that "the modal personality type among female therapists is depressive, among male therapists, schizoid trends predominate" (p. 3). Later on, she notes that "the professional practice of analysis and the psychoanalytic therapies offer an attractive resolution of the central conflict about closeness and distance that pervades schizoid psychology" (McWilliams, 2006, p. 5, cf. Wheelis, 1956). While she identifies this trend as specifically connected to psychoanalytically oriented therapies, the same might be said of the therapeutic relationship in general. Might not individuals who crave the contact with other human beings but resist the engulfment that characterizes schizoid relational patterns gravitate toward the intimate confessional nature of therapy, where one shares the privileged access to another's life without having to be in that life as a participant? In contrast to this (if I am able to evoke another self-state of my own) is the sense that the moments of genuine connectedness that routinely occurs between patient and therapist transcend the situation, the left brain analytic reductionism which cynically views therapy as a form of paid friendship.

These reflections paradoxically were crucial to my understanding of Richard's experience. In the beginning, our interactions felt one-sided, as if I was indeed simply a recorder, a mute witness to his monologues. Later, particularly in my responses to his self-denigrating messages, both written and verbal (letters and answering machine messages that would stream in, almost as a meta commentary on our sessions), I began to notice a shift, the image of the angry parent that he was imagining me to be, giving way to an authentic engagement with me as an actual human being. In a particular session after he expressed relief at the fact that that I was not angry with him for a missed session, we discussed the fact he had stopped recording himself.

"I mean, after all, I can come here. I don't have to talk to myself anymore."

Part of me reacted to this statement, a flicker of the irritation that I had felt at certain points in the past, moments where my presence in the room was unacknowledged, almost unnecessary. I thought that this was not entirely my perception, but a consequence of a lifetime of self-protective behavior on his part. I tried to verbalize this experience without reinforcing his guardedness.

> I can understand why you feel like it is necessary to keep people at a distance. Sometimes I get the feeling that you feel the same way here, like you have to entertain me, or keep me at arm's length.

He sighed, his voice breaking as if fighting back some strong emotion.

> I know I do that. Almost like I make the world around me disappear. Then when I'm not paying attention it's like I wake up and you're there in the room. I know I come in here sometimes and I just kind of throw everything out at you and then when I get home I beat myself up, like I shouldn't have said so much… God damn it.

He seemed about to launch into another bout of self-flagellation, but stopped himself. Regaining some of his composure, he finished.

"But, then we talk about it, and it's not as bad as I thought."

"That's different then the camera. You never go back to it and work through it. It just stays there in a box somewhere. Here, we get to unpack it." There was a mutual laugh at the literal box inadvertently morphing into metaphorical one.

Afterwards he began to go through his routine, including his daily trip to the local library to hunt for new movies (as well as his contact with the librarian and the tales of her heroin addict daughter). I mentioned a movie about the street artist Banksy (*Exit through the Gift Shop*, 2010) that I had seen earlier in the week that had reminded me of him. In the movie, one of the artist's fans, in a similar fashion to Richard, had been chronicling every moment in his daily life on videotape. In the course of our discussion, Richard disclosed for the first time that in addition to taping himself, he had also written a novel about his experiences, again placing it in a box in the back of his basement apartment, never to be seen again. As with his videotapes, he expressed that he had no interest in ever reading it or publishing it. We talked more about his literary interests, and I related a story that had entered my mind as he spoke, about Franz Kafka (an author whose emotionally abusive relationship with his father Hermann, chronicled in a despairing, 47 page letter, paralleled Richard's own experiences). As he was dying, Kafka had instructed his friend Max Brod to destroy all of his unpublished work. I mused that perhaps the famously inscrutable author of *The Metamorphosis* had used his writing as a kind of mirror, some sort of proof that he existed. It didn't matter if anyone else read it, it was for him and him alone. Once he was dead, it was no longer necessary. Richard seemed keenly interested in this idea. We talked about how he was not truly acknowledged by his parents as someone with a separate identity and will, his only purpose seemed to cater to his father's endless list of demands. His mother, similarly preoccupied with religious matters and the need to please her ill and bitter spouse, failed to see Richard's pain and protect him from the abuse he suffered at home and at school. All of this was on top of his efforts throughout his childhood to be a perfect Christian, in spite of his struggles over being gay, and hence unacceptable in the eyes of the church. To be seen for who he is rather than for what the viewer wants him to be; this was what seemed to lurk behind the relentless self-scrutiny and documentation.

"But, it's not like when I first landed here haha, you know, like I'm talking to the camera. Coming here, I know I don't have to feel that way anymore. You're not just a camera, you're a real person."

As he said it I felt that it was true for him in a way that was unexpected for both of us, that in my challenging him about my status as mere spectator, I had ceased to be one. As we ended the session he turned to me.

"So what happened? he asked. After a moment he noticed my confusion.

"I mean with Kafka, did his friend burn everything?"

"No, he didn't. He refused. I think the implication is they both knew he wouldn't do it."

Afterwards, I reflected on this moment between us. I realized that this seeming diversion into literary discussion had been a moment of recognition. The disclosure of frustration over my status as mute witness to his monologues, and our subsequent discussion about Kafka, had given way to a recognition that therapy was not just another instance of recording the past. His handing over of his life experiences was not simply to consign it to the flames. Somewhere in the process, I would ignore his request to discard it and respond to the unvoiced desire to help him rescue something valuable from it. Bromberg notes the healing power of this type of here and now engagement within psychotherapy, "the potential for the coexistence of selfhood and otherness becomes not only more possible, but also gradually begins to take place with greater spontaneity, with less shame, and without affective destabilization" (Bromberg, 2012, p. 27). Despite the impairment in the capacity for mentalization in some individuals with developmental trauma, moments of authentic relatedness can allow this dissociated material to be made an object of reflection in the therapeutic relationship.

Conclusion

Often in treatment, there is no sense of a definitive ending and one's sense of progress is often ambiguous. The fear of his psychiatrist's wrath and my efforts to reinforce the importance of regular attendance, coupled with his mother's worsening condition ultimately resulted in Richard leaving treatment, precisely at the moment when I suspected he would need it the most. The anticipated rejection served to reinforce the codependent dynamic with his ailing mother. Unable to relegate certain responsibilities regarding her care to healthcare providers, he remained in a state of fear and hyper-vigilance over something happening while he was away at an appointment, in effect protecting his mother by moving away from his angry and rejecting treatment providers. On the other side of this was a recognition that this "problem" was not mine to solve. My efforts to protect him from the wrath of the father/psychiatrist most likely had the opposite of its intended effect. If the preferred state of an individual with this type of attachment style is one of relief at having escaped the intrusive and unwanted connection to another, any attempt at repair may in effect be a further rupture/misattunement.

These dynamics should be considered when adopting a Gay Affirmative stance in therapy with survivors of sexual abuse and other types of complex trauma. Certain approaches emphasize a somewhat directive approach in regards to bolstering the patient's attitudes regarding sexual orientation. It has been my experience that in some cases of extreme internal conflict (for instance ego dystonic sexual desires in individuals whose deeply held religious convictions or cultural traditions that prohibit homosexuality), any attempt at directly challenging their conflicts may backfire, causing them to retreat from therapy before work can be done to help them come to terms with their orientation. In a similar way, too challenging of an approach to Richard's defensive attachment strategies, pushing him toward a premature acceptance, would likely have resulted in retreat from yet another controlling attachment figure. In a very real sense, it is the person (who in any case may not possess a firm sense of their own identity, given the vast array of possibilities open to those with a more fluid sense of desire, or as in the case with complex trauma, multiple unintegrated self-states with contradictory attitudes related to sex) who must be the driving force for change, even in instances where internalized homophobia is an obstacle to self-acceptance. The therapist cannot ultimately be the agent of change, but only a collaborator or guide in the process.

Close Reading Questions

1. What is disorganized attachment? In this case study, how does the experience of trauma affect attachment to the therapist and to others?
2. What does Jarrette-Kenney mean when he writes, "When developmental factors impede self-regulation, dissociative states become the central means of self-preservation, but at great cost to the individual, laying the groundwork for the development of later psychopathology" (Schore, 2007)?
3. What is EMDR? Summarize how it was helpful in Jarrette-Kenney's collaboration with his client.

Prompts for Writing

1. Discuss how Gay Affirmative Therapy frames internalized self-hatred as a reflection of the dominant culture. Compare how Jarrette-Kenney and Healy practice Gay Affirmative Therapy in their respective chapters.
2. How would you describe Richard's mind-body connection? How do his illnesses reflect other forms of the embodiment of trauma in this book, as in Conti or Hartman?
3. Why do you think Richard is particularly prone to addiction and self-harm? What are some possible connections between addiction and self-harm after the experience of sexual trauma? Relate these questions to McGuire's case of Angela.

References

Bailey, J. M., Vasey, P. L., Diamond, L. M., Breedlove, S. M., Vilain, E., & Epprecht, M. (2016). Sexual orientation, controversy, and science. *Psychological Science in the Public Interest, 17*, 45–101.

Banksy (Director), DCruz, J., (Producer), & Ifans, R. (Writer). (2010). *Exit through the gift shop* [Video file].

Blizard, R. A. (2001). Masochistic and sadistic ego states. *Journal of Trauma & Dissociation, 2*(4), 37–58.

Bromberg, P. M. (1996). Standing in the spaces. *Contemporary Psychoanalysis, 32*(4), 509–535.

Bromberg, P. M. (2006). *Awakening the dreamer: Clinical journeys*. Hillsdale, NJ: Analytic Press.

Bromberg, P. M. (2012). *The shadow of the tsunami: And the growth of the relational mind*. London: Routledge.

Breuer, J., & Freud, S. (1895/2000). *Studies on hysteria*. New York, NY: Basic Books Classics.

Diamond, L. M. (2003). What does sexual orientation orient? A biobehavioral model distinguishing romantic love and sexual desire. *Psychological Review, 110*(1), 173–192.

Diamond, L. M. (2016, October 13). *Just how different are male and female sexual orientations?* Presentation at Cornell University, Ithaca, NY. Retrieved from https://www.youtube.com/watch?v=m2rTHDOuUBw

Etengoff, C., & Daiute, C. (2014). Clinicians' perspective of the relational processes for family and individual development during the mediation of religious and sexual identity disclosure. *Journal of Homosexuality, 62*(3), 394–426. doi:10.1080/00918369.2014.977115

Hacking, I. (1999). *The social construction of what?* Cambridge, MA: Harvard University Press.

Irish, L., Kobayashi, I., & Delahanty, D. L. (2010). Long-term physical health consequences of childhood sexual abuse: A meta-analytic review. *Journal of Pediatric Psychology, 35*(5), 450–461. doi:10.1093/jpepsy/jsp118

McWilliams, N. (2006). Some thoughts about schizoid dynamics. *Psychoanalytic Review, 93*, 1–24 and appears here with the permission of the National Psychological Association for Psychoanalysis.

Ngun, T. C., & Vilain, E. (2014). The biological basis of human sexual orientation: Is there a role for epigenetics? In D. Yamamoto (Ed.), *Epigenetic shaping of sociosexual interactions: From plants to humans* (pp. 167–184). Cambridge, MA: Elsevier.

Ouimette, P. C., Kimerling, R., Shaw, J., & Moos, R. H. (2000). Physical and sexual abuse among women and men with substance use disorders. *Alcoholism Treatment Quarterly, 18*(3), 7–17.

Reich, D. B., & Zanarini, M. C. (2008). Sexual orientation and relationship choice in borderline personality disorder over ten years of prospective follow-up. *Journal of Personality Disorders, 22*(6), 564–572. doi:10.1521/pedi.2008.22.6.564

Schore, A. (2007). Review of *Awakening the dreamer: Clinical journeys* by Philip M. Bromberg. *Psychoanalytic Dialogues, 17*(5), 753–767.

Schore, A., & Schore, J. (2008). Modern attachment theory: The central role of affect regulation in attachment and treatment. *Journal of Clinical Social Work, 36*, 9–20.

Shapiro, F. (2001). *Eye movement desensitization and reprocessing (EMDR): Basic principles, protocols, and procedures.* New York, NY: Guilford Press.
Van der Kolk, B. A. (2014). *The body keeps the score: Brain, mind, and body in the healing of trauma.* New York, NY: Viking.
Van der Hart, O., Nijenhuis, E. R. S., & Steele, K. (2006). *The Haunted Self: Structural Dissociation and the Treatment of Chronic Traumatization.* New York, NY: Norton.
Whyte, L. L. (1960). *The unconscious before Freud.* Garden City, NY: Anchor Books.

9

EFFECTIVE USE OF GAY AFFIRMATIVE THERAPY IN A FORENSIC CASE OF SEXUAL TRAUMA

Russell Healy

Pre-Reading Questions

1. What do you know about Gay Affirmative Treatment (GAT)? Might the personal disclosure of the therapist's gender and sexuality help to form the therapeutic alliance in GAT? Do you think that a gay therapist would be a better practitioner of GAT? Why or why not?
2. How have non-heteronormative lifestyles been subject to legal management and criminal accusations? Have LGBTQ folk been historically linked to sexual offense?
3. How might homophobia and misogyny be analogous?

Introduction

The purpose of this chapter is to examine the use of a gay affirmative treatment (GAT) approach in a case involving a gay man who was a victim of sexual assault in adolescence. The case example will explore when to introduce GAT, how to introduce GAT, and to what degree to use GAT. Prior to treatment, the client had never disclosed his orientation to family or friends. Additionally, he was convicted of a sex offense himself, and was Court-mandated to attend and complete behavioral health treatment.

The term "gay affirmative therapy" (GAT) first appeared in 1982, in "Psychotherapeutic Implications of Internalized Homophobia in Gay Men," by psychologist Alan Malyon. He states that, "Gay affirmative psychotherapy is not an independent system of psychotherapy. Rather, it represents a special range of psychological knowledge which challenges the traditional view that homosexual desire and fixed homosexual orientations are pathological" (1982, p. 69). Interestingly, his article appeared two years after the category "ego dystonic homosexuality" was added to the third revision of the Diagnostic and Statistical Manual of Mental Disorders (DSM). The ego dystonic homosexual is one whose same sex attractions are unwanted, and cause distress:

> This category is reserved for those homosexuals for whom changing sexual orientations is a persistent concern, and should be avoided in cases where the desire to change sexual orientations may be a brief, temporary manifestation of an individual's difficulty in adjusting to a new awareness of his or her homo-sexual impulses.
>
> *(APA, 1980, p. 281)*

Thus, The American Psychiatric Association suggested the lived experience of the ego dystonic homosexual was characterized by shame, loneliness, guilt, depression, and anxiety.[1] Malyon never mentions ego-dystonic homosexuality specifically, but it seems clear that internalized homophobia and ego-dystonic homosexuality are the same phenomena.

Malyon believed that homosexual men are subjected to a homophobic "biased socialization" (1982, p. 61), one that creates obstacles against healthy identity development. Being socialized in a homophobic social context can cause gay men to develop "internalized homophobia" (p. 60). If the internalized homophobia is too powerful, opportunities to correct the damage during adolescence or young adulthood may be missed or avoided. Malyon clarified that this is not the fate for all gay men: "the developmental significance of any particular aspect of the socialization experience is determined by the special vulnerabilities, needs, and defensive strategies, of each individual" (p. 62). Malyon approached his work with gay men from a psycho-dynamic perspective, but acknowledged that integrating other techniques such as correcting cognitive distortions and role modeling by an openly gay therapist, or an informed non-gay therapist, are important healing factors.

Malyon was a psychologist, and for many years psychology took the lead in developing and articulating GAT. Many of those psychologists were British, as the US and England took a lead in the emergence of GAT. In 1984, social worker Theresa DeCrescenzo published a study on the *Attitudes of Mental Health Professionals towards Homosexuality*, which found that social workers were more homophobic than their counterparts in psychology. This did not surprise me. When I was an MSW student in the mid 1980s, many of the faculty in my program viewed homosexuality as pathology. Their positions were informed by classical psychoanalytic theory. None of the faculty were openly lesbian or gay, and I was advised to keep my identification to myself (I did not).

Gay affirmative treatment is more of a stance than a stand-alone model of therapeutic work. As such, GAT can be integrated into a number of established models of clinical work. The stance is simply that there is nothing pathological about having a homosexual or bisexual orientation. What clients do, or do not do, with their orientations is part of what determines a client's happiness and sense of agency. Our role as social workers is to assist gay clients with internalized homophobia to be fully expressed and self-embracing. A gay affirming stance requires a commitment to be fully educated about gay experience.

In the late 1980s and into the late 1990s, GAT was about the removal of internalized homophobia, and developing and consolidating a gay identity. Several models of identity development were produced by psychology (Cass, 1979; Coleman, 1982). My literature search on GAT revealed that much of the literature on GAT in the recent past has been from a psychodynamic perspective. With the onset of outcome-driven and research-based treatments, that trend has changed. GAT can be integrated into most approaches easily, even in the context of Court-mandated, relapse prevention focused treatment, as I will demonstrate.

In the late 1990s, social worker John Lebolt published a qualitative study on the experiences of gay men in GAT. He used phenomenological methods to gather data from a small sample of gay men in GAT. Lebolt also used aspects of feminist research methodology, because he believed homophobia and misogyny to be analogous. He was looking to get more in-depth data from a small sample, because of the "complex, intersubjective" nature of the therapeutic relationship, which he thought may be hard to quantify (1999, p. 3).

Lebolt found different variables of effectiveness in openly gay therapists and non-gay therapists. Gay therapists could function more effectively as role models for gay men who are working to develop positive gay relationships. Non-gay therapists who had experience with the gay community (the study was conducted during the HIV epidemic; the non-gay therapists often did HIV-related casework), and who were "sensitive and imaginative" played a healing role through simple, genuine, non-judgmental acceptance (1999, p. 13).

Other useful techniques identified included: therapist self-disclosure regarding their own sexual identity, supporting their clients in self-affirmation, and the therapist's ability to identify external as well as internal homophobia. Group therapy was found to be a useful approach, especially for men in the early stages of identity development, as it allowed them to be immersed in a gay experience that reflected the wide diversity of the gay male community at that time (1999, p. 12). That was my experience as a clinician. I facilitated therapy groups for gay men from the early 1990s until 2013. In the 1990s, gay men were actively seeking group experiences for help with socialization issues, relational issues, and the chance to experience solidarity. As the internet emerged as a way to gain social connectedness, I noticed there was less interest in supportive process groups. Another hypothesis is that society has changed, at least in metropolitan regions. Younger gay people have an easier time in general living openly "queer" lives, hopefully because of activism on the part of older generations of gay persons. More will be said about group therapy in the case study.

Social worker Catherine Crisp calls GAT "gay affirming practice" (GAP). She considers GAP to be a best practices approach, one that is culturally competent. She uses the term practice instead of treatment or psychotherapy because social workers practice in a variety of settings (2006, p. 7). Crisp also developed the Gay Affirmative Practice Scale as a way to measure competence in clinical work with lesbian, gay, and bisexual persons (2006). Crisp believes that a GAP approach is consistent with social work perspectives, specifically, person-in-environment (PIE), emphasis on strengths, and cultural competence. The PIE approach does not locate pathology in an individual without taking into consideration the impact of the social environment on the client. Since gay[2] clients endure a biased socialization, they may have internalized homophobic beliefs about their lives. A strengths perspective respects a client's need for self-determination, and is a health-based outlook. Cultural competence requires us to acquire knowledge, explore our attitudes (and correct where needed), and improve our skills in our work with client's whose experience is different than ours (2006, pp. 2–3).

In 2005, Crisp published, "Homophobia and Use of Gay Affirmative Practice in a Sample of Social Workers and Psychologists." Countering DeCrescenzo's findings, she discovered little difference between the two professions, suggesting social work has progressed in the area of GAP. She used her GAP scale, and two other previously developed scales designed to measure homophobic attitudes. Again, I'm not surprised, but pleased instead by the results. My former MSW program now has a number of openly gay faculty and staff, and its current curriculum is gay affirming.

Before the 21st century, GAT concerned itself with internalized homophobia. Now, GAT concerns itself with heterosexism. Joe Kort is a nationally recognized social worker with expertise in GAT. Kort asserts that, "it is prejudice to be only gay friendly. You must be gay informed" (2008, p. 17). Kort posits two fundamentals of GAT. The first is we must understand, recognize, and combat heterosexism. The second is that if we are to practice according GAT, we must understand heterosexual privilege. Kort acknowledges these are socio-political constructs, but asserts the impact of the biased socialization gay people experience has psychological consequences. Those consequences inform our work as GAT/GAP clinicians. For Kort, heterosexism denies children and adolescents the possibility they might be, or are, gay. A heterosexist socialization creates a developmental obstacle for gay youth. Rather than seeing "becoming gay" as an unremarkable, normal experience, youth must endure a coming out process that non-gay youth never have to consider. Even today, coming out can be a needlessly painful "right-of-passage" for gay youth. When an adult identifies as gay, they often lose their heterosexual privilege. This can trigger grief, or mental health disorders ranging from an adjustment disorder to depression (2008, pp. 19–20).

Social work has continued to study and evaluate what makes GAT effective. Recently, a study published by Alessi, Dillon, and Kim suggested, "therapist engagement in affirmative practice is determined by a multitude of factors, including affirmative counseling self-efficacy and beliefs." They concluded, "training and education that focuses on improving attitudes may only be the first step toward ensuring that therapists practice affirmatively" (2015, p. 9). This is an important finding for social work, because self-efficacy is essential for client self-determination.

As a clinical social worker, I value the principle of self-determination. Also, I do not believe in therapeutic neutrality. In my role as a clinician, I have positions and opinions. One opinion is that gay people always benefit from freedom from shame. Another is that individuality and individual expression is essential to having a healthy sense of self, and the ability to be self-determined. Persons that are self-determined value themselves, and respect and value others. Those are important therapeutic outcomes. They outweigh whether or not someone develops an identity that fits externally designated norms. A therapeutically neutral approach runs counter to GAT, because it does not allow for the clinician to act as a role model or take a stance.

I believe an overemphasis on the socio-political elements of establishing a gay identity can burden individuality. Homosexuality is simply an orientation. Openly identifying as gay is what some gay persons do with their orientations. Persons are complex, and have many ideological, religious, and ethnic loyalties. In over 30 years of GAP, I have noticed that for some of my clients, gay identity is primary; for others, it is secondary. The latter cohort tends to be people of color and those with strong, traditional ethnic and family ties. They have reported they feel alienated by metropolitan gay life-norms. Some have been religiously or politically conservative, or come from Black or Latino communities that do not share the educated, white, liberal identity criteria that can define much of how today's media represents the gay community.

Philosopher Kwame Anthony Appiah has been complicating the concept of identity for over 30 years. He believes that identities come, "with labels and ideas about why and to whom they should be applied… identity shapes (our) thoughts about how (we) should behave, and… it affects the way other people treat (us)." But, identity is not as simple as all that. He points out that, "dimensions of identity are contestable, always up for dispute: who's in, what they are like, how they should behave and be treated" (2018, p. 12). Appiah began by thinking about nationality, class, culture, and religion as sources of identity, but added sexual orientation and gender. Appiah's father is African (Ghanaian), and his mother was British. Appiah's parents were the first high-society inter-racial marriages in England; Appiah speculates that his parent's relationship formed the basis of the film *Guess Who's Coming to Dinner.* He was born in England, but was raised in Ghana and educated in British boarding schools during adolescence. His father was an attorney and his mother a novelist and philanthropist. He spent many summers at his maternal grandmother's home in the English countryside. Professor Appiah is married to a man, and is highly educated. As he grew up, he became aware that people were often confused about how to think about him and treat him. This formed the basis of his inquiry into the nature and ethics of identity.

Some identities are subordinate, others are dominant. Subordinate identities can be burdensome, because they are at the effect of dominant identities who can abuse their power. To counter this dynamic, Appiah advocates for a cosmopolitan world view, one that makes us all "citizens of the world." He favors intersectionality, because it demonstrates how multiple identities "interact to produce effects that are not simply the sum of each of them" (2018, p. 19). Consider Appiah himself. He is of mixed-race descent, which is an identity group here in the States, but less so in Europe. His father was African, Appiah was raised in both Ghana and England, and was educated in English boarding schools. His speech is impeccable, he can have a British accent, which has created interesting dilemmas for him when he travels. He notices that people want to label him, to place him regionally and ethnically, and in terms of class. Finally, he is married to a man.[3] Does that simply make him a gay man? Not likely, Appiah might say. He does not perform being gay any more than he performs being African. As he points out, LGBTQ norms can depend on race and gender (p. 19). He downplays his many identifications to make his case for a cosmopolitan world view. A clinician who only offers GAT would miss the opportunity to see Dr. Appiah as a full, complex person. Certainly, we identify with groups for reasons of solidarity and social connectedness. But, if our group identifications define us, we can lose our autonomy. Without autonomy, we cannot be self-determined.

This is a paradox of GAT: it has utility because it decisively affirms a sexual minority, which has been historically subjected to marginalization and stigma (Herek, 2007). But, affirmation alone is more than our gay clients need at this time in history. In the preceding pages I offered a brief overview and history of GAT. Next, I will use a case example to show how GAT can be integrated into a therapeutic alliance.

Case Study Context

The case I will discuss came from a period in my career when I was working in a private practice with a forensic psychologist who specialized in assessing and treating sex offenders. He was a dedicated behaviorist, but recognized that a lot of his clients had homosexual arousal/orientations. He thought those offenders would benefit from a GAT, and brought me in to work with offenders that had male victims. I learned how to use cognitive-behavioral and relapse prevention approaches with my clients, and integrated a gay affirming stance. I practiced as openly gay, and was direct in my belief that their internalized homophobia would be part of what would contribute to relapse. Most of the clients passed as heterosexual, which allowed them privilege and access to adolescent, and in some cases, pre-adolescent males. My theory was that their arrest and conviction subjected them to the stigma of being a sex offender. Developing a gay identity and a gay social life might mitigate their stigma, and give them an opportunity to live a more authentic life, one in which they would have more skills to prevent a relapse of sexually abusive behavior. For the most part, I was successful in helping them prevent relapse. Some of them went on to develop more rewarding interpersonal lives in the gay community, while others preferred to live quietly with the support of a small group of friends and family. The work was difficult at times, and long-term by nature of their lengthy Court orders. Over 20 years later, I still keep in touch with a number of them. The ones that remained in treatment and "successfully completed a full course of sex-offender specific therapy" did not relapse.

What sets this case apart from the cohort of sex offenders I was treating at that time is that he was a victim of abuse in adolescence, and his conviction placed him only on the border of being an actual offender. That gave me a wider range of choices in how I could assist the client I am about to present.

Introduction: The Case of Hal

Hal was referred to me by my supervisor and employer, Dr. White, the forensic psychologist. Hal's attorney had just arranged for Hal to plead guilty in an Alford Plea. Cornell Law School's legal dictionary defines an Alford Plea as one which registers neither a formal claim of guilt nor innocence toward charges brought against a defendant in criminal court. In practice, an Alford plea allows for the prosecution to claim a win in exchange for a reduction in the sentence (e.g. probation, not prison). The plea is somewhat controversial among legal scholars, because it can backfire, especially in cases where the defendant continues to assert innocence after the plea has been accepted by the Court. It can also function as a way to move defendants quickly through the Courts, with less attention given to issues of justice (Bibas, 2002; Ward, 2006). Another problem with the plea is that it can accompany, or require, an expression of remorse. Remorse is highly subjective, and can be a mitigating factor when expressed, or an aggravating factor if absent. There are reasons why a truly remorseful defendant will not, or cannot, show remorse. A deferential defendant will follow their attorney's instructions to the letter to say nothing and do nothing. A defendant with mental health or neurological problems may not know how to show such emotions (e.g. someone on the autism spectrum). In other cases, a savvy criminal defendant may be able to play the system by acting remorseful, but not feeling remorseful, in hope of a favorable outcome (Ward, 2006).

In Hal's case, the charges against him were lessened to a fourth-degree offense, which does not carry the assumption of incarceration. To receive this arrangement, he plead guilty to a lesser offense, agreed to undergo therapy, and reported to a probation officer. Hal was one of those deferential clients. He allowed his attorney to manage his entire case, and his attorney told him to say nothing about his charges to anyone. I would be the first person to hear the entire truth about what occurred on the night he was accused of molesting his best friend's five-year-old son.

Dr. White and I were concerned about Hal. Because he was able to get an attorney immediately, he never had to confess to any investigating officers (many of the offenders I saw were relieved to be apprehended, and gave full confessions at the time of their arrest). The problem with this was it made Hal look guilty of more serious charges. Mostly, the guilty get lawyers before they are brought in for questioning. The only written information we had about Hal was the Court mandated psychological evaluation Hal initially underwent. Following his attorney's instructions, Hal revealed very little to the psychologist assigned to evaluate him. No sexual history, no relational history. To the psychologist, Hal looked like just another pedophile who lived in his mother's home. Despite being diagnosed with pedophilia, Hal still received the favorable plea bargain. Dr. White acknowledged that the Court appointed psychologist's evaluation was poorly done, and was willing to evaluate Hal to see what level of care he would require.

Fortunately for Hal, he revealed more to Dr. White. His attorney told him to be more candid, because we were going to help him. Hal told Dr. White that he had been living as a closeted gay man at his mother's home, because it fell to him to look after his mother. He was the unmarried sibling in a large, traditional family of Eastern European origin, in an ethnic, urban neighborhood. Hal could not explain what happened on the night he was at his friend's house. He had not been alone with the child that evening, and claimed that he accepted the plea because he wanted to spare his friend and the son the stress and embarrassment of a lengthy criminal investigation. That was enough for Dr. White, who determined that Hal could be managed in the community with outpatient treatment. I contacted Hal and scheduled a first appointment.

Hal arrived early. He was a slender, shy, and nervous man in his early thirties. He was clearly anxious and had to leave the session for a few moments because his stomach was upset. He claimed that "this whole experience" gave him irritable bowel syndrome (IBS). I was the first clinician he had ever met, and was worried about how to comport himself. His attorney told him to be open, but not to claim innocence, because that could ruin the Alford Plea bargain. Hal was afraid that I would contact his attorney, or his probation officer, to tell them he is denying his guilt and asserting innocence. I explained to Hal that I couldn't do that capriciously or without his permission. Yes, I would have to work with his probation officer, but limited to confirming his compliance with therapy, not about the content of his sessions. I recall that Hal seemed only slightly relieved, so I decided to tell him I'm gay (I could sense he would not ask). I explained I simply wanted to help him through this period of his life and avoid future trouble with the Courts. This proved to be the right gay affirming move; Hal was visibly relieved.

I asked Hal why he did not identify as gay, explaining that he might have looked less like a pedophile and more like an adult with an adult's sexuality. His first response was "my attorney told me not to." His second response was that he assumed his family and friends in the neighborhood knew he liked men, but he had never come out to them. His ethnic sub-culture was traditional, Catholic (Orthodox), and as such preferred a "don't ask, don't tell" approach to matters of sexual behavior. At that time, Hal did not believe he could be gay on his own terms. He still attended Mass and held conservative political views. He thought the gay community would reject a conservative person of faith, not the other way around. We continued talking about therapy, and explored how it could help him. I left him thinking about the utility of coming out, at least to his mother. I also suggested that there might be a way for him to maintain his faith and be a member of a welcoming gay community.

After that visit, I began to formulate a conceptualization of Hal. He had internalized the homophobic messages of his biased upbringing, and would need support and encouragement around the goal of becoming gay on his own terms. That could look like any number of ways of being, but the point was to integrate a positive sexual identity, and begin to live a more fulfilling, self-determined life. Still, there was the question of what happened with the boy he was accused of molesting. I could not recommend a treatment plan without fully understanding what happened. If he had an attraction to minors, then his therapy would need to have a primary sex offense-specific focus.

Hal also seemed to have the kind of coping strategies and defense mechanisms of someone who had experienced trauma. He was comfortable living a double life, suggestive of dissociation and compartmentalization. He was avoidant, repressed, and vigilant, as if he expected danger around every corner. In his *Gay Affirmative Therapy for the Straight Clinician: The Essential Guide* (2008), Joe Kort writes that growing up lesbian or gay can produce a form of post-traumatic stress disorder (PTSD). He is suggesting that what Malyon termed a biased socialization, is in fact a process through which gay persons are slowly, chronically exposed to threats of a loss of physical integrity, emotional integrity, and rejection. Such threats are embedded in our culture, covertly and overtly, and easily perceived by young gay persons at a vulnerable time in development. Also, these threats may induce a feeling of helplessness, horror, and fear. Kort cites noted trauma expert Bessel van der Kolk: "the younger the age at which the trauma occurred, and the longer its duration, the more likely people (are) to have long term problems with regulation of anger, anxiety, and sexual impulses" (1996, p. 187). Kort describes the trauma of growing up gay as "insidious and chronic." Kort further hypothesizes that the trauma of growing up gay manifests in "sexual secret keeping." He further proposes that the trauma of growing up gay can produce social isolation, and "settling for very little" (2008, pp. 71–88). Sexual secret keeping, isolation, and settling for very little certainly described Hal when I first met him.

I needed more from Hal to be able to recommend a sound treatment plan. In our second visit, I addressed the issue of his allegations directly. I showed him the copy of the first psychological evaluation, in which he was diagnosed as a pedophile. Of course, being avoidant, he hadn't read it. Hal was very upset by the unfavorable tone of the evaluation. I pointed out to him that he admitted to not disclosing anything to the evaluator, leaving the psychologist no other choice than to fill in the blanks with what little information was available in the discovery packet. I suggested to Hal that his attorney may not have given him the best advice. According to Hal, he came out to his attorney, who then told Hal that everyone in the Courts are homophobic. Frightened even further, Hal agreed to follow his attorney's advice to the letter.

I asked Hal to tell me what happened. He told me that he was at his best friend's house as usual, on a Sunday afternoon for dinner, at a gathering with friends and family from the neighborhood. This occurred most Sundays, and was a major part of Hal's otherwise wan social life. Hal's friend's wife had always been cordial toward Hal (everyone in this network went to the same Catholic High School together), but not effusive or warm. Her brother even less so; he was several years older, and Hal remembers being bullied by him when they were in school.[4] The brother was not a weekly fixture at these gatherings, but this Sunday he made an appearance. When he arrived, the five-year-old boy, ran up to him. Instead of greeting him with a hug, he punched his Uncle in the groin. When asked why he did that, the boy said, "Uncle Hal does that to me."

Hal was not certain of every detail that followed. Essentially, his friend, the boy's father, told Hal to come with him for a drive. Back at the house, people were alarmed. Hal's friend knew that his brother-in-law would call the police, and warned Hal to get a lawyer. He drove Hal home. That was the last time Hal would ever talk with his now former best friend. Hal called an attorney, a criminal defense lawyer on the internet who promised an immediate reply 24 hours a day, 7 days a week. Given it was Sunday, Hal felt his choices were limited. But he did make the call, and was immediately represented. The police had been notified, but the attorney was able to intervene and prevent an arrest at Hal's house. Hal and the attorney appeared at the police station the next day, where Hal was processed. His attorney did not permit Hal to be interrogated.

I asked Hal what he thought of the boy's behavior. Hal offered his speculation. Because Hal was a trusted member of the boy's extended family, he would sometimes baby-sit while his friend and the friend's wife would go out. Hal would be entrusted to bathe the child and put him to bed. Sometimes, Hal said, he would "blow raspberries" on the child's stomach. He said everyone played with the boy like that, including the Uncle. That was the extent of Hal's explanation. I was skeptical, certainly. But, being a clinician and not a detective, I wanted to balance my skepticism with curiosity.

In our next visit, I returned to the question of his relationship with his friend's son. Hal consistently described a close-knit, if not tense and repressed, circle of neighborhood family and friends. I was curious—was he angry at his friend for not intervening, for not using his authority as a father? Hal denied anger, in fact, at that time he still expected to be friends with this group. I decided it was time to take a sexual history. It turned out that Hal had quite a sexual history, albeit a secret one. He would go into the gay neighborhood of a nearby city to look for men for sex. Also, there was a park near his neighborhood where men would cruise for sex. He spent a lot of time there. I was surprised he never got arrested in a raid. Hal knew how to handle himself, he was more street-wise than I first assumed. The kind of sexual partner Hal claimed to prefer was a man older than him, more dominant, and Black or Latino. Given his traditional values, Hal was surprisingly open. I suspect he trusted me because I came out to him.

After getting Hal's sexual history, I decided on a course of treatment for him. With his history, I did not believe he had any pedophilic arousal at all. His narrative of his sex life had veracity. So did his denial of pedophilic arousal. I had enough clinical experience with gay men and offenders to be able to intuit as much. I believed that Hal needed to be immersed in a gay social milieu. As only a part of my practice was forensic, I had resources to offer Hal. I also worked with gay men with mental health and relationship issues, and had a therapy group comprised of gay men. This group had a strong working core, one that I expected would be non-judgmental and accepting of Hal. Instead of placing Hal in an offender's group, I recommended he join the gay men's therapy group in addition to individual sessions with me.

First Critical Incident: The Secret

Hal joined the group, and continued to see me for individual sessions. As I expected, the group welcomed Hal and was very supportive toward him. They were not concerned about his Court-mandated status, in fact, they told him that he was a victim of the Uncle's homophobia. They believed he was wrongly convicted before I did. Seeing Hal in both settings allowed me to address issues raised in the group setting. I told Hal that I wasn't ready to take the position that his conviction was wrong. There were holes in his narrative that I wanted clarified. He was disappointed, and I used his disappointment as therapeutic leverage. I asked him to tell me more about his best friend, and the friend group. It took several sessions, but I learned what kept Hal connected to his friend for so many years. It wasn't the group of friends. Hal tolerated them because they and his best friend, whom I will call Bob, continued to be friends.

What kept Hal in relationship with Bob was sex. This was Hal's big secret, one that, when kept, made him look so suspicious. Hal and Bob began having sex together when they were both 15. As things evolved, Bob began dating girls but still expected sexual favors from Hal, who was beginning to fall in love with Bob. At that time in his treatment, Hal could not see that Bob was using him for sex. The girls he was dating were also part of their faith community and would not be sexually active until marriage. From Bob's perspective, he and Hal had a secret arrangement. From Hal's perspective, he and Bob had a special relationship that had to remain secret because of their shared community and faith values. Hal was willing to accommodate Bob.

According to Hal, the sex became unwanted and routine. The focus was on Bob's needs. Hal continued to be with Bob sexually, because he thought he had to in order to maintain the relationship. Hal described a pattern. Bob tended to be rough during sex and would flood with guilt afterwards. Consequently, he would push Hal away after they had sex. Hal told me that after a few days would pass, Bob would initiate sexual contact again. Bob knew how to manipulate Hal emotionally: promising he wouldn't push Hal away, spending one-on-one time together, acknowledging the importance of the relationship between them. To Hal, time alone with Bob felt like dates. But, those times would never occur on a weekend, because that was when Bob saw his girlfriend. Once he sensed Hal was trusting or compliant again, Bob would initiate sexual activity. Bob was the first one to get his own car, so many of their assignations would occur there. Hal began to find the sex unpleasant, but he acquiesced.

I pointed out the obvious to Hal. If Hal was female, Bob's behavior would be considered abusive. Hal had not considered that. He thought what he and Bob were doing was "gay," and thought gay men rarely had successful relationships, because being gay was only about sex. This was an opportunity for a gay affirming practice moment. Malyon might say that Hal's biased upbringing was informed by homophobia, which caused him to accept a powerless position in a relationship with a man who passed easily as straight. Kort might argue that Hal settled for less because he was used to a heterosexist dynamic in his relationship with Bob. Furthermore, Kort would say that Hal was a victim of "covert cultural sexual abuse," which has its roots in heterosexism. Kort posited that, "covert cultural sexual abuse is the expression of heterosexism, a belief in mainstream society that demands that all people be - or pretend to be - heterosexual" (2008, p. 48). In Kort's view, homophobia is a product of heterosexism, and is used against the development of healthy gay identities. Hal could not, in his adolescence, see a way for another kind of acculturation. He was willing to settle for a relationship that was informed by homophobia in the form of sexual secret keeping, and one of the worst norms of heterosexism, specifically, a dominant-subordinate interpersonal power dynamic.

The intervention was easy. Hal had become a full and active participant in his group, so I asked him to tell the group what he had told me. The group was not surprised, after all, they experienced the same kind of biased socialization in their lives. But, they were angry that Hal's secret had caused him to be labeled with a felony conviction. One member pointed out that all he had to do was reveal the history of the relationship with Bob, which may have led to a simple child protection evaluation instead of a conviction. At that time, Hal could not imagine any other way of handling the situation. Even though the sex between them ended when Bob married, Hal felt loyal. Would the revelation have caused distress for Bob and his family? Certainly, but Hal would have his autonomy intact. The group continued to press Hal for more details. They kept pointing out the role homophobia played in this situation. Hal was beginning to understand, from the group's gay affirming perspective, that he could live a happier life.

As more details about his relationship with Bob, and Bob's family and their friends emerged, I could see how Hal had been wrongly convicted. Unless very well-kept, secrets are not sustainable. The keeping of secrets catches up with people, because eventually they look suspicious. Bob's wife had always been uncomfortable with Hal and Bob's relationship, and her brother even more so. I believe what Bob's son did the night his Uncle visited became an opportunity for them to have Hal removed from their lives. In retrospect, Hal admitted he thought everyone in his social network was suspicious of Hal and Bob. Once Bob married things fell into a more traditional pattern. Hal began having anonymous sexual encounters in secret. He said he was glad sex with Bob ended. He told himself he could enjoy being an extended member of Bob's family and still have what he thought of as a gay sex life, albeit a secret one. It would be awhile before Hal recognized the sequelae of his abusive and exploitive relationship with Bob.

Second Critical Incident: Self Determination

Hal's treatment began to take off after he revealed his secret to me and the group. Most evenings after group ended the members would go out for coffee. Hal began joining them. He began to seem happy. He hadn't made any new friends since High School. Hal worked as a printer, and there were no co-workers with whom he shared any common interests. His relationship with his mother was good, but Hal still could not come out to her. One of Hal's sisters lived nearby and began to help Hal with his mother's care on a more frequent basis, freeing Hal to stay out late with the group, or spend more time exploring parts of the city he had never seen. His nascent interest in fashion and theater began to bloom. A member of the group gave Hal a book by designer Cecil Beaton. Hal was hooked, and began scouring used bookstores and the Internet for more such books. He even began attending theater events on his own.

Hal also began visiting gay bars, and on one such trip he met a man whom he liked very much. But, this was different than his previous experiences with cruising for anonymous, single encounters. Perhaps because Hal was developing a stronger, more defined self, as well as an identity as a gay man, he was able to be more interpersonally present. Hal and the man he met (I'll call him Jose) did not have sex the night they met. Instead, they talked, and discovered they had much in common other than being gay. Both Hal and Jose were close with their mothers and siblings. Both were Catholic and did not want to abandon their faith. Many of the values they learned from going to Catholic schools mattered to each of them. They were able to make a distinction between dogma and Catholic teachings regarding peace, compassion, and the need to care for the poor.

One big difference between them was that Jose had his own apartment, in an area of the nearby city which featured more diversity. Hal began to realize that living with his mother, in the neighborhood in which he was raised, and, near to where Bob and his family lived, was simply not good for him. Hal and Jose began dating exclusively, with Hal spending more and more time at Jose's apartment. They enjoyed a full, satisfying sex life. However, Hal could not allow himself to spend a full night with Jose because he felt responsible for his mother's care.

The group actively encouraged Hal to change his relationship with his mother. Specifically, they believed, as I did, that Hal should tell his mother and sisters that he is gay. I attempted to correct his cognitive distortions, and suggest alternate, more positive forecasts than his. We role-played various strategies. Hal began to believe he could come out to his mother, but, as he got closer and closer to telling her, his IBS got worse. I contacted a Social Service agency in Hal's county that provided services to the elderly. As it turned out, Hal's mother was eligible for substantial supportive care and case management. Enough for Hal to move out of his mother's home and into his own apartment. This was easier for Hal to manage; coming out to his mother was still an overwhelming task for him. He found an apartment near enough to his mother's home and closer to the city.

Hal and Jose continued dating. Now that they could spend full evenings together, their relationship strengthened. Hal spent more time attending theatrical events in the city. He carried himself with more confidence. He presented as a much happier person. In spite of the fact he was still living two separate lives, he was no longer living a secret life of furtive, anonymous encounters. He was able to reflect on that time in his life and concluded that anonymous sex was as unpleasant as his sex was with Bob. I explained that people who have been abused often re-enact their abuse until they are able to begin the recovery process. This made sense to Hal. Despite all of his progress, his IBS continued to get worse. I recall thinking, now that Hal's life was more self-determined, his symptoms should abate somewhat.

Critical Incident Three: Premature Termination

By all measures, Hal's treatment was successful. His probation ended without incident, and Hal was not placed on the State's registry of sex offenders. This was a real gift, and a just one. Hal was free to live his new life fully, without the unfair stigma of being labeled a sex offender. As his therapist, I felt satisfied that I had made the right decision to treat Hal from a GAT perspective rather than from a sex offender-specific treatment perspective. He continued to attend group sessions with only occasional individual visits. Hal was in a maintenance phase of therapy. He was no longer ordered by the Court to attend therapy, so I did not pay close attention to the fact that his attendance was less regular. Hal's IBS was still an issue for him. I assumed he was working with his doctor to find the right treatment.

He was working with a physician, but IBS was not the problem. Hal had an advanced form of esophageal cancer. He had assumed he had IBS because it ran in his family, and he thought of himself as an anxious person in general. Hal was admitted to the hospital because his symptoms had become unmanageable. His cancer was discovered while hospitalized. He never left the hospital. Hal died after three weeks of inpatient treatment for cancer. His disease was just too advanced for any kind of meaningful recovery. We spoke once by phone, I told myself that I should visit him, but did not get the chance.

His therapy group was devastated, as was I. There was only small comfort in the notion that Hal enjoyed life as self-determined, more authentic, and fully expressed person before he died. I spoke with his mother to offer my condolences. She seemed like a very kind person. I chose to reveal one aspect of Hal's therapy to her. I told her that I believed he was innocent of abusing Bob's child. I explained that he took a guilty plea to spare his friend's family the stress of a trial. She thanked me, and said she came to the same conclusion herself. To this day, the inequity Hal experienced remains unresolved for me.

Discussion and Conclusion

Readers who are familiar with the tenets of sex offender-specific treatment may take issue with how easily I chose to emphasize a GAT over an offender-specific approach. Likewise, those who are victim advocates or trauma specialists may think my approach did not adequately address the sequelae of Hal's abusive and exploitive relationship with Bob. My first response to both of those potential critiques is ethical, not clinical. NASW's Code of Ethics declare that both *Social Justice* and *Dignity and Worth of the Person* are two foundational ethical principles of the profession (2017). Hal was vulnerable to stigmatization which could result in loss of employment and discrimination with regards to finding employment. Fortunately, his employer did not find out about his conviction. That was a function of luck on Hal's part. As a clinician concerned with the principle of Social Justice, I believed that I was obligated to provide a service and resources consistent with his unique situation. I believed that a gay affirming approach to treatment would serve him best. Additionally, I thought that Hal deserved treatment that would afford him dignity and help him discover his worth.

From a clinical perspective, I felt that GAT would serve him better than sex offender-specific treatment (SOST). SOST is based on relapse prevention and is designed to address sexually deviant and abusive behavior. Such an approach could unintentionally serve to reinforce Hal's internalized homophobia. Moreover, I wanted to help Hal prevent a relapse of any behavior or situation or consequence of living a secret life. Helping him find a way to live an authentic gay life, on his terms, would be the most effective form of relapse prevention.

Regarding Hal's victimization, I also believe that a gay affirming approach was the best clinical frame in which to address his history of victimization and exploitation. His relationship with Bob occurred in an exploitive, secret, and heterosexist context. As referred to earlier, Kort argues that growing up gay can create a unique form of PTSD because of covert cultural sexual abuse. Hal learned to settle for less, and to keep sexual secrets. I believe this is what led to his arrest and conviction. In my mind, the best way to help him recover from abuse was to employ a gay affirming treatment.

If Hal had abused Bob's son, his treatment would still have a GAT component. I would have placed him in an offender's group I facilitated which consisted of men with exclusively young male victims. That group was created to offer an environment free of homophobic shame and stigma, with the intent of providing an opportunity for male-target offenders to work on developing a gay identity as a way of exiting their cycles of sexual offending behavior. The composition and dynamics of the offender's group were very different than the gay men's group, but Hal would still have the opportunity to do his work in an environment with gay affirming norms. Moreover, if Hal evidenced trauma symptoms such as severe dissociation, I would have referred him to someone who specialized in treatment such as eye movement desensitization and reprocessing (EMDR). Hal responded so well to the gay men's therapy group that I did not have to consider any additional treatments.

Finally, by acting as a gay role model for Hal, and offering him a gay therapeutic and social experience with peers, I was able to provide Hal with a second opportunity to have an unbiased socialization that could correct his earlier, heterosexist, biased experiences. The case of Hal was chosen because he reflected a relatively complex clinical scenario that was successfully treated with a primarily gay affirming approach. Hal was also an easy person with whom to work. He was friendly, sincere, and open. He did not reject my attempts to correct his distorted beliefs about gay life. In fact, he welcomed them. In retrospect, Hal had managed to keep an undamaged part of himself available in case a safe and affirming opportunity emerged. I also chose Hal for this case study as a way to honor his life. To this day, I admire his courage and his gracious nature. I wish he was around still. I expect his life would be inspirational.

Close Reading Questions

1. Summarize Appiah's counter to the dynamic including subordinate identity. How does this theory manifest in Healy's work with Hal?
2. Healy cites Kort's idea that growing up gay can cause PTSD. Why does Healy cite Kort here? Did Hal have symptoms of PTSD? How important is that diagnosis to understanding this case?
3. What did you learn from Hal's experience in group therapy? What did you learn from Healy's approach to establishing a therapeutic alliance and upholding his client's right to self-determination?

Prompts for Writing

1. How does this case make you think of forensics and sex offender work differently than you did before? In what ways does it remind you of the clinical work in Kahn and Alessi's chapter on Gender and Sexual Minority Asylum Seekers?
2. Healy writes that Hal thought that the gay community would reject a person of faith and not the other way around. What do you make of Hal's assumption? How does it compare to Jerrod's assumptions in Goldblatt Hyatt's chapter?
3. What were your thoughts when Hal learned that in a heterosexual relationship, Bob's behavior would have been considered abusive?

Notes

1 In 1973, homosexuality's status as a psychopathology was de-classified by the APA, and removed from subsequent revisions of the DSM. Ego dystonic homosexuality was removed from the DSM in 1987, because it was acknowledged that ego dystonic homosexuality is the result of growing up in a homophobic society.

2 The case example used in this chapter is about a gay man. However, when the term gay is used in a broader context, it is meant to include lesbians, bisexuals, and those who identify as queer.

3 For more information on this fascinating Philosopher, go to Appiah.net.

4 Talk about settling for less. This was Hal's only social network, complete with all the leftover baggage and tension that can come with such long-term friendships, in a small, ethnically homogenous enclave.

References

Alessi, E. J., Dillon, F. R., & Kim, H. M. S. (2015). Determinants of lesbian and gay affirmative practice among heterosexual therapists. *Psychotherapy, 52*(3), 298.

American Psychiatric Association. (1980). *Diagnostic and statistical manual of mental disorders* (3rd ed.). Washington, DC: American Psychiatric Association.

Appiah, K. A. (2018). *The lies that bind: Rethinking identity.* London: Profile Books.

Bibas, S. (2002). Bringing moral values into a flawed plea-bargaining system. *Cornell Law Review, 88*, 1425.

Cass, V. C. (1979). Homosexuality identity formation: A theoretical model. *Journal of Homosexuality, 4*(3), 219–235.

Coleman, E. PhD. (1982). Developmental stages of the coming out process. *Journal of Homosexuality,* 7(2–3), 31–43. doi:10.1300/J082v07n02 06

Crisp, C. (2005). Homophobia and use of gay affirmative practice in a sample of social workers and psychologists. *Journal of Gay & Lesbian Social Services, 18*(1), 51–70.

Crisp, C. (2006). The gay affirmative practice scale (GAP): A new measure for assessing cultural competence with gay and lesbian clients. *Social Work, 51*(2), 115–126. doi:10.1300/J041v18n01_05

DeCrescenzo, T. (1984). Homophobia: A study of the attitudes of mental health professionals toward homosexuality. In R. Schoenberg, R. Goldberg, & D. Shore (Eds.), *With compassion toward some: Homosexuality and social work in America* (pp. 115–136). New York, NY: Harrington Park.

Herek, G. M. (2007). Confronting sexual stigma and prejudice: Theory and practice. *Journal of Social Issues, 63*(4), 905–925. doi:10.1111/j.1540-4560.2007.00544.x

Kort, J. (2008). *Gay affirmative therapy for the straight clinician: The essential guide.* New York, NY: W.W. Norton & Company.

Lebolt, J. (1999). Gay affirmative psychotherapy: A phenomenological study. *Clinical Social Work Journal, 27*(4), 355–370.

Malyon, A. K. (1982). Psychotherapeutic implications of internalized homophobia in gay men. *Journal of Homosexuality,* 7(2–3), 59–69. doi:10.1300/J082v07n02_08

Ward, B. H. (2006). Sentencing without remorse. *Loyola University Chicago Law Journal, 38*, 131.

INDEX

Taylor & Francis Group
an informa business

Taylor & Francis eBooks

www.taylorfrancis.com

A single destination for eBooks from Taylor & Francis with increased functionality and an improved user experience to meet the needs of our customers.

90,000+ eBooks of award-winning academic content in Humanities, Social Science, Science, Technology, Engineering, and Medical written by a global network of editors and authors.

TAYLOR & FRANCIS EBOOKS OFFERS:

A streamlined experience for our library customers

A single point of discovery for all of our eBook content

Improved search and discovery of content at both book and chapter level

REQUEST A FREE TRIAL

support@taylorfrancis.com

Routledge
Taylor & Francis Group

CRC Press
Taylor & Francis Group

For Product Safety Concerns and Information please contact our EU representative GPSR@taylorandfrancis.com Taylor & Francis Verlag GmbH, Kaufingerstraße 24, 80331 München, Germany